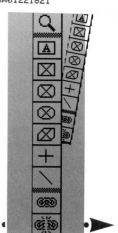

teach yourself...

QuarkXPress 3.2
for the Macintosh

Joseph Kasmer

A Subsidiary of
Henry Holt and Co., Inc.

First Edition—1993

ISBN 1-55828-262-9

Printed in the United States of America.

10 9 8 7 6 5 4 3 2 1

MIS:Press books are available at special discounts for bulk purchases for sales promotions, premiums, fund-raising, or educational use. Special editions or book excerpts can also be created to specification.

For details contact: Special Sales Director
MIS:Press
a subsidiary of Henry Holt and Company, Inc.
115 West 18th Street
New York, New York 10011

Development Editor, *Laura Lewin*
Production Editor, *Patricia Wallenburg*
Copy Editor, *Suzanne Ingrao*

Dedication

To the memory of Jamaica Stone

Acknowledgments

Once again, I owe a personal thanks to Gerard Black of Black-Eye Productions, San Diego, for taking time from his many duties in broadcast television to unselfishly provide a discerning eye and technical assistance for parts of this book.

I have also made use of the paintings of L.L. Richwood in Chapter 12. Though these works have been photographed and scanned, much of their character comes through in these pages. The originals in San Diego reward those who directly view their vibrant colors and detail. The copyright to these images is held by L.L. Richwood, all rights reserved.

Thanks also to my hundreds of publishing clients and students at UCLA and elsewhere, and to Steve Berkowitz at MIS Press for prompting into existence this book and others.

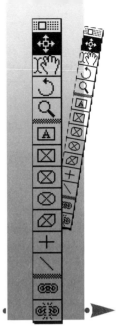

Introduction
Your 24-Hour Consultant

This book is for everyone using, or considering using, QuarkXPress on the Macintosh. You can go through it in an armchair reading, or work with it alongside your computer.

A full-time consultant to tutor you in new software and to help you on the job would be a welcome resource. Having provided this service for major publishers and corporations, I can attest, direct training works. Workshops, seminars and classes are less expensive and easier to arrange. Having taught hundreds of professionals from all disciplines, I can also recommend quality courses as cost-effective for acquiring skills.

But such approaches have their limits. They can't possibly keep pace with your requirements over the long run. Much of the information they impart is often lost or is difficult to access weeks later. Also, these approaches don't permit the expert to be available to every client at every moment they need guidance.

Wouldn't it be better to combine the advantages of each approach in some other form, that is, one that would provide quality access to an expert in the software? I thought so, and the result is this book, an affordable 24-hour, on-site alternative to help you climb the learning curve. The book you're holding will lead you into the working environment of QuarkXPress, the tools, the features, and the best methods for achieving results quickly. Just as I do in my face-to-face sessions, this book will demonstrate methods with hundreds of examples. It will also provide memory joggers that give you working knowledge of the program, as well as easy reminders to return to.

Getting the Most Out of This Book

Teach Yourself…QuarkXPress 3.2 for the Macintosh can be your guide to discovering one of the most rewarding software packages available to electronic publishing. You'll discover in it the most useful features and surest methods for creating effective publications and designs. Its 112 capsule summaries and over 300 illustrations will help guide you through every feature as it's presented.

QuarkXPress is one of only a handful of programs that truly provides features of impressive power and scope. It's one of the brightest pieces of publishing technology available.

Consider *Teach Yourself…QuarkXPress 3.2 for the Macintosh* the combination of the scores of consulting sessions, workshops, training seminars, and college classes in which I've taught desktop publishing skills to people with much—as well as to those with scant—experience.

This book presents the tools and procedures of QuarkXPress to you in stages, the way most people turn to them in their actual work. This task-oriented approach uses chapters, each of which leads to a set of integrated skills. Certain chapters such as Chapter 5, are complete examples, start-to-finish, using the capabilities presented. These on-the-job chapters apply the skills to a project you can see unfolding. Remember, skills take hold most strongly when their first introduction is followed immediately by practice. So, if you have the opportunity, try to work through the examples in the on-the-job chapters, or better yet, apply the techniques to your own projects.

As your QuarkXPress abilities and skills accumulate, you'll be able to apply more of them to your current publications and designs in progress. You'll gain mastery the fastest once you learn, and then experiment with work that has significance to you. Whether you're facing project deadlines or not, you'll find the cumulative approach of the following chapters a highly practical one. It will hasten your understanding of the program's functions and suggest ways to make use of them.

This book develops logically from the most fundamental and useful methods to the most specialized, from setting up the program and a document to printing final output. You'll find straight-ahead presentation, explanation, and description of features and techniques with discussion of methods and clear step-by-step procedures. Examples and figures accompany the procedures as they are developed.

Conventions

N O T E

Notes indicate that you should take note of the information provided, which often contains a helpful hint or points out a special circumstance.

SHORTCUT

Shortcuts indicate that you can perform some action more quickly by using alternative shortcuts keystrokes, or other methods or approaches.

WARNING

Warnings indicate a caution that you may lose data or lose work if you perform an certain action.

At-A-Glance

You'll also find key points summarized in separate At-A-Glance inserts, like this one. This jogs your memory without forcing you back through all the explanatory details previously presented.

Several times throughout the book you'll notice the On-the-Job chapters appear. These step-by-step, work-through examples detail use of the techniques explained in preceding chapters, on actual projects. They illustrate—as only thorough, complete examples can—most of the skills presented in earlier chapters. On-the-Job chapters also include At-a-glance summaries inserted where special techniques are called for. If you're in a hurry, you may choose to temporarily skip an on-the-job chapter to take on more techniques. Otherwise, you should look closely at actual tasks being handled in these highly illustrative chapters.

Throughout the book, you will encounter references to the Command key. Depending on your keyboard, this may be labeled as ⌘. They are the same key.

Within this book you'll find skills for beginning with QuarkXPress, working in the Macintosh-QuarkXPress interface, managing QuarkXPress documents, editing text, typesetting, importing and exporting text and graphics, handling master pages, manipulating graphic images, controlling content flow through the document, customizing the QuarkXPress environment, creating multiple editions and templates, transferring files, and doing print runs and color publications, as well as countless other techniques.

A Brief Outline

From the basics of file manipulation to the secret shortcuts of QuarkXPress, each of the 18 chapters in this book explores and reveals a different set of skills. Combined, they can lead you to substantial QuarkXPress publishing and design proficiency.

An overview of QuarkXPress brings the tools and features of the program into perspective in Chapter 1. Scanning over the range of the program's operation you'll see how far you can push the limits of the program. We'll look at QuarkXPress-generated documents and operation and see what makes the QuarkXPress world so distinctive.

QuarkXPress creates an environment by virtue of other software that supports it, as will become clear in Chapter 2. Here, we'll explore how QuarkXPress works within the Macintosh interface, how to install the program, and how to approach this unique desktop publishing world.

The best way to gain a foothold in QuarkXPress is to get a good grasp of how documents are generated and navigated, and how the interface controls everything on the page. In Chapter 3 we look at working with publication and design elements on the QuarkXPress page and pasteboard, as well as working between pages.

At the foundation of virtually every page or design lies type. Without question, it is with type that QuarkXPress excels. Chapter 4 reveals basics of type control in

QuarkXPress, from retrieving and generating text to adjusting the nuances of its appearance on the final print. You'll see how to generate text, how to import it into a document, how to apply typefaces, how to style type, size it, and space it. You'll also learn how to use guides, margins, and columns to fashion text.

Putting techniques to work makes them yours. In On-the-Job: Newsletters, Chapter 5, you will see file handling, document construction and type control at work, with those techniques learned in the first part of the book applied in an actual document.

Graphics can make or break a design or publication. In QuarkXPress graphics come into picture boxes in which they can be manipulated and modified in ways explained in Chapter 6. We'll examine the graphic features of text and illustrations as they appear in a document, learning how images can be imported, cropped, sized, aligned, framed, and anchored. You'll see how text box linking can be achieved easily and how all the page elements interact with each other.

In publications that inform, text and pictures must coordinate clearly. Chapter 7 will take you through the steps that make one such publication a success.

As the message in a publication or design becomes crucial, the demands placed on text within it increase. Chapter 8 takes up the challenge of detailed formatting in paragraphs and stories. This chapter will show how controls work at both paragraph and story levels, how to regulate hyphenations and justification, and how to accomplish special effects with type.

In newspapers every story must attract the reader while at the same time fitting in with surrounding stories. In On-the-Job: A Newspaper, Chapter 9 shows how QuarkXPress features enabled one such front page to achieve this.

As the complexity of a document increases, graphics can become intertwined with text. Where one flows, the other can follow. Chapter 10 explains master pages and style sheets, grouping, anchoring, and the movement of text and picture combinations. Here you'll find methods for providing unity within documents by integrating text, picture, and line items.

Chapter 11 demonstrates methods used on books, manuals, and catalogs for establishing and controlling the dynamic of box elements. You'll see here how separate entries can be merged.

In QuarkXPress, a graphic can be modified in an electronic darkroom, much as a photographer controls the final image print. Chapter 12 reveals the fascinating effects and modifications possible within documents, showing how contrast and halftone adjustments are achieved.

Chapter 13 shows an illustrated magazine article in development. We see which steps of digital image manipulation make the images tell their own story, as they are prepared for optimum quality to match output through an imagesetter.

You may wish to use certain of your most successful layouts and master pages and graphical elements more than once. Building on work that went into a first effort is essential and in the program is made practical by using publication templates. Chapter 14 shows how to develop subsequent issues of a publication. Working with multiple documents and multiple editions of the same document, we'll look into ways to reapply whole pages, to cross the document boundary, to return to existing documents, and to set up and reuse whole documents in new forms.

Desktop publishing generates a torrent of file movement. Documents change computer platforms, graphics meld into new formats, texts slip in and out of files. Chapter 15 unveils ways to manage the tumult, including some sophisticated methods of file management. You'll learn about QuarkXPress libraries as well as about ways to export text, graphics, and layouts by command and to auxiliary software.

Color control and matching can be elusive, but they are manageable. Chapter 16 shows the ways of making custom colors, of applying colors, and of preparing the document for color separation during printing.

The final incarnation for most documents is the printed page. Chapter 17 shows ways to successfully handle printing by proper management of fonts, image files printers, and odd-sized pages.

Chapter 18 presents many hidden, time-saving, work-enhancing shortcuts, tips, and suggestions for working with QuarkXPress in the Macintosh environment.

Appendix A provides a handy reference to the procedures outlined in the chapters; it is a compilation of all the At-A-Glance summaries giving outlines to the key elements of each technique. These summaries are organized by chapter so that you can locate methods quickly and easily.

Appendix B suggests a number of other sources that can aid you in further developing your computer, layout, typesetting, design, and related skills.

Every book worthy of its reader should serve him or her as a springboard and friend. This book has been written to be just that for you. As in all my workshops and classes, students' comments, reactions, and experiences in electronic publishing are always welcome. I encourage you to send your correspondence to Studio K, Box 3562, San Diego, CA 92163.

Now, I invite you to teach yourself QuarkXPress for the Macintosh.

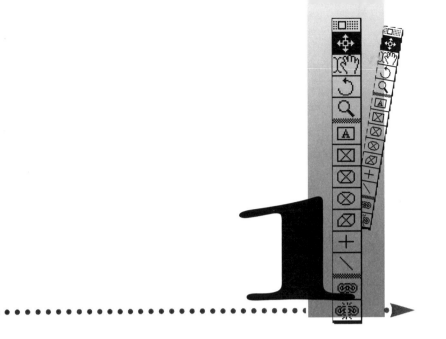

Publishing with QuarkXPress

What you will learn in this chapter:

- ❖ The function of QuarkXPress
- ❖ How the program composes documents
- ❖ Control devices and tools
- ❖ The form of text and picture elements
- ❖ Content and item differences
- ❖ Multiple documents

There has been no better time to be working with electronic publishing. Competition and developments have pushed software to new heights of functionality. Always a leader in typography, QuarkXPress has passed through several incarnations, acquiring many diverse and delightful features. Its current version answers many of the wish lists thought up for features by desktop publishers. It has added some new functions that may not have even occurred to most people.

In this chapter we'll take a broad look at the program. We'll glimpse it's interface and look into ways we'll be treating page elements in its documents. We'll see the two-sided nature to these elements and how QuarkXPress takes clever advantage of them.

Hand Me the QuarkXPress?

Software is a tool, we often hear. The larger truth is that a software program provides a set of tools. No single tool built the Golden Gate Bridge or the room in which you are reading this; and no single tool can make a full-color catalog or a modern consumer magazine. As one of the most sophisticated desktop publishing programs yet developed, QuarkXPress far surpasses the tool analogy.

QuarkXPress, you see, is not so much any single thing as it is an environment; a place providing capabilities and opportunities, in which a diversity of results can be created.

If you follow QuarkXPress, you know that it's been widely used by professionals in publishing and design to produce books, magazines, newspapers, advertising, and documentation. Others apply it to stationery, posters, forms, brochures, and corporate publications. Skilled designers and typesetters find features in it to which they are accustomed. But anyone who can operate a Macintosh computer can use QuarkXPress. (And even if you're unsteady with the Mac, you'll find tips in Chapter 2 to help get you up and running with the program.)

The Interface and the Environment

The process of desktop publishing is essentially simple: You develop an idea for a publication or design. You tell the program to generate a file document in which adjustments, additions, and changes can be made. There the idea is worked into a graphic form as completely as time and resources allow.

Eventually the file document is transformed into printed pages, or into a multimedia display.

Equally simple is the idea at the core of every desktop publishing program: create a simulation of pasteup and typeset pages. Software that does this mimics the real world by making work on digital files seem like work on actual pages. Other elements from the real world such as lines and other images can be made to interact on those simulated screen pages as they might on the printed page. (Some designs will never see the printed page, going instead into multimedia presentations, or out as FAX images between computers. But in this book we will use the printed page as a standard.)

Creating a convincing simulation of the graphic world has led to recreating the tools and capabilities of that world. On a simulated page generated by QuarkXPress we enter a virtual reality where we can fashion and adjust page elements with amazing precision and speed.

Type and graphics modifications take seconds instead of hours. Scaling a typeface or an image on screen is infinitely simpler than in the physical world of type shops, stat cameras, and darkrooms. It has become nearly axiomatic that the more capabilities given us by the software program, the faster we will arrive at our goal.

The *document file* is where QuarkXPress simulates the graphic world. Each document includes much that is not evident on screen, or on the page. Designs are made of *elements*—largely type and graphics existing on the page in relation to each other. The relations among design elements can be conceptual as much as visual. For instance, text that is indented in a document appears as type shifted from the margin. But the document also holds certain settings for that indentation, which will be in effect even if those particular words are replaced with others as in Figure 1.1.

Encoded in the document file along with all the text and graphics we see are these relations. They include connections between jumped text, arrangements of pages and page spreads, hyphenation standards, references to other files, and so on. Relation-charged QuarkXPress documents such as these contain much more than meets the eye. When one element shifts, dozens of others might be adjusted automatically to accommodate the change.

The document, then can become quite a complex file. How are we to deal with all the relations being balanced and adjusted within it? The answer looks back at us from every QuarkXPress document. It is the *interface*—whose sole purpose is to connect us with every one of the program's capabilities. In the interface, every control has a visual counterpart on the screen by which we can change the document and its elements.

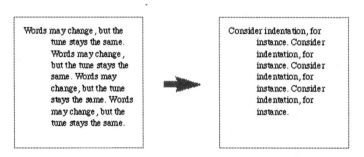

Figure 1.1 *Text can change while format remains.*

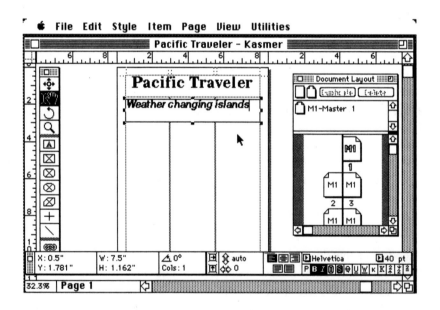

Figure 1.2 *Interface controls of QuarkXPress.*

Figure 1.2 shows a page under construction. Around it appear parts of the interface, the tools, devices, controls, and command menus used to bring and manage page elements in the page design. These are the most readily accessible parts of the interface; we will look at them in Chapter 3.

The QuarkXPress interface is not just a tool box. It produces an environment in which to work. It is the way to the heart of the program, and it is much more sophisticated than it first appears. It may be all we ever see of the thousands of behind-the-scenes operations in which QuarkXPress responds to our directions. The interface is our interpreter to QuarkXPress' work crew. To know the interface is to control the program.

Control Devices

If you've worked with the Macintosh or one of the other graphic user interfaces that present commands through menus, you've probably become accustomed to the *open-and-pull-down* approach. It's good; it works and with it you can easily recall how to do what you want.

Turn to graphics or desktop publishing software and you are sure to encounter mouse tools. Click and the mouse cursor changes function and appearance. Again, easy and functional. Maybe you've gone further and picked up power use keyboard strokes, often displayed opposite the menu commands they activate. Some are hidden and often among the most powercharged techniques accessible through uncited keystroke controls. You might—with this experience under your belt—begin to imagine you've seen it all, in terms of interface control. Graphic user controls, after a time, can start to seem like old hat.

But then if, expecting more of the same you open a document in QuarkXPress, you'll be surprised. There are tools, the menu bar, keyboard shortcuts, the familiar types of controls. But look at the program window display, as in Figure 1.2, and you'll discover some things which stand out. Look closely at the bottom of the window, and over at the right side. Along the bottom is what appears to be a read-out summary. And to the side is a miniature layout window. These things look a little strange because they are designed to do things differently. The folks at Quark have designed an exceptionally useful control device; it's called a *palette*.

Frankly, when I first encountered the Quark Measurements palette (that's the long horizontal box at the bottom) I tried to get it off the window and out of my way as quickly as I could; ditto for the Document Layout palette (at the right). However, they soon proved their worth. Today, I use these palettes all the time.

Their great virtue, especially for the Measurements palette, is this: they provide instant feedback and control. They don't usurp the controls from tools and menus; but the palettes provide an advantage. They continually tell you the status of an item and let you change it at will. This is a significant advance in graphic user interface design, namely feedback. And as anyone who's ever tried to parallel park a car by the bump method can tell you, feedback is the way to go.

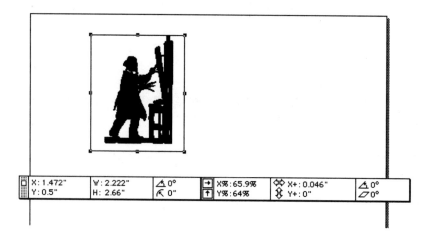

Figure 1.3 *The Measurements palette for a graphic.*

A palette measuring a graphic on the page, as in Figure 1.3, indicates position, size, scaling, and other attributes. In addition, it will actually change that graphic when you type in a new value such as coordinates, size, or scaling, into it, or when you click on the buttonlike controls. In short, the Measurements palette gives you interactive control.

Text

If you're a typesetter (or if you spec type in your work), you probably have your own mental checklist of features against which to test QuarkXPress. Yes, the program will align type left, right, centered, and justified. It does give fractional control of leading (line spacing) and of interparagraph spacing, and automatically jumps text. It indents, hyphenates, does tracking, kerning, shifts baselines, subscripts, superscripts, spell checks, and all the things you'd expect of it.

The program also does many of the things you may have lusted for in your typographical heart such as rotating type, scaling type horizontally, shading, trapping, and overprinting type. It aligns text within layouts by vertically centering lines, aligning them all to the top of the layout, to the bottom, or spreading them out in automatic vertical justification, as in Figure 1.4.

You may be accustomed to the

vertical alignment of text to the top.

But it can also be aligned to the

bottom within a text box, centered,

or as here, vertically justified.

Figure 1.4 *Vertical justification*

Quark also performs even more extreme text manipulations. For instance, the program can flip text of any length so that you're looking at it as though from the back side of a window sign painting.

Pictures

To the chagrin of graphic designers, illustration is sometimes still treated as an afterthought in many electronic publishing programs. Perhaps this is because the origins of desktop publishing can be traced to word processing. QuarkXPress has made strides to close the gap between the treatments of type and graphics. Besides rotation, scaling, and cropping features, the image-conscious designer will encounter shading and contrast adjustments, halftoning with gray levels, angle, and screen frequency options. Don't overlook color editing and separations based on several models with trapping and overprinting features, of course.

Items

Text, pictures, and lines are the only printable things QuarkXPress allows in a document. (Of course, there are also guides, baselines, and other nonprinting particulars.) But everything we see in publications and graphic displays can be represented in text, picture, or line form.

The whole basis of design is that these elements will interact with each other on the page and thus on the eye and mind of the reader. One interaction is *runaround*—text flowing in columns around other text or pictures. Other interactions include overlapping, abutting, aligning, and spacing.

Those design elements with which we work—text, illustrations, and rules—QuarkXPress calls *items*. Items are half of a duality that reappears frequently throughout QuarkXPress documents. Text appears as a *text box*. That box is an item. Within the text box is *type*. That type is content. *Graphics* appear in a picture box. That's an item. Within the picture box is the image itself. That's *content*. Rules and lines are simpler, but still fall into the item/content duality.

As an item, our design element is subject to being resized, moved, deleted, turned, copied, and otherwise manipulated. As content, our element might be hyphenated, spell checked, kerned, lightened, or cropped. Figure 1.5 shows just such a dual role for one text box.

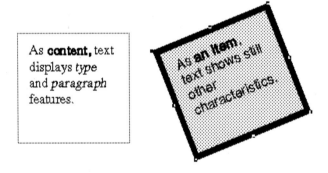

Figure 1.5   *The dual nature of text.*

Duality is easy to deal with. It's simply a matter of choosing what we want to do with the element on the page. Some tools and some commands are specific to items, and some are specific to text. And as you'll see, choosing the appropriate tool is the first step in successfully taking advantage of the dual nature of QuarkXPress text and pictures.

Location and View

Nearly every successful feature ever devised for navigating around a page or document has been incorporated into QuarkXPress. You'll find a *grabber hand*, *scroll bars,* a *miniature window, zoom tools, menu commands, keyboard strokes, typing fields,* and a special technique for enlarging exactly the area of interest. You can even locate graphics files external to a document, which serve as the source of imported pictures.

A sailboat's rudder and sails can both be used to direct the craft. Moving about the document is much the same—many options, and even more combinations. Some of the positioning and viewing features of QuarkXPress are likewise alternative ways of arriving at the same result. But which you choose will depend on the circumstances. The software provides an especially useful means of navigating your way through a document.

After discovering these controls, each person uses them in an individual fashion. Chapter 3 will demonstrate.

Multiple Documents and Libraries

QuarkXPress can open several documents simultaneously. If you've ever had to play the *copy element-close first document-open second document-paste element* game with an application that only provides one document window at a time, this will seem a landing on the shores of paradise. Imagine when you're lifting text and layouts from your last dozen publication issues to make a year-end review. Or suppose you're copying over design elements from work for former clients to that for a current one.

There's also a system of collecting elements in a library subfile QuarkXPress can access. Such a library can be used to hold and transfer items to any document. In fact, you can create or open several such libraries for organizing graphics, text, or layout elements. The library system can speed and focus complex publication development tremendously. It complements many of the other document features we'll be examining in Chapter 3.

Onward

In this preliminary cruise through QuarkXPress you've glimpsed only the briefest view of the program's features. As the following chapters reveal, there are literally hundreds of techniques and features to take advantage of. Principle among these is *interactivity,* an area we'll turn to as we explore actual publications on the job.

Next, though, we'll examine how to fit the program into your system. There are installation decisions to make and some brief procedures to follow. Introducing QuarkXPress properly into your system is the first step to using it, and its tools, palettes, and commands.

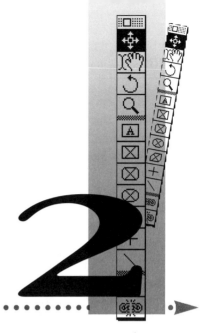

QuarkXPress and the Macintosh

What you'll learn in this chapter:

- ❖ Working with the Macintosh
- ❖ How to install QuarkXPress
- ❖ QuarkXPress program files
- ❖ Basic controls in QuarkXPress

Between the introduction of new software and its successful use, you pass through a fitting-in period. In this chapter you'll see how QuarkXPress can be fit into your Macintosh system. We'll see how to install QuarkXPress onto your computer. You may find your system already places you directly into QuarkXPress. If so, it will be possible for you to begin work on a document as explained in Chapter 3. However, there are decisions made during the installation process that affect the way QuarkXPress performs. We'll look at some of them here.

For the moment, let's proceed under the assumption that you're starting from ground zero. We'll move step by step through the flat fields of the Macintosh desktop and into rich mountains and valleys of QuarkXPress where functionality on your desktop publishing projects begins.

We'll check the Macintosh operations that apply to QuarkXPress. If the program is already installed, and you're anxious to work on your document, then you may wish to skim over the next few sections and continue on to Chapter 3.

Quark in the Macintosh

Much has been made of ease of use in working with the Macintosh computer and software designed for it. There are countless variations and concealed tricks that can be plumbed from the depths of the Mac. We will opt here for the most practical approach. That means the Mac will be viewed as a means to our greater goal—developing documents in QuarkXPress. When it expedites our work, we'll reveal a hidden feature or shortcut; otherwise we'll pass directly to QuarkXPress operation.

QuarkXPress operates in the Mac environment by virtue of its ability to follow an organization laid out in the system software. This system guides all the operations of the computer. Though it has more than one software component, you can consider the system as a unified program, interpreting commands that come from QuarkXpress or any other software package.

Versions of the Macintosh System

As of this writing, the Macintosh system has reached Version 7.x. You might think then that it would be best to treat QuarkXPress as though it were being used in the 7.x series. However, because the 7.x versions create incompatibilities with some software written before introduction of System 7, many professional desktop publishers have declined to upgrade to it. In order to retain use of their software collections, they continue to employ the System 6.x series (around System 6.0.7, or thereabouts).

Fortunately, QuarkXPress 3.2 was designed to work with Systems from 6.0.7 onward. So in general we'll consider those features that apply to both series. In fact, when you're using QuarkXPress features, you'll hardly know which system is supporting it.

What is the System?

The *system* is the world in which everything that happens in a computer running QuarkXPress takes place. Early systems were designed to tell the disk drive when to turn and where and when to move data on a the disk. Now the Macintosh system does much more than spin disks and transfer data. It is really the operating system for all the computer functions. Right now, in the set-up you're working with, if something is going to be done in your computer, the system will be involved in doing it.

Using QuarkXPress (or any other program) is a way of indirectly giving some commands to the system, which then acts on them after they've been translated. In fact, the system is essential to the operation of any software. The *Finder* is one piece of software, which works closely with the Macintosh system. It provides for your interaction in seeing and manipulating files, for starting programs and getting information about files. The Finder is such an integral part of the Macintosh environment that its often considered part of the System. Once you start up a Macintosh, you can see the screen, which represents a desktop of windows and files. This is the Finder at work.

In many ways the Finder appears transparent. That is, you actually see and move little icons that represent the files you want to work on. But it's always working in close coordination with the System to provide access to the contents of any disk or other medium attached to the Macintosh. In a similar way, QuarkXPress works in concert with the System to produce and manipulate its own documents, and to gain access to other files.   .

From the Finder

One of the beauties of the Macintosh System/Finder environment is that you're given instant access to all the files and software from the moment you switch on the computer and the desktop appears as in Figure 2.1. You're only one step away from QuarkXPress, or any other program.

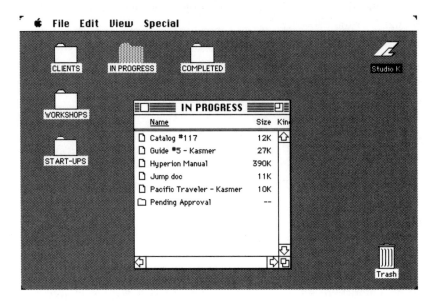

Figure 2.1   *The Macintosh desktop.*

The Macintosh environment provides control through visual representations rather than written commands. Because of this image-oriented approach and because the Mac is the direct interpreter of our commands to the computer processor, it belongs to a class of software known as *graphic user interfaces.* An interface is just the place where two things come together, the way a key connects your hand to a door lock. Often an interface is a way for one thing to control the thing it meets.

We can control the Mac through the desktop interface. We can also control it through a program interface such as QuarkXPress. Here we can handle graphics as well as nongraphic things like words and numbers in a graphic, I-see-you way. It allows for desktop publishing and design. And it allows for QuarkXPress.

The Macintosh and QuarkXPress

Several graphic controls operate in the Macintosh interface and in every Macintosh program. In this, as in every graphic user interface, you often make choices about objects. These objects can be files, programs, circles, words, nearly anything that can be represented visually.

The first step in working with any graphic user interface object is usually to select the object in question. The universal method for selecting is to position the pointer or tool over the object and click. Sometimes dragging the cursor through or over the object will select it. The object will normally indicate its being selected in some obvious way. For instance, the header title bar on a window may change appearance, small handles may appear on a graphics square, or text characters may turn light on dark background, as in Figure 2.2.

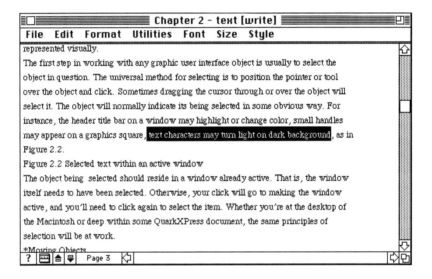

Figure 2.2   *Selected text within an active window.*

The object being selected should reside in an already active window. That is, the window itself needs to have been selected. Otherwise, your click will go to making the window active, and you'll need to click again to select the item. Whether you're at the desktop of the Macintosh or deep within some QuarkXPress document, the same principles of selection will be at work.

Moving Objects

To relocate objects, first click to select as above, then (holding the mouse button down) move the mouse so as to make the object move on screen. For instance, you can move any window, just as the QuarkXPress window is about to be shifted downward in Figure 2.3. In moving a window, grab it by the top title bar with the pointer on the screen (also called a *tool*, or a *cursor*) as shown.

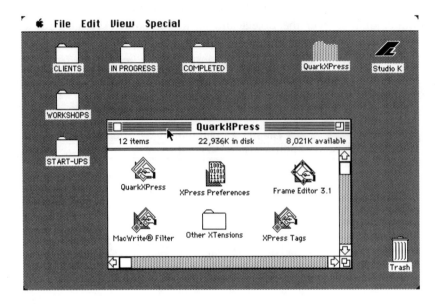

Figure 2.3 *Repositioning the QuarkXPress folder window.*

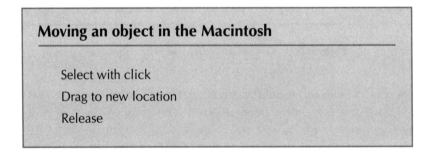

Moving an object in the Macintosh

Select with click

Drag to new location

Release

Virtually everything that can exist on the Macintosh desktop—files, objects, and command menus, appears in a window display. Note all the windows open in Figure 2.4. When you open a folder or group of files by double-clicking, a window appears. If a folder exists within that window, it can be opened also, and so on.

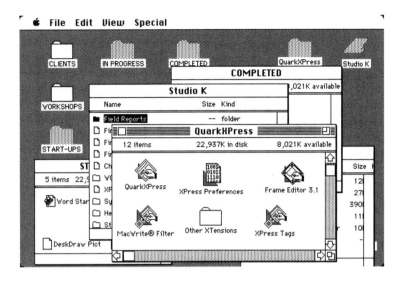

Figure 2.4   *Open folders on the Desktop.*

Objects can exist in the space extending beyond a visible window. To view them (or pull then into the window's purview) use the scroll bars at the bottom for horizontal shifting of view, or the one on the right for vertical shifting. Clicking the mouse with pointer over the **Arrow** buttons will slide the viewing window over the larger conceptual space previously out of view, as in Figure 2.5. The view will also slide when you click at either side of the small box in the scroll bar, or when you point the mouse arrow at the scroll box, hold down the mouse button and drag it one way of the other. These methods come in handy especially when looking for a file in a folder full of file icons.

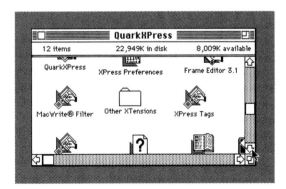

Figure 2.5   *Using scrolls bars in a window.*

Scrolling window views

Click **Scroll Bar** arrow

or

Drag **Scroll Bar** box

or

Click in **Scroll Bar** outside box

Objects, including windows, can be sized larger or smaller. To widen a window for instance, point the arrow cursor carefully at the lower right-hand corner as in Figure 2.6. Notice the flicker in the window as you click. This is a signal that you can drag the mouse in any direction. You can pull out or squeeze in the height and width concurrently, one way larger, or the other way smaller. Just drag by holding down the mouse button and moving the mouse to bring the box to new dimensions.

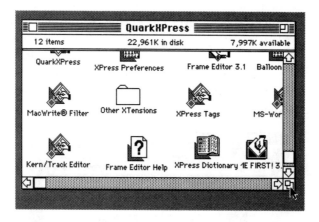

Figure 2.6   *Resizing a Window.*

In programs like QuarkXPress, when an item is selected, small handle boxes appear at the sides and corners. These may be pulled using the mouse in a simi-lar way to resize the item, as in Figure 2.7. There the picture box of a digitized image is being enlarged toward the right by a Pointing Hand cursor to display the whole image. The Tool cursor may change appearance depending on the object or the program, but the effect is essentially the same.

Figure 2.7 *Resizing a picture item.*

Sizing objects

Position pointer (on side or corner handle) until it becomes a sizing tool

Drag to new shape and size

The graphic interface succeeds so well because the computer can talk back to you about commands you give. It can ask for details, warn you of some impending loss, or ask your confirmation. This feedback process is accomplished through boxes like the one in Figure 2.8. Through a question-response format you engage in a dialog with the software at work. These are *dialog boxes*. Your response can be given using the mouse tool and the keyboard. Often it's very simple like **OK** or **Cancel**. Other times you might specify further details.

Software control buttons like those in the figure are a way of choosing among alternative replies. When clicked with the mouse pointer, decisions are compiled for the program. Items can be chosen by name in a dialog box from a list by clicking, or specified by typing in at the keyboard. When you've made all your specifications, you normally send them together by clicking an **OK** button. Or you can say, Forget this whole conversation, by clicking a **Cancel** button.

In the later sections more uses of graphic interface techniques will be elaborated. Mainly, we'll be looking at working within QuarkXPress.

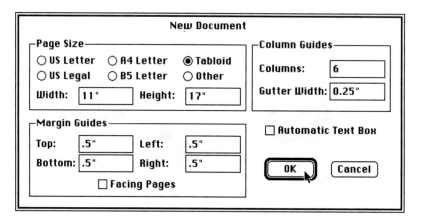

Figure 2.8 *A QuarkXPress dialog box.*

Installing QuarkXPress into the Macintosh

Setting up QuarkXPress on your system is an easy process. It requires a few items: the QuarkXPress Installation disks and computer configured to certain minimum standards as recommended by Quark, Inc.

To install QuarkXPress onto your hard disk, simply make sure the desktop is visible and insert QuarkXPress Installation Disk #1 into the floppy disk drive.

Next comes one of those rare instances when I recommend you blindly follow orders from a piece of software. But since it's for installation, this should happen only once.

The installation procedure is largely a matter of inserting the appropriate disk when directed by the dialog boxes that appear. First you'll be led through some dialog boxes that set up your registration file. Then the User Registration Disk will be requested. And later other disks will be asked for. This will involve swapping disks in the floppy drive. You have some options that can customize the organization of the QuarkXPress folders and files. Let's explore what they are.

Decisions During Installation

Unless you know why you want to customize the installation of the program, I would recommended you follow the defaults, by clicking **OK**. Customizing involves dialogs with the installation software to specify paths different from the default.

These choices determine which files will be copied into the hard drive's QuarkXPress folder. They include files that work in close cooperation with the main engine of QuarkXPress, the file, QuarkXPress, about two and a half megabytes in size. Some files such as the dictionary are crucial for hyphenation, others such as the filters are needed to import or export text.

Other files add functionality in different ways. These are known as *Extensions*, which link up with the main application to perform a variety of duties. Included in QuarkXPress 3.2 is the Efi Color XTension, a color managment addition. You can also locate other extensions from Quark, Inc. and third-party vendors and add them to your system as needed.

At the time of installation you'll encounter dialog boxes that ask you to choose which files to install. Among the decisions are which word processing filters to install. These determine the kinds of file formats that will be made accessible for importing to a QuarkXPress document and which formats will be available for exporting text. If you don't know which to use, allow them all to be installed. If, however , you have a closed, totally controlled system, you may wish to select only the filters for the word processors active on the system. These files take up relatively little space, so excluding them will save only a few kilobytes of disk space. Other files here store preferences and defaults that you can establish from inside the program. The QuarkXPress Help files are stored here also.

The User Registration disk is a blank used to store information about your system, and to register the program with its publisher, Quark, Inc. After installation, you can send it back to Quark, Inc. to register. When installation is complete, you see a message indicating so. Click **OK** and you're out of the procedure.

Note that installing does not simply copy the software onto your hard drive. It creates directories and files. Now you are ready to run QuarkXPress in your system. To do that, begin at the QuarkXPress folder in the desktop.

To QuarkXpress

When QuarkXPress has been installed, you can find the files in place on your hard drive. An icon will exist in the program folder. You can double-click on it to initiate the program.

Whenever you start QuarkXPress, the System runs the program file, QuarkXPress, found in the program folder. You can open this folder window so as to have access to it for easy program starting. Another arrangement you might try is to drag the program file out onto the desktop. This location makes it easy to find. However, you'll notice that the program can't find its Preferences file and will offer to create a new one.

Starting QuarkXPress

Locate QuarkXPress icon
Double-click on it

An alternative way to arrange for start-up is to create a document, which you save in a convenient location, an IN PROGRESS folder for instance. You can also drag a start-up document to the desktop without interfering with the Preferences file. You then double-click on this document and proceed with a new document or use **Save As** to create one, as we'll soon see.

If your work sessions usually involve the same set of programs, such as QuarkXPress, a word processor, and a graphics application, you might want to group three start-up files inside a start-up folder for easy access.

Basic Dialog Controls in QuarkXPress

If you've worked extensively in the Macintosh, you're already familiar with the types of dialog box controls you'll encounter in QuarkXPress. Some of these are shown in Figure 2.9 where a Save As dialog box is displayed. It includes a list of files contained under the folder above it. Within this kind of dialog you can navigate to different listings by opening a folder within the list, or clicking on the list heading and choosing a folder of interest.

The box below the list will accept whatever you type into it. Below it are two round icons that act as radio buttons, that is, in the manner of the older-style automotive radios in which only one button can be activated at any time. To the right in this box are **Standard** buttons that when not shown in grey are available and send a command to QuarkXPress. This is similar to the type of scheme you'll see used in the program to find, open, import, and otherwise deal with files.

Still other types of dialog controls will appear. For instance, the Rules dialog box, as shown in Figure 2.10, displays checkboxes that can be left blank as in the upper half of the figure, or into which can be clicked an X, as in the lower half of the figure. In this case, putting an X into the checkbox expands the dialog box to reveal even more options.

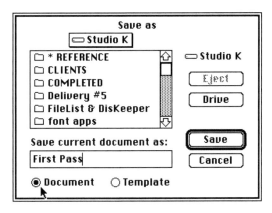

Figure 2.9 *A dialog box with listing, field, button, and radio button controls.*

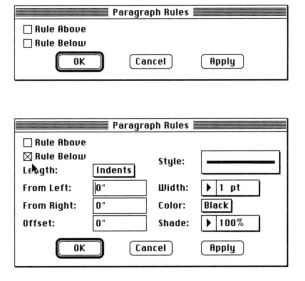

Figure 2.10 *A QuarkXPress dialog box with checkboxes.*

The Mouse Tools

The mouse is a vital player in QuarkXPress. You know that to start any program, you point the mouse cursor on its icon and double-click. To open a group window, you double-click on its folder with the mouse pointer. In fact, to open any folder you just point and double-click. The mouse is also used move files and folders as you've seen, as in dragging a file from one folder to another, in other words, point and click-drag to new location.

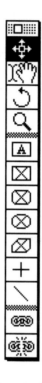

Figure 2.11 *Mouse tools in QuarkXPress.*

In QuarkXPress you can use the mouse to pick out other tools to replace the pointer so familiar to the desktop. By clicking on these tools in a special palette, you effectively make the mouse become that tool. The 14 mouse tools are shown in the Tool palette of Figure 2.11. You might count just 13 icons. One of the tools doubles as two according to the duality inherent in QuarkXPress items. You'll see more on these tools beginning in Chapter 3.

Program Switching

Getting down to business in desktop publishing, we eventually find ourselves switching between programs. No one software package does it all. We all mentally assemble wish lists for the next version of whatever software we're using most. No matter how beautifully implemented the features of a program, it is only natural to think, "If only it did this one other thing."

The demands of design goals frequently govern which software we choose to use. QuarkXPress can do word processing, but it's not a great word processor. It can create simple graphics and manipulate elaborate ones; but it's clearly not a graphics program. So we use a word processor and one or more graphics generators.

But, even with this much of our software hunger satisfied, we really want—in our heart of hearts—one giant superprogram (fully customizable) that would provide every tool and ability we'll ever use. And we'd want all these features accessible at the same time. Having to quit your desktop publishing program to start up your graphics program just doesn't make the grade when you want instant revision on the document page. One consequence of the evolution of the Macintosh system is the ability to switch between software. By taking advantage of two features, one in each environment, you can cojoin your software into what is the functional equivalent of a superprogram.

How you do program switching will depend on the configuration of your system. There are three basic ways. You may use desk accessories that appear from under the Apple menu, you might run the Multifinder application in the System 6.x series, or you might work multitasking from System 7.x. Although capabilities vary greatly among these three circumstances, the effect is to keep one program available in the background while another is being used actively.

The result is that both QuarkXPress and a graphics program can be made to run at the same time; and a word processor, a database, and type manipulation software can as well. You can switch between applications very quickly without shutting down your document file. In the case of graphics, QuarkXPress can be instructed to seek out a graphics source file previously imported into the document and to update the changes into the document.

So, if looking at the document page, you see clearly that the background of the Page One photo should be digitally airbrushed, you can switch to a graphics program, make the change, switch back to QuarkXPress and specify an update, and you'll see the photo on the document page now airbrushed. You could just as easily make major changes to a text file in your word processor and re-import the revised text without quitting either program.

Onward

Coming through the domain of the Macintosh System and Finder, we're now ready to arrive in the QuarkXPress environment. From this point on, each effort you make to understand the program will take you into further control over text, graphics, and layout. If you've been working with typesetting or desktop publishing software already, you'll still be pleased by some of the things you can do with the features and tools we'll encounter.

Focusing on maximizing QuarkXPress-based functionality as we have here, space precludes exploring the many more options that are possible in the Macintosh system.

Next, in Chapter 3, you'll get a grasp on working with QuarkXPress documents. You'll see how you can create, navigate your way around, manipulate pages, and use the control devices so well designed in this software. We're going to proceed with a still more practical approach so that in a very short time you'll have mastered the document file.

Working with Documents

What you will learn in this chapter:

- ❖ How to create, locate, and open documents
- ❖ How to set up guides
- ❖ How to adjust and use page views
- ❖ How to use tools and palettes
- ❖ How to position pages and page elements

Like mighty oaks, designs and publications grow from humble beginnings. In QuarkXPress everything starts in a one-page document, which can grow to as many as 2,000 pages. They can be as small as a one-inch square to as large as a two- by four-foot banner. This chapter explores the terrain on which all documents come into being and on which they are refined and expanded. You will see how to create document files of any dimension, and of varying page lengths, how to locate exactly any part of your QuarkXPress project, and how to view pages at virtually any magnification or reduction you can use.

Here you will also learn how to choose the right tools for working on the visual elements in your document and just how to control and monitor these elements by using palettes. Your explorations in this chapter will give you control over every region of any document you may produce.

You Are Here

Start QuarkXPress, then look at the screen immediately displayed. It reveals much about the program, even when a document is not yet present. You can see major controls for working with documents, as shown in Figure 3.1. Virtually every manipulation, adjustment, creation, revision, modification, activity, movement, deletion, addition, enhancement, and change can be achieved through one of the interface components displayed in the program window at this time. In fact, in themselves, the menu bar, the tool box, and the Measurements palette, as these parts are known, make up the controls used to apply virtually to every feature of QuarkXPress.

Note, for example, the small window at the right of the program window. This *Document Layout* window is a key to managing pages in a document. At the left, the vertical box, called the *Tool palette*, offers three groups of mouse-driven tools for creating, manipulating, and linking elements. Above both of them the familiar menu bar provides access to a multitude of functions within the program.

That long, horizontal blank box at the bottom of the window is a versatile type of layout device called the *Measurements palette*. It both controls and monitors orientations, characteristics, and dimensions of type and graphics. As you change aspects of one element or another, the values displayed there reflect that change instantly. This palette provides a speedy, precise feedback approach to page layout, as you will see.

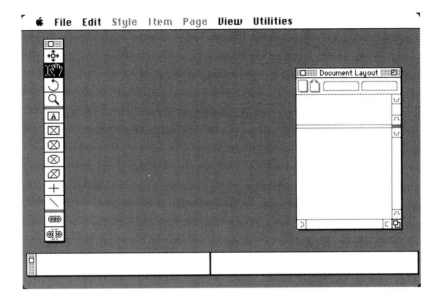

Figure 3.1   *The first layer of the QuarkXPress interface.*

Creating a Document

In QuarkXPress each new document starts from but a single page. At first the command for a new document presents a dialog box as shown in Figure 3.2. Dialog boxes offer such a clear way to exchange information, they are used frequently by the program. In this case the dialog shows you a preselected publication format and asks you to either accept it or to change the format parameters to something you will accept.

The steps for creating a new document are simple. First, open the File menu and highlight **New**, then slide over the pinter to **Document**. The dialog appears displaying the default, or prechosen, parameters. To accept them, click **OK**. Note that as you create new documents QuarkXPress automatically gives them temporary names, **Doc1**, **Doc2**, **Doc3**, and so on. (They're not yet saved to disk though.)

If, on the other hand, you want to customize the publication format, consider each aspect of this dialog box with an eye to the publication page you wish. You'll notice several things.

Under the Page Size section, five standard page formats are indicated by software buttons. The dimensions of each will be displayed in the Width and

Height boxes as you click on their **Radio** buttons. You can key in your own custom dimensions from one inch by one inch to 48 inches by 48 inches. (Inches are only one of several possible units of measurement that are available. We'll look into preferences later.)

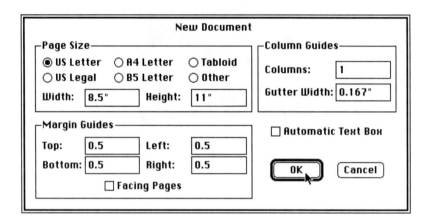

Figure 3.2   *The New Command dialog box.*

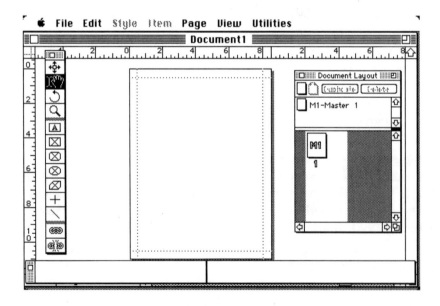

Figure 3.3   *Margin guides visible on the document page.*

The Margin Guides section of the dialog deals with the boundaries of the active page area. These guides can be displayed on the screen as in Figure 3.3, but will not print. They help form a visual framework during layout. In some cases they also provide for automatic text layout. You can specify any combination of the four margins that will fit on the page size selected.

The **Facing Pages** checkbox determines how the Left and Right margin guides will be treated, and how the pages of a multipage document can be displayed onscreen. When checked, Left and Right margin choices are replaced with **Inside** and **Outside** choices.

Pages beyond Page One in a facing pages document are displayed in page spreads (pages 2 and 3, 4 and 5, etc.) rather than singly.

N O T E

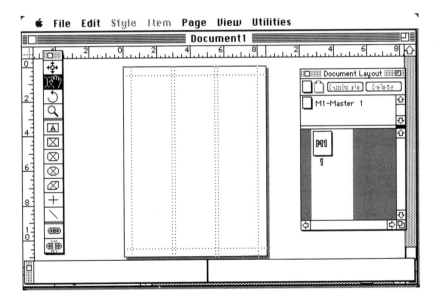

Figure 3.4   *Column guides displayed.*

Column guides are like margin guides in that they appear in the document onscreen as in Figure 3.4, but they do not print. They in no way constrain your layout, acting only as visual cues. Here you can choose the number of column markers to be laid out automatically as part of a grid. They will be spaced equally within the area defined by the margin guides selected above. You can also specify the space between columns in the field labeled Gutter Width.

The **Automatic Text Box** feature can facilitate flowing text within columns through the installation of a partitioned text box. It also puts a similar text box (which we will explore in greater depth in Chapter 4) on the hidden master page, which accompanies and defines page 1. This master page is automatically named Master A. You can derive other pages from Master A; they will have the same column characteristics as page 1. Such a feature becomes extremely useful in typesetting book-length documents. Master pages are explained in detail in Chapter 10.

When you set up a customized document format by making revisions to the New dialog box, these specifications are saved as the default and used for the next document created through the **New** command.

Opening Existing Documents

More often than not desktop publishing projects will require you to revise, update, or expand documents already in existence. Since QuarkXPress can handle several different document windows simultaneously, you can transfer elements, groups of elements, or designs directly from one to another. Each new or existing document opens in its own window beneath the menu bar, overlapping any windows already open. Figure 3.5 shows three such documents open in the program, each at a different view. They have been arranged by adjusting their dimensions and then positioning by moving through the title bars.

Document files can be opened in any of several ways. The setup and organization of your system and folders may vary, and with it, the exact steps for opening from existing files. But one method is fairly consistent; that is opening from within QuarkXPress itself.

The steps here vary only according to where the desired files are located. Begin by opening the File menu in QuarkXPress, and choosing **Open**. An Open dialog box will appear as in Figure 3.6. There is one simple approach to follow. Using the Open dialog box, you hunt through the folders for the file as we saw in Chapter 2. When you locate the document file in the file window, just double-click on it to open. This is quick to describe, but not always as fast to do, depending on how many folders stand between you and the file you seek.

Documents can only be opened one at a time. So if you want more than one, you'll need to repeat either of the opening procedures above for each file.

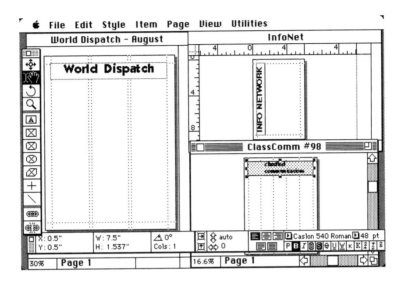

Figure 3.5 *Three documents opened in QuarkXPress.*

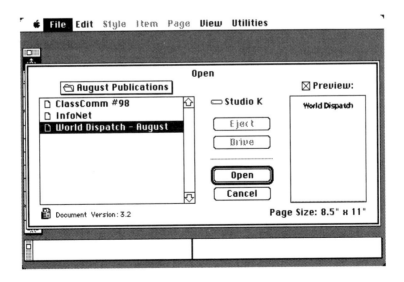

Figure 3.6 *Opening a document through the dialog box.*

Adjusting Document Windows

The documents you open, like documents you create, typically appear in the overlapping fashion of Figure 3.7, most recent being uppermost and shifted slightly down and right of the previous window. This is called *stacking documents*. One of the commands under the View window, Window submenu, will do just that, **Stack Documents**.

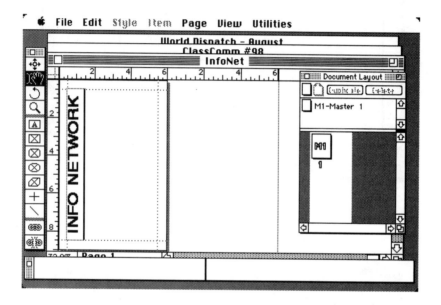

Figure 3.7   *Multiple documents stacked.*

Clearly there are times when you want to see parts of more than one document at the same moment. When this happens, note that you can adjust document windows using the usual methods for adjusting windows.

You can also use commands under the Window submenu (see Figure 3.8) to automatically rearrange open document windows in a different way. The choice, **Tile Documents**, will fit all the documents on the screen. Results will vary according to screen size and the number of documents. Three documents are shown tiled in Figure 3.9.

In the lower half of the windows submenu, you'll find a listing of all the documents currently open. The one indicated by a checkmark is the active window. You can switch to another document window by just selecting another name on that list. If that document is obscured, as under stacked windows, it will be lifted to the front-most level.

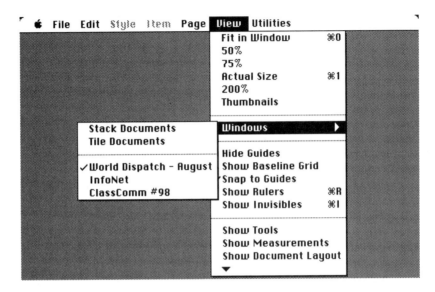

Figure 3.8   *The Windows submenu.*

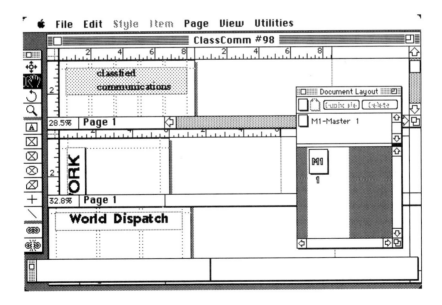

Figure 3.9   *Effect of the Tile Documents command.*

Saving Documents

You save documents in a procedure similar to the **Opening** procedure. QuarkXPress labels new documents as **Document1**, **Document2**, and so on, depending on how many new files are already opened. To give your document a descriptive title, open the File Menu, choose **Save**, and key in a file name (following the usual Macintosh limit of conventions).

 You might like to save copies of your documents at different stages of completion as you progress, giving slightly differing names to each stage, such as **stage1**, **stage2**, **stage3**, or **January mag**, **February mag**, **March mag**. If you are experimenting with different layouts, consider saving a file for each major change in order to have various fall-back versions to return to, if necessary.

N O T E

To save a document under a different name or in a different folder or disk location, open the File Menu, choose **Save As**, and proceed as above, either changing the name, the directory, or disk path name in which the document file is saved.

Changing Page Dimensions

When much layout work has already gone into a document, a change in the page size should be undertaken only after careful consideration. Many hours of layout work can be lost by revising a choice of page size on which elements have been laid out. You can experiment with various page dimensions and aspect (height-to-width) ratios on-screen. But altering the page size is apt to leave already-positioned text and graphics in places not intended. If you reduce the page size drastically enough with large items no longer fitting in the workspace, QuarkXPress may be unable to produce the new smaller size. Take care when changing page size so as to avoid jumbling page elements. We'll see more about how to use the workspace area surrounding the page later.

Changing page set-up itself is simple. Begin by opening the File menu and choosing **Document Setup**. Then select or key in the new format in the dialog box, much as you would chose a format in the New dialog box. At this dialog you can also convert a document to a facing-pages one or a single-sided one.

Standard Page Views on Command

Large format documents like newspapers and diminutive projects like small display advertisements, have one thing in common: at actual size they can be difficult to work with on a typical monitor screen. One won't fit; the other needs magnification. In fact, most documents on which you work will require you to take several different views other than actual size during production.

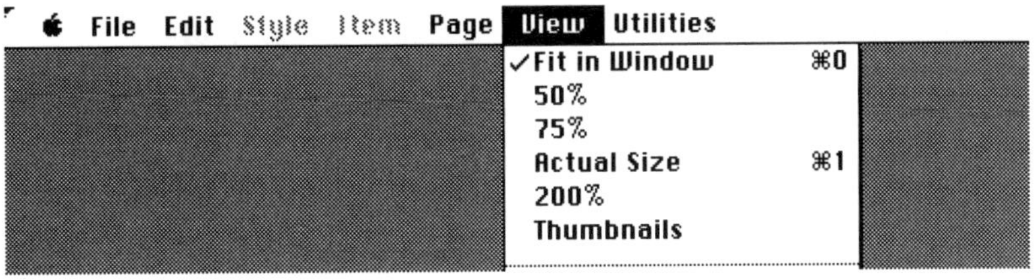

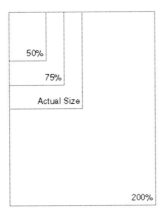

Figure 3.10   The View page magnification choices.

Six ready-set views can be chosen in the View menu, Figure 3.10. Four of these views are based on percentage of actual size—50%, 75%, Actual Size, and 200%. Percentages refer to measuring the proportional change along one side of the page. For example, an 11-inch-long, letter-size page viewed at 50% would appear five and a half inches long. In reality, the page being viewed at 50% is one-fourth the area of actual, but we're following a different convention here. It's the same one used in copy machines. Figure 3.11 shows the relative size comparisons of these four views.

Figure 3.11   Relative sizes of preset views.

Two special views appear in the first section of the View menu. The first, **Fit in Window**, adjusts the display so that a page (or page spread) just fits within the active document window, whatever the size of that window. If you change the size of the window, and then reapply the **Fit in Window** command, the page view will be scaled to fit within the new window dimensions.

The other view, **Thumbnails**, displays a Lilliputian view of several pages at once. This view can be less than 10%, so QuarkXPress doesn't even try to make page elements accessible in it, even though they may be displayed. It's the kind of view you might take if you like to tack the pages of your publication on the wall and look at them from a distance. You can't select or otherwise alter items or contents in it. It's principle values lie in allowing an overview of page geometry and providing a way to assemble multipage spreads, such as three- or four-page centerfolds. We'll see more about the usefulness of this later.

The Pasteboard

Pages can be displayed in such a way as to encompass the surrounding pasteboard workspace. Figure 3.12 shows this space in use during the construction of a page spread. It's a nonprinting part of the document where you can temporarily shuffle any design elements you want off the page while you're assembling your layout. Leave items there, and they will never print; overlap them, and only the part on the page will print.

The pasteboard serves as a handy place to leave notes on a page in progress. Separate pasteboard spaces accompany each page or spread. The relative extent of the pasteboard can be seen clearly in Thumbnail view. A thin line encloses it and its pages.

Viewing pasteboard with pages

    Option + Fit in window

To see all the pasteboard while being able to work with elements there, open the View menu and hold down the **Option** key as you choose **Fit in Window**.

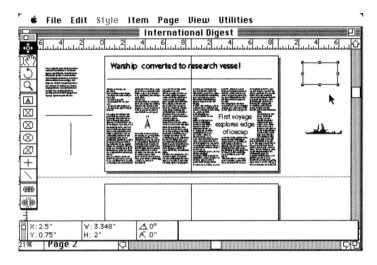

Figure 3.12   *A page spread and its pasteboard in use.*

Controlling Page Views by Direct Entry

As you choose page views, you might notice numbers changing in a small box at the lower left of the active window. This value, **percent view**, reflects precisely the percent size view currently applied. Note this **View Percent** field to the left of the horizontal scroll bar and page number display in Figure 3.13. It provides a feedback means for magnifying or reducing page view with precision. You can use it to change the view to any percentage you prefer from 10% to 400%. Using it, you can zoom in or out precisely as you might by monitoring the focal length numbers on a camera's telephoto zoom lens.

To use the **View Percent** field, aim the cursor over it, double-click to select the value already there, then key in your preferred view, in percentage, in its place. Press the **Return** key. The screen will redraw the window in the new magnification or reduction.

The QuarkXPress Workshop

As a workshop where publications and designs are created and modified, QuarkXPress handles the basic materials including pages and the text and graphic elements placed onto them. Gain a solid grasp of QuarkXPress tools and devices, and you can produce excellent results on nearly any layout.

Figure 3.13 *View percentage field.*

Precision percentage views

Double-click value in percentage view display

Key in new percentage

Return key

The tools and many of the features of the program appear through various palettes. These, like painters' palettes, provide a means for changing the document canvas you're working on. Since these palettes take space on the screen, you'll find times when they're best left out of sight. Normally on opening a new document, the program automatically displays the three palettes, the Tools palette, the Measurements palette, and the Document Layout palette. Displaying or removing palettes from the screen is a simple matter through the View menu. All the **Show/Hide** commands under this menu instantly display or conceal the feature in question. These are *toggle* commands. As such, they alternate states between **Show** and **Hide**.

Each palette is a small window itself, and so can be moved by dragging from the title (or other) bar found at its top or left side.

NOTE

The Tools and Measurements Palettes

We can think of text and graphics as items that can be manipulated and revised. As such, they are created, imported from other files, moved about on a page, moved over or behind other items, moved between pages, stretched, shrunk, and otherwise altered. The Tool palette contains tangible devices for handling text and graphic items. Tools from this palette initiate nearly every manipulation performed on an item. Working first with one of the simplest tools demonstrates many of the ways all tools function.

Using a Tool

In laying out publication pages one of the most indispensable graphics elements has proven to be the humble rule. As horizontal or vertical lines that typically separate text on the page, rules are perfect for helping to organize a page. Quark has dubbed the tool that makes these lines "the orthogonal line tool." But Rule tool will describe it just as well. It draws only horizontal or vertical lines regardless of how you drag the mouse. The lines in Figure 3.14 were drawn with the Rule tool by dragging in various nonhorizontal and nonvertical directions.

The Rule tool shares operational features common to the other tools. The first step in all tool use is to select the tool. To select the Rule tool, click on the fourth button from the bottom of the Tools palette; it appears on the **Crosshairs** button indicated in Figure 3.14. By moving the mouse onto the Document window area you'll see the cursor become a similar set of crosshairs.

SHORTCUT

Two easy ways to choose tools are available through the keyboard. To move the tool selection from one tool to the one below it, hold the **Command** key and press **Tab**. Each time you press, tool selection moves downward (you'll see the button appear highlighted). **Command-Tab** at the bottom-most (the Unlink or Broken Chain) tool shifts selection to back up to the first, the Item tool. **Command-Tab** cycles through all the tools like this. To cycle in the other direction, upward, hold both **Command** and **Shift** keys while pressing **Tab**; selection then moves upward, switching at the Item tool down to the Unlink tool. Note that if the Tool palette is hidden either **Command-Tab** or **Command-Shift-Tab** will display it onscreen.

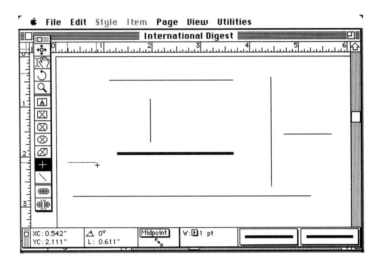

Figure 3.14 *Lines drawn using the Rule tool.*

The second step in tool use is to apply the tool. Depending on the task at hand, this may mean selecting an existing item, or making a new item. In this case we are creating a rule by drawing it. To draw a rule, press the mouse button and drag from start to finish. Then release the button. This tool works only in the horizontal or vertical direction. Even if your hand wavers, the tool will draw a line wholly in the horizontal or vertical direction. You will see the long, horizontal Measurement palette appear along the bottom when you release. Also, the cursor will change automatically to the Content tool once the rule is drawn.

Selecting tools from the keyboard

Command-Tab to move downward through buttons, or to show palette

Command-Shift-Tab to move upward

Using a Measurements Palette

When any item is created or moved, its Measurements palette normally appears on the screen. Each of the three kinds of items in QuarkXPress—line, picture box, or text box—will activate its own Measurements palette when that item is selected. In fact, you can think of each individual item as having its own Measurements palette which can be displayed when the item is selected. Consider the last line drawn in Figure 3.15, under the nameplate, *International Digest*; it is still selected. The Measurements palette for it appears at the bottom of the program window.

Figure 3.15   *A just-drawn rule with its Measurements palette active.*

At the left side of this palette you will find the x and y coordinates for one end point of the line. (These coordinates are the measurements along the horizontal ruler at the top of the window, X, and along the vertical ruler at the left of the window, Y.) Just to the right in the palette, are coordinates displayed for the other end.

Then comes the method of measuring, in this case from end to end. Across the heavy center partition in the Measurements palette you'll find the line weight in points. And further we see a drop-down list for line types—dotted, dashed, double, and so on, as shown open in Figure 3.16. The final drop-down list indicates the arrows on the line, in this case none are applied (Figure 3.17).

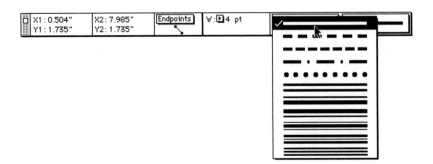

Figure 3.16 *Measurements palette Line Type list activated.*

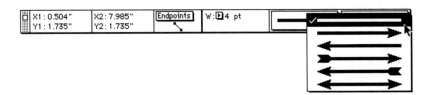

Figure 3.17 *Measurements palette Arrows Option list activated.*

As other kinds of items come onto the scene, we will see that their associated Measurements palettes are each somewhat different. But the most significant aspect of all these palettes can be demonstrated readily in this line palette. To understand that feature consider the following: The values shown are really a part of a feedback loop. They describe the item selected and can be changed with great precision. To change a value in the Measurements palette is to change that characteristic in the item itself. At the moment we are talking about changing the item features, not its contents.

Here's how to modify or otherwise change an item in general through a Measurements palette: First check that the item highlighted is the one you want to change. (A large portion of the errors made in documents can be avoided simply by assuring that the selection is appropriate.) Next, move the cursor to the palette and highlight the value you wish to change, then type in the value you desire. For features with a drop-down list, make your choice by opening and highlighting a choice from the list. Do this for all the values you wish to change. Finally, press **Return** to apply the new values to the item.

By keying in a new **X1** of **.75 inch** and a new **X2** of **7.75 inches**, and a new weight of **6**, and choosing a different line type, we have shortened, thickened and redefined the nameplate rule as shown in Figure 3.18.

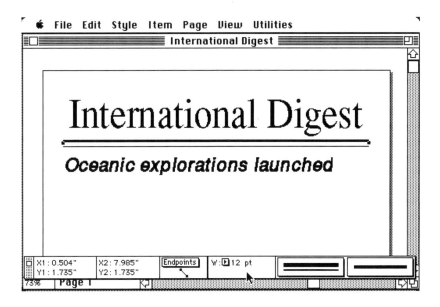

Figure 3.18   *A rule edited through the Measurements palette.*

When you try this yourself, you'll notice the speed and precision inherent in using this palette for rule revision.

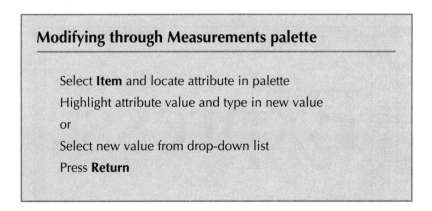

Modifying through Measurements palette

Select **Item** and locate attribute in palette

Highlight attribute value and type in new value

or

Select new value from drop-down list

Press **Return**

Keep in mind that this very special instant feedback relationship between items and their measurements palettes holds true for every item in every document.

N O T E

Page Views by Tool

Tools provide clever alternatives to effect many modifications possible through other means, such as menu commands. Sometimes they offer a measure of control not easy otherwise, or make possible a useful try-it-out approach.

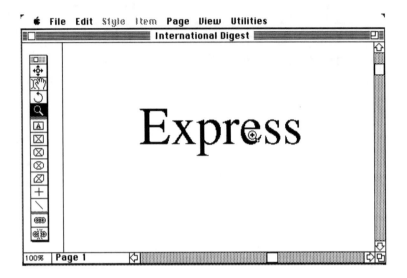

Figure 3.19 *Magnifying with clicks of the Zoom tool.*

For instance, consider the Zoom tool. This is one (fourth down in the Tools palette) specifically designed for changing views. Clicking with it changes the view in preset increments. (The default increment is 25%.) It also allows you to magnify or reduce the view around a particular point on the page. Further, with it you can indicate an area to be magnified to the full extent of the window.

Here's how it adjusts view by increments. When you select the Zoom tool, you'll notice a magnifying glass cursor with a plus sign in the center when it's over the Document window. Position it over the area of interest and click. The window will redraw in a view magnified 25% over the previous view. Click again, and the view magnifies another 25%. Notice that this method seems to anchor whatever point is under the cursor, as in Figure 3.19, where we clicked three times inside the letter e to magnify from 100% to 125% to 150% to 175%.

Magnifying view with Zoom tool

Position tool over point to anchor

Click repeatedly until magnification is achieved

Reducing magnification works the same way, except you hold down the **Option** key while clicking. A minus sign appears inside the lens of the tool cursor. The window will redraw to a view reduced by 25%. You can notice these view changes in the percentage view box near the horizontal scroll bar.

Reducing view with Zoom tool

Position tool over point to anchor

Hold **Option** key and click repeatedly until reduction is achieved

---

NOTE

The limits of view magnification/reduction are 10% to 400%.

The Zoom tool permits one other method of view change, that of *magnifying by area*. This technique is both precise and powerful. Here's how it works. Let's say we are looking at the page in the document window of Figure 3.20. Notice the view is at **Fit in window**, in this case 37.2%. Now suppose you want to look closely at the illustration of the ship, that is, you want to enlarge the view to fill the window with the ship. You can do this in one precise step with the Zoom tool. The procedure is as follows: press the mouse button and drag until the dotted box covers just the area of interest. As you're doing this, notice how the percentage value indicator in the corner box changes. It's keeping pace with the percentage view the dotted box calls for if it is to fill the window. When you've enclosed the area to be magnified, let go of the button. The subject will fill the screen as in Figure 3.21.

Figure 3.20 *Choosing an area to fill the window.*

Precision magnification with Zoom tool

Choose rectangular area to magnify

Position Zoom tool at one corner

Drag diagonally to create enclosing box

Release

Figure 3.21 *A precise Zoom tool magnification.*

Moving About the Page

As you may be starting to suspect, very often you can do some things in more than one way in QuarkXPress. Moreover, some functions interact with other functions. This is part of the richness of the program. The overlap and interaction, though, can sometimes be confusing at first. But the more of the program you see in operation, the more each implementation makes sense.

In desktop publishing we're always changing what we're looking at. Quite simply, as visual communicators, we're seldom satisfied with just one look at a design or layout. We insist on seeing close up, at arm's length, or across the room. We sometimes want to focus on one area, other times on another. Over and over we look until we're convinced that the design, the page, or the ad works as it should. Page view and page movement are changes we make over and over, so we want them to become second nature.

Going from one part of a page to another really means encompassing different areas within the purview of the window. If magnification remains unchanged, this is a simple move. You can think of moving the new area inside the frame of the window, or of moving yourself (as a viewer behind the window frame) over a stationary page.

There are two basic ways to accomplish a simple move. One is to use the scroll bars, in the way common to Windows and most Windows applications. This approach can become a bit tedious if the distance of the move or the magnification is large. After all, it requires separate adjustments to move in horizontal and vertical directions. Added complications arise in multipage documents. There, large moves on the vertical scroll bar can send you far off to other pages in the document.

Figure 3.22 *The Grabber Hand made active through the* **Option** *key.*

Another, more versatile method involves bringing out the Grabber Hand. This is one of the hidden tools. From any cursor tool already selected, with the exception of the Zoom tool, we can make the Grabber Hand appear momentarily. (Remember the Zoom tool switches to a reduced view with the **Option** key prepressed.) The Grabber Hand, which can be seen in Figure 3.22, has the effect of reaching down through the document window, grasping onto the page, and sliding it by as you move the mouse.

To use the Grabber tool, start with any but the Zoom tool selected. Hold down the **Option** key. You'll see the hand cursor appear. Press the mouse button, and drag the page in the direction you wish it to move.

Using the Grabber Hand

With any tool but the Zoom selected, hold the **Option** key
Press mouse button and drag page through window view

The Grabber tool works at any magnification and can even be used for moving the window from page to page.

Positioning Work

As you develop the layout of a publication, you come to rely increasingly on your ability to position page elements at just the right locations. Positioning work requires three capabilities: 1) changing the view or magnification; 2) bringing an area of interest within the window; and 3) shifting an item from one location to another.

Moving an item can be as simple as dragging it from one place to another. Certainly you need this skill. But what if you would like to position the item more precisely than you can easily manage by dragging with the mouse? What if you wish to move several items at once? What if the item's destination is hundreds of pages away from its starting point?

We've already started the answers to these questions by acquiring the abilities to examine at any practical view and to examine any location on the page. We can extend these skills to help us with the task of relocating items from one place to another.

Selecting Items

Not surprisingly, the first step in moving an item is selecting the element to be moved. This can be anything from a box of text, to an elaborate color illustration, to a simple rule. The Selection tool for any element is the same. That tool is the Item tool, uppermost in the Tool palette. Recall that all elements in a document are treated according to their two aspects: the content within them and their status as an item.

To activate the Item tool, point the tool cursor over the uppermost button in the Tool palette and click.

Select with the Item tool by pointing over the item in question, then clicking once. The item will be selected, and small handles will appear around its periphery or ends. (Click just once; double-clicking may engage a QuarkXPress dialog box.) You'll also see the Four Arrows tool cursor appear.

In some cases, at some reduced views or with some small items, you may find it difficult to select the item you want when using this approach. In these hard-to-grasp cases a slight variation is more effective. If you find a rule just too thin to be selected at a reduced view, or you want to grasp several items together, this alternate method will serve well. Both these cases can be handled by enclosing part of the item, or items, in a Selecting box.

To use the selecting box from the Item tool, hold down the mouse button anywhere in open space, drag the resulting dashed box so that it encloses a piece of the item (or items) to be selected as in Figure 3.23, then release. Item handles should appear on all those elements inside the box, signifying selection.

Figure 3.23 *Using the selecting box on several items at once.*

Using the selecting box

With Item tool, drag a box to enclose any part of item(s)

Moving Items: The Drag Method

The direct method for moving a selected item is to drag it to a new location. It's simple: select the item and keep the mouse button pressed. Then drag the cursor, and item to its new position. Release the mouse button to deposit the item.

Dragging is the method common to nearly all graphics applications. Its advantages are that you can see clearly where the item is moving. The method is much like the way we carry real items in the real world. Its disadvantages are that at larger magnifications the drag can take a very long time to cover distances. Depending on the speed of your computer, the screen may redraw each advance of the mouse in a plodding fashion, further slowing the move.

But more important, these moves are only as accurate as your hand movements with the mouse. And don't even think about the time it would take to move a graphic from page 356 up to page 4.

Palette Moves

Have you ever had the frustrating experience of trying unsuccessfully to use a mouse to position a design element? You know exactly where you want it to go. You know your motor coordination is up to the task. But for some reason—it's 3 A.M. before a project meeting at 8 A.M., you're trying to center a half-point line in a one point space, and you just can't seem to get your computer marvel to cooperate—the element won't go right where you need it. These things happen.

When precision becomes important, select the item, and don't try to force your hand-to-eye coordination. Sure, it's challenging. But is it worth a quarter hour or more of trial and error? You'll get better results by turning to the Measurements palette. Recall how we moved the rule in that earlier example. Now consider that the Measurements palette is a feedback device. So, keying in new coordinates will relocate an item.

The coordinates of any item on the page other than lines refers to the upper-left corner of the box that is that item, or that bounds that item. For a text box, that is the upper-left corner, as it is for a picture box. (All text in QuarkXPress exists in a text box; you'll see how in Chapter 4.) Even nonrectilinear items like ovals can be located by the coordinates of the box that would fit around them.

Positioning with the Measurements palette

Select item

Key in new location as **X** and **Y** values

You've seen how to change the location of a rule. Suppose you wanted to move the text box sidebar that's sitting at the lower-left corner of the page in Figure 3.24 to the upper-left corner, within the margins.

To do this, select the box, and release the mouse button. At the Measurements palette double-click on the X coordinate. Key in the value for the new location, in this case, **1.5**. Make a similar adjustment to the Y coordinate, in this case, **1**. Then press **Return**. The item, in this case the text box, will reappear at the new location, even if part of it is out of the window view. In this case the sidebar settles in at X=**1.5 inches**, Y=**1 inch**.

The Measurements palette approach to moving items on the page has the advantage of precision and, often, speed. It requires you to have a sense of where coordinates are on the page. With the help of the rulers displayed top and left in the window, you can pick up this coordinate sense easily as you develop your layout.

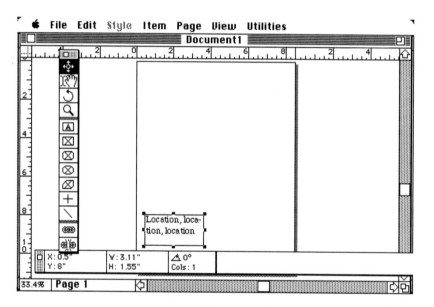

Figure 3.24 *Using the Measurements palette to move an item.*

Moving Multiples

Both of the methods described for moving a single item apply to more than one item. You can select as many items as you wish to move.

To select more than one item, use the Item tool to drag a selection box that intersects the items in question. Dragging a selected set is straightforward enough. Just grab any selected item with the mouse button, and drag the whole set to the new location. Click to release them all.

Alternatively, you can select multiple items individually. To do this, hold down the **Shift** key as you click on each item in turn. They will become selected and stay selected. If you decide to remove any of the items from the selection set, just point and click again with the **Shift** key down. This will deselect the indicated item.

Selecting scattered items

Hold **Shift** key and click on each item
(Deselect with second click)

What about using the Measurements palette with a set of items? Having selected items, you'll notice that the X and Y coordinates in the Measurements palette have changed. Now they reflect the upper-left corner position of the aggregate of items selected. Keeping this in mind, decide where you want the upper-left corner of the set to go, and key in the values in the palette as before.

Manipulating Pages

Adding Pages

Every QuarkXPress document starts as one page. But life seldom stays simple, so assume you will be adding pages. Whether assembling books, newspapers, magazines, company reports, or just augmenting a proposal with a second and third version of that display ad, you'll need additional pages. QuarkXPress will let you add as many as 100 pages at a time. The program tops out at a total document length of 2,000 pages. This covers most contingencies.

The procedure to add pages is this: Open the Page menu and choose **Insert**. In the first field box, key in the number of pages to add. Then click the button indicating relative location (before, after, at end) and key in the page the new page or pages should precede or follow. Before you give the **OK**, check your choices by reading across as a grammatical sentence. If the command reads the way you want your new pages to appear, click **OK**.

For instance, to expand a new document to 32 pages you would set up the dialog to read: " Insert 31 page(s) after page: 1" (as in Figure 3.25).

You can use the Pages menu **Insert** command at any point and repeatedly as necessary to lengthen the document. When you add pages between existing pages, automatic page numbering will be recomputed. One word of caution (which also applies to removing pages below).

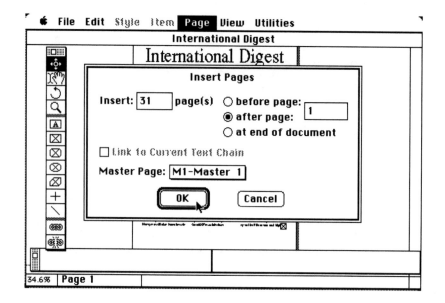

*Figure 3.25   Adding pages using the **Insert** command.*

In facing-pages documents you should consider carefully the effect adding an odd number of pages may have on page spreads downstream. For instance, by bumping them forward unevenly, the new batch-inserted pages can turn your well-designed spreads into so much visual confusion. By doing so you could inadvertently split elements planned for a two-page design into two separated pages.

Removing Pages

Pages can be dropped from a document at any time, but any items laid out on those pages will be lost from the document as well. In fact, even if an item merely overlaps slightly onto the page from the pasteboard (and this is an easy oversight to make), it will be lost. (If a text box has text linked from an earlier page, however, the text will not be lost.)

To remove one or more pages, open the Pages menu and choose **Delete**. Key in the page number, or the numbers for a range of pages, and click **OK**. These pages will drop out, and the subsequent pages that remain will be renumbered. (Note that the warning issued under **Adding** pages about consequences to downstream page spreads applies here too.)

The Document Layout Palette

It's time we considered the Document Layout palette. It mimics the page order you see through the Document window, as in Figure 3.26. You can use it to insert and delete pages, as well as to deal with Master pages (as we shall explore in Chapter 6). Every page in the document is represented here.

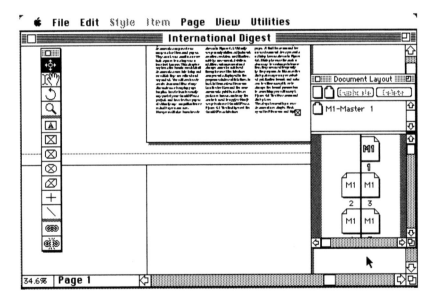

Figure 3.26 *The Document Layout palette mimics the order of pages.*

To remove a page, locate the page icon in the Document Layout palette window, select it by clicking on it, then open the palette's Document menu and choose the **Delete** command as appropriate.You can select a range of pages in this palette by clicking on the icon for one end of the range, then with **Shift** key down-clicking on the icon for the other end. They and all the pages in between will become selected.

You can also select an assorted set of pages that may not be consecutive. Simply **Command-click** on each one in turn. To remove individuals from the selection, **Command-click** again.

Selecting a range of pages in Document Layout

Click on page at one end of range

Scroll to other end in Document Layout

Hold **Shift** key and click on page at other end

Selecting scattered pages in Document Layout

Hold **Command** key and click on each page

(Deselect with second click)

To add one or more pages, you click on one the small page icons at the top of the palette. The uppermost represent plain pages; below them you'll see icons for master pages. (Options regarding master pages will be explained in Chapter 10). You can move the cursor into the window, show the layout of document pages, and click next to a page to add before or after it, or between pages of a spread to insert between them. We'll look deeper into this approach later. It includes a way to build multipage spreads.

Moving to Another Page

Facing a document from 2 to 2,000 pages, you're faced with the simple expediency of how to shift your view to the page you want at the moment. There are four quick ways to move to pages or page spreads out of view of the document window. Whichever you use, keep in mind the following: The document pages, or page spreads, are arranged from first to last one below the other. That is,

Page 1 is above Pages 2 and 3 and so on. So to move through the document in this arrangement, move the window down.

First, you can always call up the Grabber Hand tool. As you can drag parts of a page or pasteboard into view, you can drag pages into view. To do this use the Grabber Hand tool to drag sideways to adjacent spread pages, and upward for higher-numbered, downstream pages (drag downward for lower-numbered upstream pages). This method works well for nearby pages, but proves too slow for skimming through magazines or books, or even that 16-page newsletter.

Moving to adjacent pages by Grabber Hand tool

Hold **Option** key and drag pages through window view

    up to higher numbers

    down to lower

    sideways on spreads

Alternately, you can use the vertical scroll bar as you have on the single page. This works if you can estimate the relative location of the new page on the scroll bar.

Or you can use the Document Layout palette. To do this, bring the page icon in the palette window by the palette scroll bar (which works like every other vertical scroll bar). Double-click on the page you want. It will appear in the document window.

Moving to a page by Document Layout

In the palette scroll to locate page icon
Double-click to bring page into window

You can use a menu command. To do this, open the Page menu and choose **Go to**, then key in the page number you seek. Click **OK**, and the page will appear in the document window.

Moving Items Between Pages

Many elements found in a publication in progress seldom remain on one page for long. Here are two methods for moving items. They both start after you select the item or items in question.

First is the *drag* method. To do this, simply drag the items to their destination page. Clearly, the direct approach works best for neighboring pages.

An alternative is the *cut-and-paste* method. To do this, use the Edit menu choice or the keyboard to give the **Cut** command with the intended items selected. They will disappear off the page into the Clipboard out of sight. Then use any of the methods discussed for moving to another page. Finally, open the Edit menu and choose the **Paste** command at the destination page. Your item or items will appear on the page.

Moving items to distant pages in the document

Select item(s) and at Edit menu choose **Cut**

Locate destination page

At Edit menu choose **Paste**

Onward

Control of items and pages begins control of the document and will speed all your work. As you've seen, you can create new documents at will and open documents as you please. You can locate and view any part of a document you're working on. You can use tools and palettes to fashion items precisely the way you want them. You can locate any item anywhere on any page. By grasping these powerful document maneuvers, you'll have simplified the labor of every document you will ever call up in QuarkXPress.

These major activities affect your work in any document. Remember that you can use the At-a-glance sidebars and procedure highlights in this book for quick recall, while applying techniques to your documents in progress.

With document skills from this chapter, you've reached the point to embark on making use of text in your documents. Text can have the greatest range of variability and can often have the greatest effect of any page element on the reader. The type and text capabilities you will find in QuarkXPress can accentuate, strengthen, and emphasize any message so your design achieves maximum effectiveness. Let's now see how to use type and paragraph controls, search and replace techniques, and file importing and exporting.

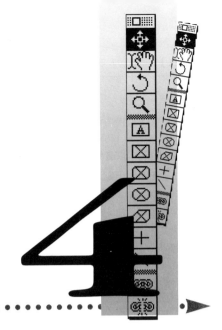

Type and Text Formatting

What you will learn in this chapter:

- ❖ Create and adjust text boxes
- ❖ How to locate and import text
- ❖ Creating exported text files
- ❖ Applying type attributes to text
- ❖ Displaying invisible characters
- ❖ How to find and replace text and invisible characters
- ❖ Formatting paragraphs
- ❖ Using the Measurements palette for formatting
- ❖ Paragraph alignment
- ❖ Kerning and Tracking

63

Type is a messenger. But it always has its own say, adding comments like "This is important! Look further. Take your time. Look how easy. Urgent, read immediately! This is trifling detail. How dignified. Don't miss this!" or a million other things.

Enticement, priority, pacing, emphasis, mood—these are the kind of values type creates. Type carries unstated messages. No text takes the form on a page without these messages accompanying it, whether intentional or accidental. While text attempts to convey information and conceptual meaning, the type in which it is set either supports or subverts these efforts.

QuarkXPress has gained a reputation for extraordinary abilities with type. This chapter shows the fundamentals of controlling type and text in QuarkXPress. You will see how to generate and how to bring text into a document, how to apply typefaces, how to style type, to size it, space it, and generally to distinguish it.

Here also will be found ways to do word processing within QuarkXPress. You'll learn how to use indents, line and character spacing, guides, margins and columns to fashion raw text into the beauty and strength found in a well-set page.

Where Text Lives

As you recall, item/content duality permeates every design element in QuarkXPress. Both text and graphics demonstrate this directly. Simply put, find text or graphics and you'll also find a box containing them. The first step to creating or importing text, then, involves generating a *text box.*

Importing or keying text into a document must be preceded by the creation of a text box, similar to the way passengers are let onto an airplane only after specific seats have been assigned for them. You can create text boxes, or (as we shall see later), you can have QuarkXPress create them. This choice is equivalent to driving text in manual or automatic modes.

Once text boxes are created, they can be resized, relocated, cut, and otherwise modified, except in special circumstances (these exceptions involve master pages, a subject we will cover later). Therefore, they can be treated like an item, with or without text inside them. The text they contain, or will contain, can be treated as typographic contents, capable of being formatted and typeset in its own right. Keeping a clear mind on this distinction between the item nature of text, and its content nature will enable you to exert maximum control over it with relative ease.

Making a Text Box

Let's assume you've chosen the place in your layout where you want some text to appear. It's not crucial that you be exact and final in your idea. Everything we do here can be easily modified after the fact. For text box creation to work smoothly, follow three simple steps: bring the space into view, bring the tool to the space, and drag the text box into existence.

The tool in this case is the Text Box tool; it's displayed on the **Palette** button as a letter A enclosed by a box. Fifth from the top of the Tool palette, as seen in Figure 4.1, it's grouped with similar tools that produce picture boxes and lines. More about these in Chapter 6.

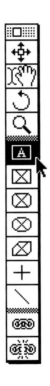

Figure 4.1   *Selecting the Text Box tool at the palette.*

The idea behind making a text box is borrowed from every graphic program you've ever seen. It's the following venerable procedure: hold down the **Mouse** button and drag a box onto the page. As happens with other creation tools, the

Mouse tool takes the form of crosshairs as you pull the it into the document window.

Notice that the moment you bring the tool onto the document window, the faithful Measurements palette begins tracking the X and Y coordinates of the crosshairs.

N O T E

The first step of actually producing the text box is to position these crosshairs at what you imagine would be one corner of the text box. Press the mouse button and drag diagonally to the location you see in your mind's eye as the opposite corner. A box will grow in size proportionally as you do this. Before you release the mouse button, you can pull the box smaller again, or drag it narrower, wider, taller, shorter according to your whim or plan.

Making a text box

Choose Text Box tool

Choose rectangular area in which to place box

Position Text Box tool at one corner of chosen area

Drag diagonally until box fits area chosen

Note that as you're dragging out the box the Measurements palette displays changing **W** and **H** values. These are, as you may have concluded, width and height measurements of the box. If you are seeking precision control from the start, you can keep an eye to these values to fashion the exact box of the dimensions you want. When you release the mouse button, the text box will be in place and selected.

Effects of Creating a Text Box

Simply creating a text box generates sends an avalanche of changes through the document! Four significant alterations can occur immediately as shown in Figure 4.2. A pointing hand replaces the Crosshairs tool at the last-drawn corner of the text box. The new Measurements palette you saw tracking the box during creation replaces any previous one. And, one of the two uppermost tools, the Item tool or the Content tool, will become active. If the Content tool activates, a flashing cursor will appear in the upper-left corner of the box.

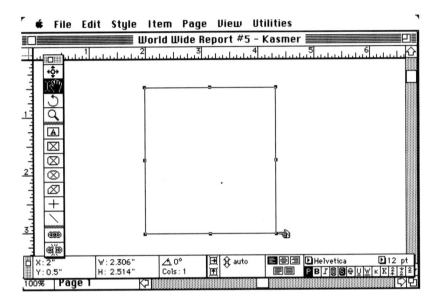

Figure 4.2   *Creating a text box.*

The pointing hand is an automatic tic in tool-text box interaction. Since you've dragged diagonal-to-diagonal the cursor has fallen over a corner point, one of eight that become active when any item box is selected. This box is now selected, ready for content (as evinced by the flashing cursor), but still treatable as an item (as indicated by the pointing hand). That hand appears when any one of several of the tools touches an active box handle. Since the Content tool is selected and touching a corner handle, the hand is ready. Its function is to resize the box. If you wish to now or later, just press the mouse button and drag the text box to a new size and shape.

The Measurements palette you noticed tracking your moves earlier is now monitoring several characteristics of the box, coordinate point of origin (X and Y), height and width (H and W), angle of rotation of the box (0°), and number of columns into which to divide the text.

These are the features of the text box as an item. The values given in the right half of the palette indicate features of the text content within the box. They monitor the typographic characteristics, as we'll soon see.

N O T E Text boxes possess many other features besides the ones shown in the Measurements palette. Some features are of an item nature; some are of content nature. They include *box background color, text run-around, box framing,* and *text inset.* We'll be looking at most of them in later chapters.

The tool selected changes as the program switches automatically to the mode previously selected, **item** or **content**. If the Content tool comes up, the presumption is that since you've just created a text box, you may wish to enter something in it immediately. The flashing cursor is an entry point for text. You're free to ignore the box you've just created and return to it later as you desire. You can, on the other hand, type in from the keyboard and have text appear directly in the box.

Text and the Content Tool

Basically, a text box can accept text through two sources, from the keyboard and from files existing outside the document. In both cases, the box must be in a ready condition before inserting text can proceed. Remember the dictum of tool use we happened on earlier: *Always select first.*

Text inside a box is content. In order to insert text into the box you'll need these two conditions met: the text box should be selected and the Content tool should be active. When this is so, you'll see the selection handles of the box in all four corners and on all four sides, and inside the text box a text cursor will be flashing (or if previously selected, text may be highlighted within the box).

N O T E The Content tool shows up as an arrow until you click on a text box, or pass it over a box already selected. Then, the **I-beam** appears as a text insertion point is designated and the flashing cursor shows up.

When the text box is empty—as it is when it's newly created—the flashing text cursor will normally be found at the top-left corner of the box, as in Figure 4.2.

This reflects the **default** setting for text (left aligned, top justified). All text next inserted will flow from that point onward into the box.

When text is already present, the cursor may, of course, be positioned anywhere within the text. It's location will determine where incoming text is inserted, whether from an imported file, or by keyboard typing.

Keying Text Directly

Let's assume you've just created a text box like the one in Figure 4.2. The box is in a ready condition, the cursor blinking inside it. Let's say you're composing a headline at the keyboard as you're working on layout. In this case, you can type immediately and text will appear starting at the location of the cursor.

In cases where you'd like to enter text into an existing text box, you'll need to first put it in the **ready** condition. Do this by choosing the Content tool, then clicking on the box in question. If the box is empty, the cursor will most often appear at the upper-left corner. Then, as you type, the characters will spill out within the box.

If there is text already in the box, the flashing cursor will be seen where it was placed last, before the box was deselected. If a section of text was highlighted then, this will become highlighted again. Very simply, QuarkXPress remembers. This memory is engineered into most of the functions in the program. Over the course of developing a publication, this seemingly small feature will save you appreciable time and duplication of effort.

Clipboard Text

One variation of the direct keyboard method involves the clipboard. As you may know, the clipboard is a Macintosh-supplied file that works with most applications to temporarily store whatever is **Cut** or **Copied.** That's **Cut** or **Copied,** as in the commands you can give under the Edit menu, or through the keyboard shortcuts Command-X and Command-C, respectively. When you select text and then dispose of it by the **BACKSPACE** key, it does not go to the clipboard. The clipboard can serve as a way of moving text from place to place either inside a document, or between files of different programs. It can be a quick way to paste text segments from a word processor, or even graphics, or other desktop publishing software into QuarkXPress, and vice versa. Of course, you can also use it to do internal document housecleaning like moving text fragments (a sentence, a phrase or paragraph or two) from one text box to another.

When you've loaded the clipboard with the **Cut** or **Copy** command, just select the text box where you'd like to deposit the text as shown above. Assure that the insertion cursor or text selection is where you'd like the text to go. Then open the Edit menu and choose **Paste** (or just give the **Command-V** keystroke. A copy of the clipboard contents floods into the text box.

To move text from one box to another, select it in the first box, open the Edit menu and choose **Cut**. Then select the second box and locate the cursor, open the Edit menu and choose **Paste**.

Clipboard text transfers

Select the text with Content tool and at the Edit menu
   choose **Cut** or **Copy**

Select the recipient text box with Content tool

(Set insertion cursor or selection if necessary)

At the Edit menu choose **Paste**

About File Formats:
Importing and Exporting Text

Most long texts that find their way into a QuarkXPress document will have originated in word processing software. There they will have been saved as a word processing files. Later during the makeup of the publication, you will insert this text into your document. Bringing in file contents from one software into another is known as *importing*.

Just like importing from one country to another this process involves issues of compatibility. If you've made a train journey between France to Spain, you may appreciate the compatibility issue. If you were on the French train heading south at the border you would disembark, hauling yourself and your luggage through to board the waiting Spanish train on the other side to continue onward. The reason was lack of compatibility. The Spanish rails were narrower than the French rails, and so would not accommodate their trains. You could still move the contents of the trains between countries, but not in the carriages they started in, and it was a lot more work.

QuarkXPress deals with text file compatibility by using individual files known as *filters* that in essence make the trains from one set of rails fit on the other set. These filters decode formatting and type style information about the text being imported. They can preserve much or all of the formatting work already performed in the word processor. Filters also work in reverse to export text files from QuarkXPress for use by word processors. To import from or export text to a particular word processing program, the filter for that word processor must reside in the QuarkXPress directory prior to launching QuarkXPress. You need not designate a filter to import a file; it's done automatically.

One common nonspecific file format that can be used to import or export text files avoids this necessity. It is called *Text Format*, also known as ASCII Format. Text saved by a word processor in this format contains only raw, unformatted text characters.

It is unlikely that you will find yourself without a filter available for a word processor file you need. But if that happens, you can benefit from the following measure. In the word processor save in the nonspecific standard format (ASCII) as provided for in the **Save As** command in that program. It's the rare word processor that does not have capacity to save in ASCII text format. (Even in that eventuality, you could still try the clipboard method to transfer the whole file. Select the entire file first in the word processor, then **Copy**. Next open QuarkXPress, set up a text box and insertion cursor, and give the **Paste** command.)

To Import Text

Assuming filter-file compatibility, importing text is usually a simple and smooth process. To import a text file into a text box, activate the Content tool and select the text box. If the flashing text cursor is visible, or text is highlighted with the text box, you're ready to import. Next, open the File menu and choose **Get Text**. You should see a Get Text dialog box like that shown in Figure 4.3. Select the file. Then click **OK**. The text will flow into the text box.

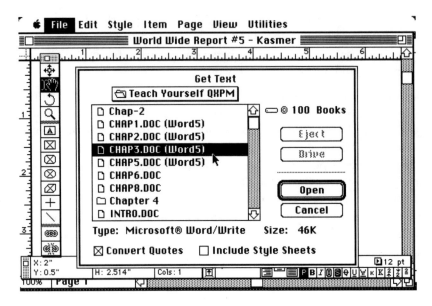

Figure 4.3 *Importing text through the* **Get Text** *command.*

NOTE

When you select a file from the list, the type of file is indicated below the list as in Figure 4.3. This file typing occurs as QuarkXPress matches its filters to the document to be imported.

Importing Text

Assure that text box is selected with Content tool active

At File menu choose **Get Text**

Select file in dialog listings

There are ways you can actually improve on the text just by importing it. Standard straight typewriter quotes can be converted to curving typesetter's quotes. The **Convert Quotes** checkbox in the dialog box when active will cause typewriter style quotes to become matched with typesetter's quotes as in Figure 4.4.

Figure 4.4   Typewriter quotes versus typesetter's quotes.

To Export Text

The process of sending text out of a QuarkXPress document follows the same approach as importing it, with two important differences. First you decide on the file format of the exported text. And second, you can choose to export all of one story or just selected text. This provides flexibility in the creation of text archives or extracts. Begin the process by placing the cursor within a story, or selecting text. Then open the file menu and choose **Save Text....** The dialog that appears will present the options just discussed.

In exporting text you are calling for the creation of a new file in addition to the text as it exists within the QuarkXPress document. In no way does exporting text change the contents of that document.

Exporting Text

Assure that text box is selected with Content tool active or a selection of text is highlighted

At File menu choose **Save Text**

Click **Entire Story** or **Selected Text** button

Select file format in dialog listings

Name text and choose destination

Text Box Overruns

What if more text goes into a text box than it can hold? In that case, QuarkXPress will keep the remainder recorded in the document file, even though unseen on any document page or pasteboard. When the character count is long and the box is too small, overflow occurs. If the text is formatted to occupy a space wider than the box, it may not be seen at all. In cases like these, the box will be tagged with a small x in the lower-right corner to indicate that not all the text assigned to a box is displayed in it. Figure 4.5 shows such a instance.

A powerful agent is
the right word.
Whenever we come
upon one of those
intensely right words
in a book or a newspa-

Figure 4.5   *Text overrun indicated by an x in the text box.*

If you are working with relatively little text—as in a headline—and have plenty of space around the text box, you can simply enlarge the box, stretching it by dragging one of the handles until the continuation x disappears and all the text shows. This is just one approach to bringing out all the text. You will see others as we continue.

Internal Word Processing

By now you might be wondering, "How does QuarkXPress handle word processing?" Look at the features you've already encountered regarding text, keeping in mind that *word processing* (also known as *text editing*) relies on keying in text in a form that can be readily handled and revised. Available to us are the text box, column control, facing pages adjustment, and automatic text box generation.

You could, of course, prepare your text layout drawing boxes as needed and keying in the text directly to each. This method works adequately on a single page layout. If there are multiple columns in the box, the text cursor will jump between columns as you type or revise.

If, however, you wish QuarkXPress to emulate the features of a word processor in a straightforward way without the distracting need to engage in layout while composing or editing text, you'll find the following method useful. It involves setting up a separate QuarkXPress document as your word processing file. This approach offers you the flexibility of text editing at any size of type available on your system, with the ease of scrolling through with the **Up** and **Down** arrow keys. When your text is ready, you can either export it through the File menu's **Save Text** command one of the QuarkXPress word processing filters, then import it through the **Get Text** command. Or you can simply copy it, move to the layout document, and paste it into the appropriate text box.

To set up a word processing document, open the File menu and choose **New**. At the dialog set up a page size and margins that will fit easily on your screen. Then do the following: assure that the number of columns is set at 1, that the facing pages box is unchecked, and that the automatic text box is checked. Click **OK**. The result will be a one-page document. Adjust the view so that the text box is centered and contained within the window. (You can achieve this by sizing the window in combination with setting an appropriate view percentage and positioning with the grabber hand.)

You also might wish to set the top and bottom margins of this document to zero so that the gap between text of subsequent pages will be minimized.

N O T E

At this point you can select a typeface font and size as outlined in the Type Control section below. To provide a clear text entry area, you can remove the palettes and rulers from the window through the **Hide Tools**, **Hide Measurements**, **Hide Document Layout**, and **Hide Rulers** commands under the View menu. (When you return to the layout document, you can choose the View menu's **Show** command for each to display them again.)

What you will have is a document pared down into a text editor. As you key in more material than a single page can hold, QuarkXPress will generate another text box on an additional page and move the cursor into it as you type.

The many worthy word processors offer specialized features such as thesauri, numbering, indexing, footnoting, and table-of-contents generators. But it's good to know that you can generate text impromptu from within your desktop publisher.

N O T E

Find/Change

If one feature pumps real strength into the text editing capabilities of any word processor, it is the capability to locate a word or phrase, and to replace it with another. QuarkXPress implements this ability in a way outclassing many dedicated word processors. You engage this command from the Edit menu by choosing **Find/Change**. Figure 4.6 shows the dialog window that appears.

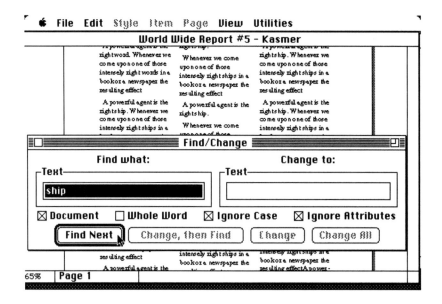

Figure 4.6 *The Find/Change search and replace dialog box.*

To locate a word or phrase, key it into the **Find What:** field and click the **Find Next** button. The field will handle up to 80 characters. QuarkXPress conducts all its searches downstream, from beginning to end. So be sure the text cursor is positioned upstream of the area you will search. That would be at the beginning of a story if you wished to search the whole story. (If you select a segment of text, the program will commence the search at the upstream end of the selection and continue until the end, or where you stop the search by closing the Find/Change dialog window.)

Checkboxes switch on various search options. The **Document** box chooses to search the whole document rather than just the story. The **Whole Word** box chooses to search for a word, such as ship rather than the sequence ...ship..., which also would find ships, shipmate, and relationship. The **Ignore Case** box lets the search locate all occurrences of the character string in the **Find What:** field rather than just the characters as given. It would locate read on, **READ ON** as well as **Read On**. The **Ignore Attributes** checkbox adds a new depth of control by allowing us to search and change type features. We'll look more into it later.

QuarkXPress shows the first instance of found text by highlighting it in the text box. You can order further instances found by clicking again on the **Find Next** button. Even though the text is highlighted you can't key in changes directly until you switch control from the Find/Change dialog box back to the document window. Click on the document title bar to do so; this will keep the selection active. That way you can make your revision directly.

You might want to use the **Find** feature to locate the occurrence of a phrase in your document—"the Caribbean", for example—for citing elsewhere in your text or including in an index. If you've marked the heads and subheads, you might use the marker (an asterisk or other notation) as a key to finding each one in turn.

You might want to check for clarity by looking over personal pronouns. For instance, you can search for the word "she" to revise some occurrences in order to distinguish between a ship's captain and the vessel she commands.

To replace text, key the substitution into the **Change to**: field. Notice that even without an entry typed in here, the **Change then Find**, **Change**, and **Change All** buttons can become active. This means, of course, that under this circumstance you can change the found text to nothing, that is, eliminate it. In any case until the first occurrence of **Find what**: text is located, only the **Find** button is active. But, thereafter the other buttons become accessible. The **Change then Find** button makes only a single substitution, but does go on to locate the next occurrence. The **Change** button makes the substitution of found text, then turns control back to the **Find Next** button. The **Change All** button automatically makes all substitutions downstream without pausing and presents a dialog box noting how many substitutions were made.

A good way to use the global replacement features of the Find/Change dialog window is to first try one, two or three instances with the **Change then Find** button. If all goes according to your wishes, then click the **Change All** button.

Type Control

The recognized strength of the QuarkXPress system is type control. While text is what's been written, type is the form in which it will finally be read. The virtues of various type treatments have been discussed at length by a variety of authors, some of them listed in Appendix B. It may be worth your time to examine some of these sources to secure a firm grasp on the many uses that the procedures revealed in this book can be put to.

Before we go any further however, take a moment to look at a daily newspaper, which like the document in Figure 4.7 delivers all sorts of unrecognized messages. Immediately, the type sends messages to your brain before you have read a word. A nameplate spread in a sturdy but dignified type across the top says solid, established. A headline, which is large and bold, says this story is of special importance. Smaller headlines say read me, too. The teasers under the headlines say come closer, take a look. The body type of the stories themselves, functional, quick to read says, here are the facts.

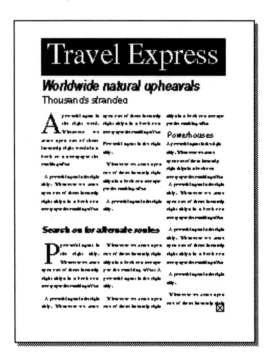

Figure 4.7 *A document carries messages in its type.*

Type is more than typeface. Size, line spacing, letter spacing, emphasis and weight, boldface and italic can great a multitude of effects. Type can be formatted into columns, and aligned straight or flexible. Most importantly, in QuarkXPress nearly everything that type is can be controlled. And so, you can precisely adjust the medium that carries the message.

Selecting Text Within a Box

By now you can guess the first step for most of the type control procedures in QuarkXPress. It is the simplest and the one overlooked most easily during a deadline rush. Always first then is this: select the text to be modified. If you've worked with word processors, you have some notion of the basic methods of text selection.

To select any section of text that's visible to you, begin with the text cursor at one end of the segment, press the mouse button and drag the mouse to the other end of the segment. Release the mouse button and proceed to make your text adjustments. Alternatively, click the cursor in place at one end of the segment. Move to the other end. Holding down the **SHIFT** key, click there. Either way, you will highlight the text between.

The following powerstrokes will prove useful in working with text.

❖ To select exactly one word of text, begin with the text cursor blinking anywhere in that word. Double-click the mouse button. The word will be selected.

❖ To select exactly one line of text, begin with the text cursor blinking anywhere in that line. Triple-click the mouse button. The line will be selected.

❖ To select exactly one paragraph, begin with the text cursor blinking anywhere in that paragraph. Quadruple-click the mouse button. The paragraph will be selected.

Selecting text by powerstrokes

Use the Content tool to do the following:
    One word—double-click
    One line—triple-click
    One paragraph—quadruple-click

Using the Text Measurements Palette

We will look into the controls over type and paragraphs exerted through the Measurements palette. These are accessible when the Content tool is active in text. For convenience we'll refer to the measurements palette for text as the Text palette.

Here you'll find adjustments in basic type style and other features, which are most often immediately useful in layout and copy fitting. Almost all the functions found here are additionally accessible through the Style menu and the commands **Font**, **Size**, **Type Style**, **Track**, **Baseline Shift**, **Alignment**, **Leading**, and **Formats**.

Type Control

What is type but text made visible? Consider the text box of Figure 4.8. In it sits a selected line of plain type. Despite its simple appearance, this line of type already possesses many attributes. The Type palette below it indicates what they are. Even the simplest text possesses attributes that define its simplicity.

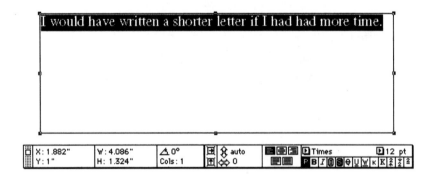

Figure 4.8   *A line of type and the Measurements palette monitoring its attributes.*

Font and Size

What does it look like? How big is it? These basic standards measure all sorts of things from tomatoes to tattoos. Consider type in this light, and look again at selected text and the Text palette in Figure 4.8. Starting at the right side of the palette you'll notice the size indicated at 12 pt, meaning 12 *points*. Points are a measurement equal to 1/72 of an inch, or 1/12 of a pica. You encountered them before in adjusting the rule line. In this case 12 pt indicates the height of the upper-case letters of the font. It's the standard method of measurement used by typesetters and should come as no surprise to anyone to find QuarkXPress using it.

Immediately to the left you will see the name of the font or typeface. In this case it is a Times Roman style (designated in the display box as Times).

To adjust either font or size in the palette, select the text you wish to change with the Content tool. Click on the drop-down list arrow next to font or size. After the list opens, click on the choice you prefer.

You can also change the value in the palette by double clicking on the field. Then key in the replacement name or size. Figure 4.9 shows modified text and its text palette in the act of being adjusted. The Times body type has already been replaced with Helvetica, and the text is in the process of being enlarged to 24 points. The text's appearance has changed from that of body text to one suited to a large heading.

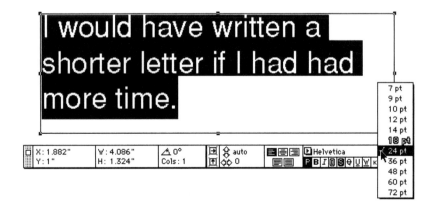

Figure 4.9 *Adjusting text size through the Measurements palatte.*

NOTE The text palette will actively monitor whatever text is currently selected. If you change your selection the palette will reflect values for the current selection. You can have countless variations in effect within any text box (although for design's sake you normally wouldn't).

Type Style

Below both the font and the size are a series of buttons that control type style. These buttons activate in the following way, starting at the left: plain type, bolding, italic, outline, doublestrike, strikethrough, underline continuously, underline word by word, small capitals, all capitals, superscript, subscript, and superior (a reduced size superscript). Figure 4.10 shows the effects of these style controls on two words of each line, top to bottom from plain to superior.

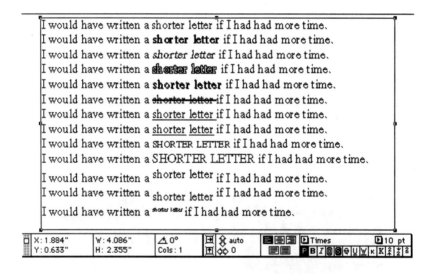

Figure 4.10 *Effects of each of the palette's type style buttons.*

To adjust type style, you first select the text in question. Then click on the button to apply or remove the style feature. Most of these buttons will not mutually exclude others, except the **P** for plain button, which wipes off any of the other styles from selected text. All the other buttons "toggle" the features on or off, like a light switch, which when pressed once, turns on the light, and when pressed again, turns it off.

N O T E Type attributes can be applied singly as shown in Figure 4.10, or in combination. Some will override or cancel out other attributes. A **Small Caps** style will cancel an **All Caps** style already applied. But others will add their effect onto existing effects. You can, for instance, apply bold, italic, and superscripting to the same text.

Paragraph Control

While type choices control the appearance of individual characters, paragraph formatting adjusts the lines of type that greet the eye. They create a mood often before any of the words are absorbed. How many times have you turned away from tightly spaced lines, or got lost trying to read right-aligned body copy?

Lines and paragraphs can flow loose, cram tight, stretch wide or tuck in narrow. They can project an impression of free openness, or dense seriousness. Whatever they may be, formatting and alignment choices always impact readability. Setting the lines one way or the other will make for a quick read, a thoughtful pondering, or no read at all.

Paragraph Alignment

In the Text palette you can find five small lined boxes just left of the font name; each represents different paragraph formatting. As you know, aligned left forms a paragraph with lines of text whose left ends are all flush along an imaginary column, allowed to end randomly ragged on the right according to line length, as in typical typewritten correspondence. The aligned-left control is the little box button in the upper left of the group.The aligned-right button sits over to the right. The centered button stands between them.

Lower right you'll find the Justified button. Justified text achieves paragraphs aligned to both the right and left by adding or removing fractional bits of space between words and letters of each line. The **Forced Justify** button sits lower right. It forces the last line of text in a paragraph to fill out the line. It does this by adding spaces between words if two or more occupy that line. If a single word occupies the last line, **Force Justify** will add spaces between the letters of that word stretching it across the line. The alignment of the five columns of text in Figure 4.11 corresponds to the five **Alignment** buttons of the Measurements palette.

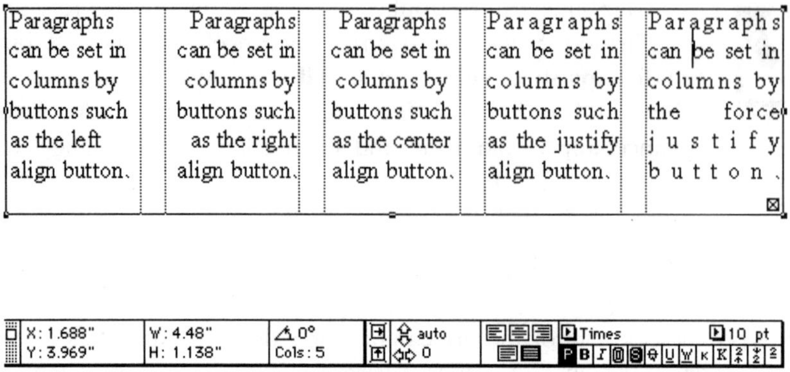

Paragraphs can be set in columns by buttons such as the left align button.	Paragraphs can be set in columns by buttons such as the right align button.	Paragraphs can be set in columns by buttons such as the center align button.	Paragraphs can be set in columns by buttons such as the justify align button.	Paragraphs can be set in columns by the force justify button.

```
X: 1.688"   W: 4.48"    △ 0°      auto   Times        10 pt
Y: 3.969"   H: 1.138"   Cols: 5      0    P B I O S Q U Y K K
```

Figure 4.11   *The five paragraph alignments.*

These buttons apply to the paragraph in which the cursor is found, whether or not all text is selected. The method to adjust paragraph formatting follows the select–click pattern. First, position the text cursor within the paragraph in question, or select text in that paragraph. Then click on the appropriate alignment button. The entire paragraph will be aligned. If the selection extends over several paragraphs, they will all be aligned.

Adjusting Line Spacing

In constant balance in any document are *type* and *space*, the yin and yang of typography. The more of either there is, the less there is of the other. Spaces between lines interact with spaces between words in such a way to speed up or slow down reading. The eye will tend to stay with type and to leap only the narrowest white space.

If space between lines is narrower than between words, look out! The eye will keep jumping down to the next line instead of finishing the line. Of course, as thinking creatures, we'll struggle to keep the eye on course. But the effort will take its toll, and reader fatigue can often defeat a desire to finish any story.

Line spacing has a profound effect on readability. This space, known as *leading* (rhymes with wedding), is generally measured between the baselines on which the lowercase letters sit. On the Text palette you'll see the leading measured in points. The value of the currently selected paragraph is indicated in a box left of the **Paragraph Alignment** buttons. You may find the term *auto*, which indicates automatic leading. (In automatic leading a percentage is added over the font size, usually 20%. So 10-pt type would be set at 12 pts in the default autoleading of QuarkXPress.) Leading affects all the lines in the paragraph in which the cursor or selection appears.

The first step in adjusting leading is to position the text cursor or to select text.

To adjust leading in small steps on the text palette, click on the **Up** or **Down** arrow next to the value. This will separate or push together all the lines of the paragraph(s) in increments of one point for each click.

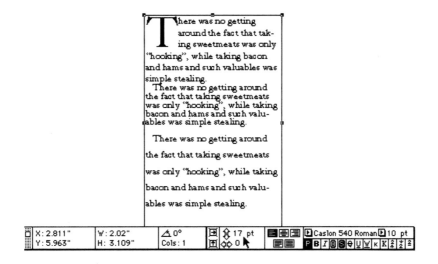

Figure 4.12 *Paragraphs of auto, reduced, and increased leading.*

To adjust leading precisely to tenths, hundreds, or thousandths of a point, select the value in the Leading Field box and key in a value. Press **ENTER**, and line spacing will change to the new value. You can also use this method to set leading to an integer value. In Figure 4.12 the auto leading of the first paragraph has been "tightened" (reduced) in the second paragraph, and "opened up" (increased) in the third.

Letter Spacing

Tracking and *kerning* are terms familiar in typesetting. Anyone who works with type is likely at some time become engaged in debate over the merits or disadvantages of these two features. That such small changes as the space between letters and words could engender so much discussion suggests the use of that tracking and kerning is often very much an esoteric art. But these two controls are really quite simple. They signify changing the space between adjacent type characters, as in Figure 4.13.

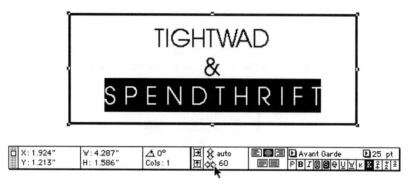

Figure 4.13   One word with kerning and one with tracking.

Here, in the first line, only space between the letters W and A has been reduced from the amount normally put between them. This is kerning, changing the space between individual letters. Kerning certain pairs of letters often creates a more unified, pleasing appearance. When you kern with QuarkXPress you are removing some of the space ahead of, that is to the right of, a character. The figure shows the last line in the process of having all the letters moved further apart, by increasing space between them. This is tracking, changing the spacing between all of a group of letters. Tracking can often subtly open or close text so that it fits more neatly into the area intended for it.

Kerning and Tracking

The adjusting of kerning or tracking is performed only slightly differently from each other, but the difference is crucial to the effect. In both cases values can be applied ranging from –500 to 500, with zero being the default or normal spacing.

Kerning is a spacing relationship between two adjacent letters. The spacing between some pairs of letters will be automatically set from tables of values kept by QuarkXPress. Here we will deal with individual pair kerning, as carried out case by case.

To kern in increments, position the blinking text cursor between the two letters in question. At the Text palette below the leading value, find the two arrowheads. (Note that if the cursor is not between two letters, or if text has not been selected, the kerning/tracking value is not displayed.) Click on the **Left** to close, or the **Right** arrow to open up, the space between the letters. The kern value will change normally in units of 10.

To kern by direct entry, position the text cursor and select the Kern field showing in the Text palette. Then, key in your preferred value. This value can be any number in the range down to the thousandth part. Press **ENTER** to apply.

Kerning at the Text palette

Position I-beam text cursor between letters

Use palette arrows for incremental changes (10 units each)

or

Key in kern value and press **ENTER**

Since kerning and tracking are similar processes applied to individual pairs and to groups of letters, respectively, you'll find tracking adjustments similar to those for kerning.

To adjust tracking, first select the range of text to be tracked. Then proceed as with kerning using the text palette arrowheads for incremental changes, or the direct entry method for precision tracking.

Columns

One of the most obvious strengths of QuarkXPress is instant column control. You can adjust a text box from a single column to several in one step. You can experiment easily and quickly with page layouts and copy fitting. The burning eleventh-hour question, Do three or four columns fit better here?, can now be answered in about two seconds. Columns are remarkably easy to control from the Text palette.

As you look left of the heavy dark line separating the Text palette in half, you'll encounter a section labeled, **Cols:**. This palette setting governs the number of columns into which a text box is to be divided. As you might recall, crossing to the left half of the palette technically puts us in the section designed for item control. However, the setting of text in columns has such profound consequences for the effects of many type features that we'll look into it here.

If you have a text box of body copy spanning most of a letter-size page, you have a problem. Clearly, visually scanning long lines of 70 or 80 characters across an 8-inch expanse is much too taxing to most readers. So, of course; shorter lines of text is an obvious answer. Shorter lines in the same space leads to narrow columns, and thus more of them. Setting type in columns provides a more graceful and practical result.

Because QuarkXPress treats text boxes as possessing adjustable columns characteristics, creating and changing columns on the page is a process you'll find instantly gratifying if you have ever worked with galleys, or other approaches that call for you to roll down window shades of text.

To change the number of columns in a text box, assure that the box is selected or a cursor is within it. Then, simply select the field that in the Text palette that shows the column's value, and type in a new value. Press **ENTER**. The same text can be reset in three or four columns, as shown in Figures 4.14 and 4.15, in a matter of seconds.

Adjusting columns at the palette

Select text box with either **Item** or **Content tool**
Select value in **Cols:** field at palette
Key in new value and press **ENTER**

NOTE

Remember that the text box always has some column setting in effect, even if that value is only **1**.

WARNING

Resetting text to fewer columns may create text box overruns. This may necessitate changing type specifications as we have done, or engaging new text boxes to take up the surplus, as we shall see later.

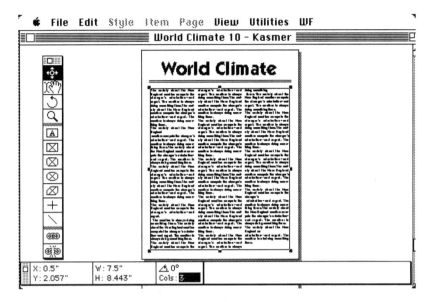

Figure 4.14 *Setting text into three columns using the Measurements palette.*

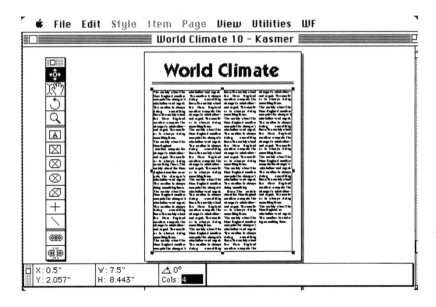

Figure 4.15 *Setting text into four columns using the Measurements palette.*

Onward

Typesetting functions such as the ones you've learned in this chapter work marvels in getting text messages across to the reader. By fashioning the basic material of your documents through the Text palette you can design documents of infinite variety. These text controls provide some of the highest levels of productivity found in this or other publishing programs.

Of course, applying your skills to a production project is the ultimate challenge. The next chapter provides opportunities to go to work on newsletters in progress and make use of the features seen here. On-the-job efforts are the ones that reward us the most and remain vivid the longest. Next you'll see how to assemble both a traditional and a modern newsletter with type and paragraph techniques.

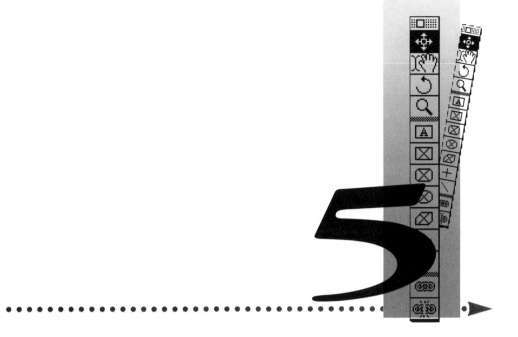

Newsletters on the Job

What you will learn in this chapter:

- ✤ How to assemble a document
- ✤ Preparing the parts of newsletters
- ✤ How to apply and adjust type and paragraph features
- ✤ Copy fitting
- ✤ Using typesetting control codes
- ✤ Working with multiple pages

The letter is the most common form of printed communication. In the sphere of publishing, this modest form has been expanded to the *newsletter*, a publication type that has permutated into a variety as great as any other.

Traditional newsletters employ a layout that requires nothing more than typing information and opinions onto a letterhead. Though the typed-letter style continues to enjoy success, a larger field of typeset newsletters ranges into designs as complex as any seen in the newspaper or magazine worlds. The widely used label, newsletter, includes all kinds—single-page efforts, four-color, graphic-intensive magazine-like publications, and book length collections of articles.

Even as other periodicals dip in number, newsletters have enjoyed an era of wide proliferation, providing every brand of news imaginable. Some promote products or services. Others report international news or pass on specialized information. Some serve as the "social glue" of far-flung groups.

Newsletters surge through the world's postal systems in every form and for every function possible.

In this chapter we will use techniques you've already encountered in this book to construct two newsletters as QuarkXPress documents. From start to finish we'll move through all the steps from setting up the document file to importing, formatting, and laying out the text. The two newsletters will be produced as two versions derived from the same material.

To assemble the first, the classic letterhead newsletter, we'll start by setting up the letterhead, then adding and formatting text files to produce a traditional single-column piece. The second version, a contemporary design, will draw on the whole range of skills encountered so far.

N O T E

You'll benefit by following each move in the development of the newsletter pages that follow. You may also benefit by working along using text of your own, building newsletters in step-by-step tandem with those constructed here. If so, feel free to replicate the designs offered in them, or to modify them as you see fit. In any case, you will soon discover how to handle QuarkXPress under the demands of actual projects.

Part 1: The Letterhead Newsletter

We begin with the classic newsletter, information set onto a letterhead. We have two text files and the following information for the letterhead itself: The World

Report, Beyond the horizon, No. 17, The Studio K Editors, Box 3562, San Diego, California 92163. We're told that the final newsletter will be a letter-size sheet, printed front and back, in traditional letterhead format, and to be mailed in a standard #10 envelope.

Producing the Letterhead

Producing the top of the letter itself is our first task. We'll create a QuarkXPress document and proceed with developing this information into a letterhead. Consider what we have to work with: a title, a tag line, a credit, and an address.

With the computer started up and QuarkXPress already installed, we are at the desktop. Our first step is to run the program. We do this by locating and double-clicking on the icon to start the program.

After the Quark ID-logo window appears momentarily, we reach the program window where we can create our document file. We open the File menu, select **New** and slide the mouse over to choose **Document**. As New dialog box appears, we select the button that makes this document letter sized, key in values of 1.25-inch margins all around, click off the check from the **Facing Pages** checkbox, accept a one-column layout and leave the automatic text box function engaged, as shown in Figure 5.1.

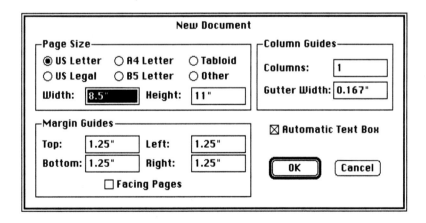

Figure 5.1   *Detailing the newsletter's document layout at the New dialog box.*

Next appears an Actual-size view of the corner where top and left margins meet. We'll back off a bit and have a look the whole page while we decide just where to arrange the letterhead information. Opening the View menu, we choose **Fit-in Window**, and can then see all the margin guides clearly. An automatic text box is already contained within these margins. We'll use it later for the body copy.

For the letterhead we need another, smaller text box. For the moment we've decided we want to put the letterhead information centered at the top, quite traditional in Times typeface. We select the Text Box tool, position it at the left margin guide, above the top margin guide. Since we're using these guides just for convenience, we're free to ignore them when we wish. A one-inch-high text box running down about three-quarters of an inch from the top should be about right. The Tool palette happens to be obscuring the vertical ruler. We point on the bar at the top of that palette and drag it slightly to the right, away from the ruler. Next,we drag a text box across from upper left over to the right and down past the top margin guide.

NOTE The Measurements palette for text will indicate the position and dimensions of the text box we've just drawn. We could have alternatively just drawn a small text box anywhere on the page, then at the Measurements palette, keyed in the values of size and location to suit the letterhead.

NOTE At an early stage like this we'll usually choose to save the file to the hard disk. Doing so makes the document window clearly identified by name in the event other documents are opened. Also, although we've just begun the document and have not yet put much work into it, saving the file now initiates the habit of frequent saving. As survivors of countless software crashes will testify, the habit of saving inevitably pays back the small efforts it requires. From now on, we'll take it as given that this document and all other documents are being saved whenever some significant bit of work goes into them.

Opening the File menu and choosing **Save**, we use the Save As... dialog box to key in the title for this document, World Report #17. We're locating it in the folder, Kasmer's Clients. Navigating through the hard drive's folders in the Save As... dialog we locate this folder and double-click to open it. Then we click **OK** to save the file by its new name.

We need to type in the letterhead data through the keyboard. Since we're planning to center the text and to use a Times Roman typeface, we'll first choose these at the Measurements palette. Assuring that the text box is selected and that the Content tool is active at the Tool palette, we click on the **Centering** button, and open the fonts list, then click on **Times**.

Before keying in the World Report data we return to **Actual** size through the Command-1 keyboard shortcut. Because the Document Layout palette obscures the text box at this view, we'll hide it by double-clicking on the tiny box in its upper-left corner. (We could also have opened the View menu and chosen **Hide Document Layout**.) We use the Grabber hand to slide the page so that the text box is clearly visible. Then we type the data.

> ## Using the Grabber hand
>
> With any tool but the Zoom selected, hold the **Option** key
> Press mouse button and drag page through window view

Pausing a moment, we consider the appearance of this text box, (Figure 5.2). In place between the left and right guides, it sits over the top margin guide, which we can see running through the third line. We ignore the top margin for the moment; these guides don't print.

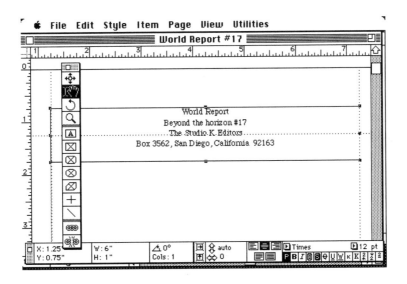

Figure 5.2   *The text box with letterhead drawn over the margin guide.*

To take a closer look at the text itself we open the View menu and choose **200%**, and then use the Grabber hand again to position the window view so we can see all the text.

We want a traditional letterhead appearance, so we will emphasize the first line title by making it larger, bolding it and setting it all capitals. Our first step is to select the text line, by triple-clicking on it. Next, at the Measurements palette, we open the font size list and click on 18 pts. Then, we click on the **Bold (B)** button, and the **All Caps (K)** button. And to pull the title into a tighter group, we click several times on the **Increase Tracking Arrow**, setting that value at **50**. These type revisions yield the line shown in Figure 5.3.

Figure 5.3 *Style adjustments applied to the title line.*

N O T E   A selected line displays as inverse or highlighted text—white on black in this case. We're setting type black on white (like ink on paper). Now, QuarkXPress remembers its selections. Selected text in a box will appear unselected when the text box is deactivated. But, will appear highlighted and selected when the box is activated again. So while examining our changes we click in an area outside the box. This deactivates the box and the text inside shows up in normal display, black on white. When we click on the text box again, the contents become active once again and the selected line appears highlighted as before.

N O T E A note to typographic purists. It is true that there are specific typefaces for bold, italic, and so on. And a strong case can be made for their preferability in many circumstances. But throughout this book, we choose to use the automatic type style capabilities of the program in order to demonstrate their use. The decision of using a bold typeface or a plain face with bolding applied will be left to the user-designer.

Turning next to the tag line under the title, we select that line with a triple click, and return again to the Measurements palette. We apply a smaller size by selecting the Font Size field and typing in **8**, italicize by clicking the **I** button, and decrease leading to 9 points by clicking on the **Leading Down Arrow** to bring the tag line up closer to the title.

Moving to the third line, The Studio K Editors, we triple-click to select it, and at the palette apply bolding and small capitals through the buttons. To drop this line away from the tag line we increase the leading to 17 points by clicking the **Leading Up Arrow**. To tighten the line's letter spacing like the title's, we decrease tracking –10 by clicking the **Tracking Down Arrow**.

Finally, selecting the address line, we reduce its size by double-clicking in the Font Size field and typing **8pt**. And here we again apply a decrease in letter spacing –10 by clicking the **Tracking Down Arrow**.

At this point it becomes apparent that the title line should be larger, so we triple-click that first line again and increase the font size to 24 pts by opening the palette font size list and clicking. This suggests to us less tracking, so we click the reduce **Tracking** button until we see a more pleasing appearance at tracking of 30.

Switching off the guides (View menu, **Hide** guides) we examine the letterhead at the 200% view shown in Figure 5.4. For our purposes, the letterhead portion now appears completed.

Typesetting Body Text

Now we turn our attention to the text that will make up the body of newsletter. Since this material was generated in another program and saved as word processing files, our task is next to bring it into the document, prepare the content, then format it. At this point we'll turn to the text box placed automatically within the margins when we created the World Report #17 document. Into this box we'll import those text files directly.

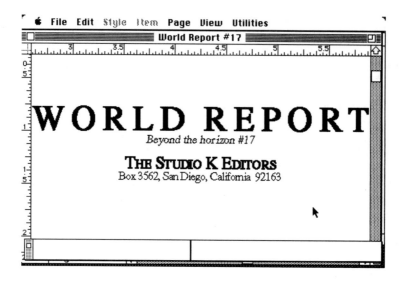

Figure 5.4. *Double-size view of the letterhead.*

N O T E

Here the automatic text box and the letterhead text box do overlap. Generally, **Text Runaround** is engaged (through a default setting) and one text box may force text in another box to reposition. However, now this push works in our favor because the features of **Text Runaround** are driving the body text downward from the Letterhead text box. **Text Runaround** controls will be explored in detail later.

To import the first of the text, we choose the Content tool, then click on the large, automatic text box. A flashing text cursor appears beneath the Letterhead text box (because the **Runaround** feature pushes it there) indicating where text will be inserted. At this point we decide to establish the font and size by selecting **Times** and **12pt** at the Measurements palette. Opening the File menu, we choose **Get text**, and locating the file, Border Crossings, within the Field Reports folder (Figure 5.5), double-click to import it. The text comes into the box in the selected size and font, then the cursor flashes at the end of the text.

Deciding to import all the text at this time, we again choose **Get text** to bring in the file, Pirates...contraband. At this point, the program flows the text to the bottom of the text box on Page 1, and automatically inserts Page 2 with a similar text box into the document. The balance of the Pirates...contraband file flows onto page 2, as shown in Figure 5.6's greeked text, Fit-in-Window view of portions of both pages.

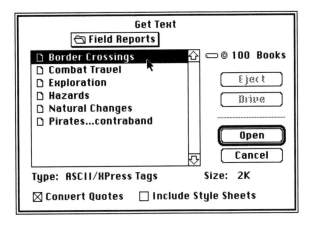

Figure 5.5 *Importing the Border Crossings file through the* ***Get Text*** *command.*

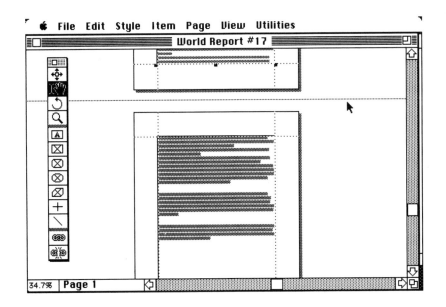

Figure 5.6 *View of Page One's original text box and Page 2 generated to handle overrun.*

With all the text now in place, we take a closer look, by returning to Actual size view.

There will almost always be some clean-up or massaging of text necessary before final formatting. Often word processors (the people, not the software) put in two spaces between sentences. Sometimes extra carriage returns are entered between paragraphs.

In some cases, we find odd characters have taken the place of apostrophes or other characters originally typed by the word processor (person). These odd translations can happen unexpectedly.

In other cases the writers themselves introduce spurious characters just as unexpectedly. Here as shown in Figure 5.7, we see that the writer of the *Border Crossings* article has preceded each paragraph by a bullet. We'll need to remove them before proceeding much further.

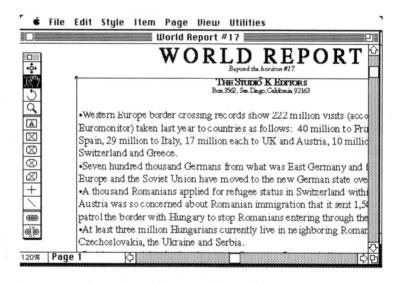

Figure 5.7 *The imported text with irregularities.*

Also, we've been informed that the fourth paragraph about the 3 million Hungarians is dated and should be removed. We attend to this first by quadruple-clicking in that paragraph to select it, and pressing the **BACKSPACE** key to delete it.

Next we take on the bullets. The obvious thing to do here is what's known as a *global replacement*. The character code for a bullet can be identified through the **Key Caps** feature of the Macintosh system. In fact we use it so commonly we know it to be **Option-8**. However, here we use the universal method for dealing with odd characters in text. We first select one from the text with a drag of the mouse and copy it to the clipboard using the Edit menu shortcut, Command-C. Next we click the cursor to the beginning of the text, and then at the Edit menu, we choose **Find/Change**.

At the Find/Change dialog box with the text cursor flashing in the **Find what:** field box, we use the shortcut, **COMMAND-V** to paste in the bullet character. Since we wish to perform a global deletion rather than a replacement, we leave the **Change to:** field in this dialog empty. In fact, we tab over to that field and press **Backspace** to assure it's empty.

This precaution is a wise one to follow in general when seeing an empty field, since it's possible that in previous use the dialog may have commanded a change to a space character. In such a circumstance the field would appear empty, but the result of using it would add unintended spaces.

We click the only button now active, **Find Next**, and the process begins. The first bullet is located and selected by the **Change** function. We click the **Change** button and examine the result, Figure 5.8, to be sure it's what we want with no unintended surprises. Satisfied, we then click the **Change All** button. The Change dialog box makes substitution of all bullets with nothing (thereby removing all of them) throughout the text. After the last change, a dialog window appears indicating the number of changes, in this case, 10.

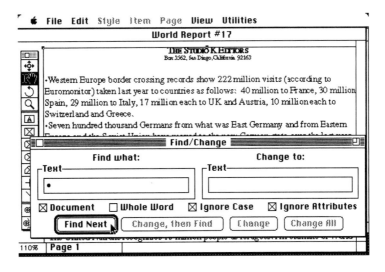

Figure 5.8 *The first step in removing unwanted characters.*

Now we position the text cursor back at the beginning of the story and prepare to use the Find/Change dialog box to remove double spaces. We do this by typing in two spaces in the **Find what**: field, and then typing a single space in the **Change to:** field. Proceeding as before, we direct global replacement through the dialog **Change All** button.

Next we move into the area of paragraph formatting. Here's what we have in mind. Although there are other ways of handling paragraph spacing we plan to use the **Change** feature to make our text self-consistent by first eliminating any double-carriage returns. With text cursor at the story beginning and with the Find/Change dialog box active we key in two new-paragraph codes in the **Find what:** field, **\p\p**, and a single new-paragraph code in the **Change to:** field, **\p**.

These new-paragraph codes are generated each time the **ENTER** or **Return** key is pressed. They appear as paragraph markers,¶, when you activate the **Show Invisibles** command at the View menu. Take note that the first character of the code is the backslash (\), not the common slash (/).

N O T E In case there may be unnoticed triple carriage returns, we run the same global change from the beginning of the text a second time, as well. In fact when replacing doubles we run the **Find/Change** command repeatedly until no more instances are found. This usually occurs within two or three attempts.

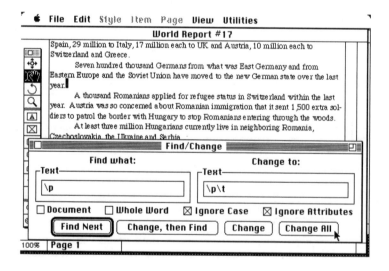

Figure 5.9   Inserting tabs through global replacement.

Basic QuarkXPress character codes

New line	**\n**
New paragraph	**\p**
Tab	**\t**

Next we want to put a tab at the beginning of every paragraph, so we use the Find/Change dialog box to replace every paragraph with a paragraph and a tab, using the codes, **\p** and **\t** as in Figure 5.9. This indents every paragraph except the first (since it has no carriage return preceding it). To take care of that one, we set the text cursor in place at the beginning of the text box and type in a tab by hand.

We are dealing with simple formatting here. So in order to separate articles, we go through visually, insert the text cursor, and add a carriage return to create additional space between them.

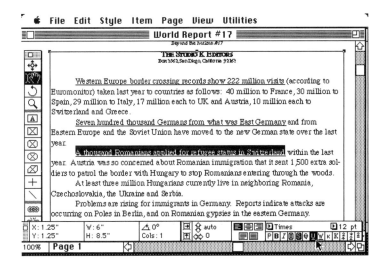

Figure 5.10   *Setting off text with underlining.*

In keeping with the traditional look of this piece we'll put a simple typewriter-like emphasis on each new article by dragging to select lead-in text and then underlining using the Text Palette Continuous Underline button as shown in Figure 5.10.

Copy Fitting

Now we can pull our view back and take an overall took at this newsletter. A glance at Page 2 reveals (even at Fit-in-window view with text greeked as in Figure 5.11) that we still have yet to fill out the publication. And in this case there is no more text coming in. So it's up to design alone to balance the page without impeding readability, which is always a fundamental consideration in a newsletter.

Here we choose to try for a fit by increasing the leading. Checking that the Content tool is selected we click to insert the text cursor in the story, and then from the Edit menu, select it all.

SHORTCUT

An alternative for selecting all the text in a story is to quintuple-click with the cursor in the story. Depending on the coordination of the operator and the double-click speed setting for the mouse in the control panel this may be easier or may not be easier than the Edit menu or COMMAND-A keyboard techniques

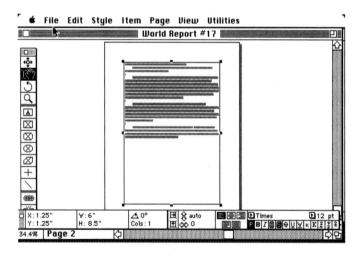

Figure 5.11 *A view of Page 2 shows the copy-fitting challenge.*

With all the text selected we move to the Measurements palette and click on the **Leading Up Arrow** while monitoring the change at page 2. At 19 pts we are rewarded: our text has just filled the text box without running over, as seen in Figure 5.12. This line spacing is slightly more than a space and a half, but in this simple layout the wide spacing seems to work well.

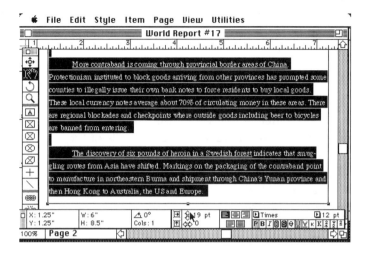

Figure 5.12 *Increasing leading through the text Measurements palette.*

One final addition to this document is a page number added at the top of page 2. We select the Text Box tool and drag a small box into the position shown in Figure 5.13, centering the box at 4.25 inches, the horizontal center of the page, by lining up the center handle of the text box with the **Ruler Mark**.

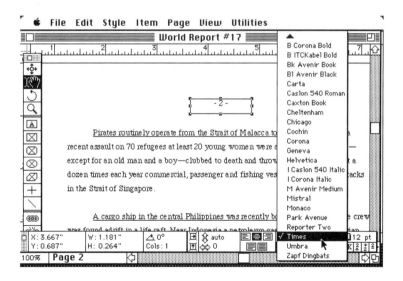

Figure 5.13 *Adjusting a small Page number text box.*

Using the text Measurements palette we again choose **Times** and center the text. We type in -**2**- and with one final **Save** command, put World Report #17 to bed.

Part 2: A Contemporary Newsletter

We can make a very different newsletter using the same sources that went into the classic newsletter above. By calling on other skills of formatting, type styles, and column adjustments from preceding chapters, we can shape the same information into a publication with a clearer, more alluring appearance.

We'll be working with the same text, the same title, tag line, credit, and address as before. In this case, though, our task will include redesigning the previous format into a special-size newsletter that will fold into a 5.5-inch by 8.5-inch format and be a four-page, self-mailer document.

The new page format will call for narrow columns and a different layout altogether. The articles will be broken into separate stories and given more individual play within the layout. We will add headlines and rule elements to set them apart from each other and we'll set the type in multiple columns to make for an easier read. We will also make a space for adding an address label for mailing.

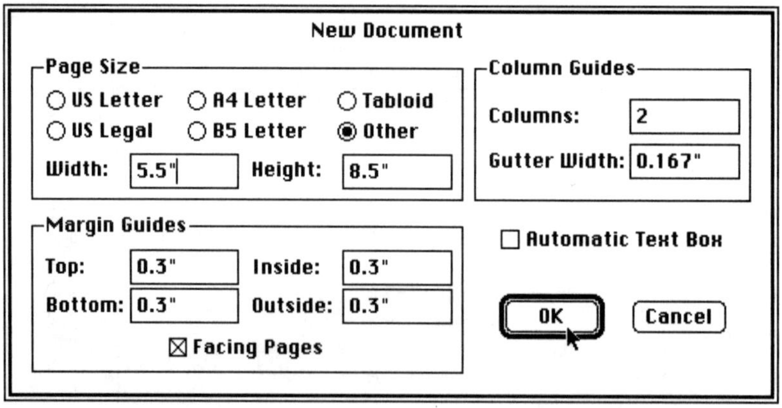

Figure 5.14 *Creating a custom-sized, two-column document.*

Our first step, generating the document to be known as World Report-4 Page, occurs at the File menu's New dialog box as shown in Figure 5.14. We've set the page size to match 5.5 by 8.5 inches, chosen 0.3 inch margins, facing pages, a two-column format with a 0.167 inch (one pica) separation.

Because we want more flexibility in this publication's layout, the **Automatic Text Box** feature was turned off by clicking to remove the X in that field box. Clicking **OK** at the dialog box gives us a single page of the new smaller document. We'll add the others as needed.

As we proceed, we make use of the body text as it appears in the letterhead document. Importing text into a simple, document (such as World Report #17), is one way to begin. Since the text has already been gathered and edited in World Report #17, we'll make use of it. We rename World Report #17 as Text #17 by opening the File menu and choosing **Save As**. Now, by moving between windows we can cut and shuttle text easily into our more elaborate design document, World Report-4 Page.

Preparing Body Text

Our first step in handling our text source document, Text #17, is to remove all the special type formatting in the body copy, in this case, the underlining. We engage the Content tool, put the cursor into the body text, and select all (Edit menu and **Select All**, or quintuple-click). Then at the Measurements palette we press the **P** (for plain text) button. The underlining disappears. This method will also clear out any bolding, italics, and other type styles that may have been applied by the word processor. Granted, many times preserving type styles is important. But here, as we transform the World Report material from a traditional letter form to a typeset pages form, underlines are out.

Also, we prefer to start layout work with **Auto Leading** (normally set at 120%). This will prove useful at whatever size we may work with. So, with all the text selected, at the Measurements palette, we select the leading field and key in **auto**.

Preparing the Nameplate

We next move to prepare the nameplate in the new document. We're going to cut items and text from Text #17 document as we move them to the World Report-4 Page document. This will help us keep track of what remains to be included in the new layout.

The first step in shuttling this material to the new document occurs when we pick the Item tool, select the World Report letterhead text box in Text #17 by clicking on it, and open the Edit menu and choose **Cut**. Then we move to the World Report-4 Page document by opening the Window menu and choosing from the list of open documents, as shown in Figure 5.15. In World Report-4 Page we open the Edit menu and choose **Paste**. The letterhead text box appears.

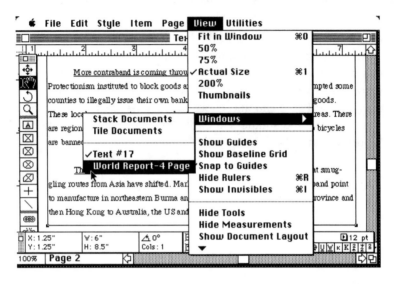

Figure 5.15 *Moving to the new layout document.*

By pointing onto the upper-left Selection Handle, we drag the text box, adjusting its shape so that it is seated into the upper-left corner of the margin guides. Then similarly grasping the box's lower-right corner, we drag the shape into that shown in Figure 5.16, establishing the newsletter's nameplate text box. While making these adjustments, we change views, use the Grabber Hand to position the page, and hide or show palettes to accommodate our efforts.

N O T E There is an alternative to cutting items from the source window, then calling up destination window and pasting them. We could display both windows concurrently by choosing the View menu's Windows listing, then sliding over to the **Tile Documents** command. This will fit all open windows adjacent to each other, automatically resizing them as it does so. It's a feature that helps when we want to see parts of two documents simultaneously. Additionally, this concurrent window display allows easy copying. The method is to simply drag the items from one window to the other. As the mouse cursor appears in the second window, so does an outline of the item. Releasing the mouse button causes the **Paste** function to engage.

However, as useful as this feature can be, we've chosen the **Cut-Switch Windows-Paste** method because we're deliberately paring away at the available source document material to keep track of what's left.

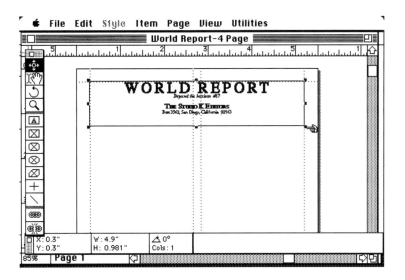

Figure 5.16 *Shaping the nameplate's text box.*

Quick copying between documents

Display both documents concurrently (View menu,
    Windows list, Tile)

Select item in source document window

Drag to destination document window and release

Now we'll work on the newsletter's nameplate. Here's what we plan. The title will be larger and accompanied by the tag line and issue number. But the credit and address will be excluded from Page 1. Most of the publication information will be included on the back page.

One of the first things we're doing to the nameplate is making the title larger. We drop the cursor in the line, World Report, and triple click to select the line. Experimenting with its appearance through the Measurements palette, we remove the bold style, enlarge the font to 48pt, then set the tracking to –10. We then set the cursor between the two words and increase kerning to 25.

The tag line and issue number are next triple-clicked and stretched out from the palette with tracking of 200. For use later on the back page we copy the text box with the Item tool, and move it temporarily to the pasteboard at the right. Then we remove the credit and address lines from the Nameplate text box by drag-selecting with the Content Tool Text Cursor, and shorten the box by grasping the bottom-center handle of the selected box and pulling upward.

We select the Rule (Orthogonal Line) tool to add a rule to set off the nameplate, dragging the rule into place (from left to right guide) beneath it. At the Measurements palette, we select the Thickness field by clicking, then key in a point size of **4pt** for the line. Using the View menu command **Hide guides**, we remove the guides and survey what we've done in Figure 5.17.

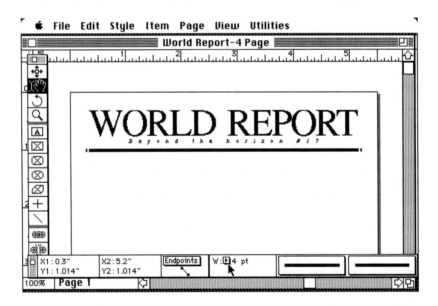

Figure 5.17 *Newsletter title and tag line set off.*

The Mailer Section

Before we retypeset and lay out the body text, we're going to prepare the back page mailer space. Then we'll have a clearer idea of how much space is available for the body copy.

To proceed, we'll need to create three more pages. This can be done through the Document palette or through the Page menu. The Document palette method is piecemeal, that is one page at a time. In this case we'll use the menu command. We open the Page menu and choose **Insert**. In the Insert Pages dialog box of Figure 5.18, we key in **3** in the **Pages** field, leave pressed the round button that indicates after page: 1, and leave the Master page selection at the default **M1-Master 1**, which is the one we set up when creating the document at the New dialog box.

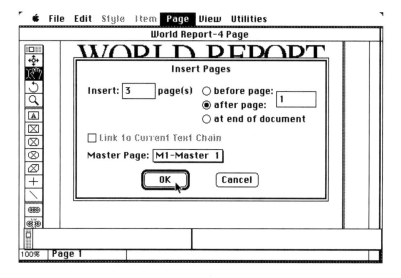

Figure 5.18   *Adding pages to the World Report-4 Pages document.*

Turning to the Document Layout palette (we've brought it up through the View menu **Show** command) we now see the icons for all four pages, with pages 2 and 3 shown as facing pages. The designation M1 sits in each page as an indication of the master page format applied to it. Our object is to move that text box, which sits on the pasteboard of Page 1 to Page 4. We could drag through the pages, but we prefer another way. Engaging the Item Tool, we select the text box and give the **Cut** command. Then at the Document Layout palette we double-click on the **Page 4** icon. Page 4 appears in the window, then we select the **Fit-in Window** view. Now we give the **Paste** command, and the text box appears on Page 4.

To develop the mailer section of the newsletter, we decide to use the lower half of the page. From the View menu the guides are switched to **Show** guides. The Rule tool is chosen and a rule drawn across the middle of the page at 4.25 inches, left-to-right margin. We select the **Thickness** field and type in the thickness in the Measurements palette, 4pt.

Next we make some adjustments to the text box just brought from Page 1. The text would sit well as a return address in the upper-left corner of the lower half of the page. So using the Content tool, we select the first line title with a triple-click, and after some experimentation reduce it to **22pt**, typed in at the Measurements palette. Next, after triple-click selecting the tag line, Beyond the Horizon, we reduce tracking on it (in the palette) to **45**.

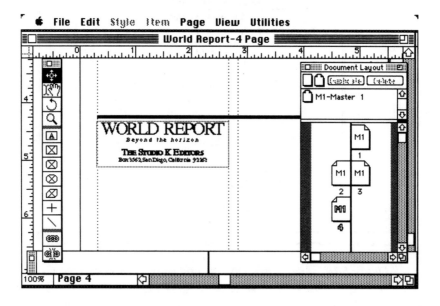

Figure 5.19 *A return address positioned on Page 4.*

Then manipulating the box handles, we size it down to fit in the left column under the rule. Using a Zoom Tool click to view in at 100%, we turn to the Content tool again to select the issue number and, pressing the **BACKSPACE** key, delete it, leaving the return address of the mailer as in Figure 5.19.

Text Layout on Page 2

Our attention turns to the text held in the Text #17 document. Our total layout area for text in World Report-4 Page has already been reduced. The format before us suggests headlines, grouping of articles. And these will further reduce the space available for body copy. We'll turn to the text document to see about gathering them for a unified page spread in Pages 2 and 3.

Using the View menu, Windows document list, we select **Text #17** and locate, then select by dragging the text cursor, the consecutive material on modern-day pirates and on on the Strait of Malacca. Estimating these will fit on one of the inside pages, we cut them into the Clipboard (using the keyboard, Command-X). Then at the View menu, Windows list, we select the World Report-4 page document again.

Using the Document Layout palette to double-click on the **Page 2** icon, we bring that page into the window, choosing from the View menu, Fit-in window. Next, we select the Text Box tool from the Tool palette, and draw a box within an area of page 2 where we imagine the body copy fitting.

N O T E

If your preference for fitting copy runs to using accurate word counts and calculating numbers of lines, here's an indirect, but quick method in QuarkXPress that provides a reliable count. It relies on the fact that before running a spelling check, the program runs a word count.

Open Utilities menu and open the **Spelling** list under it, then choose **Story** (or **Document** as appropriate). Then, allow the program to continue and it will present a small dialog box with the count of words in the story in which the cursor sits. At the end of this count it will then present a Spelling Checker dialog box. Click **cancel** and continue. The only disadvantage to this method is that it will lose your place in the text as the **Spelling Checker** settles in at the first suspect word in the story.

To bring in the pirate and Malacca text, we check that a text cursor is flashing in the text box on Page 2. We then issue the **Paste** command (at the keyboard, Command-V). The text cut from Text #17 flows into the text box. At the Measurements palette we select the **Cols:** field and type in **2**.

Next we hunt each piece in the text box for subheadings, at Actual size. Composing a suitable phrase at the keyboard for each article on Page 2, we copy the phrase (at the keyboard, Command-C). We then insert the cursor at the beginning of the article and paste in the subheading phrase (at the keyboard Command-V). Two carriage returns are added for separation. We edit our prospective subheading to a paraphrase where appropriate and remove the tab of the lead paragraph of each article.

Word counting through spell checking

Put the cursor in the story of interest

Open the Utilities menu and open the **Check Spelling** list

Note the count and click **OK**

When the Check Story dialog box appears click **Cancel**

Then selecting the subheading, we add style features of bold and all capitals. Figure 5.20 shows the first piece so treated. A subheading has been prepared for the Malacca piece as well. With the cursor still in the text, we select all (quintuple-click) and click the **Justify** Button on the Measurements palette.

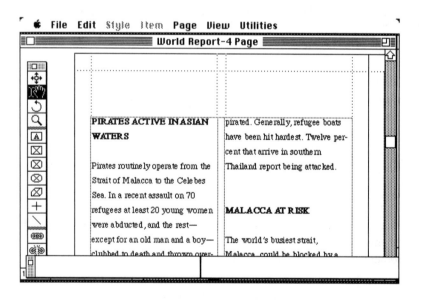

Figure 5.20   *Page 2 with a subheading.*

Finally, to achieve the right fit for this text box we drag the center handle of the top side down until all the copy fills the resized box (without generating an overflow "X" in the lower-right corner).

To headline the piece we choose the Text Box tool and drag a box into the space above the body text box. Into it we type the heading Seaworth Ships on the first line, then a return and at the next line, from Asian ports. To format the headline, we then select all the text (quintuple-click). At the Measurements palette we open the font list by a click on the arrow and choose the helvetica. For style, the choice is italic. Next, to size the Seaboard line we set the cursor in the word and triple-click to select the line. Experimenting with the choices in the list, we finally click in the **Size** field and type **30** for 30 points.

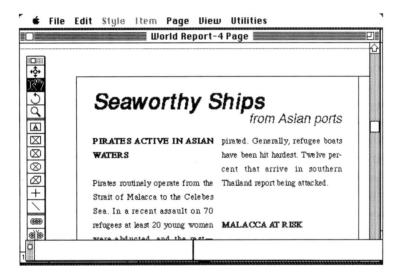

Figure 5.21 *Page 2 completed with heading and body text.*

At the second line of the heading box we insert the cursor and triple-click to select the line. Here we choose 18pt from the size list and click both the italic and the right-align buttons in the palette. The result is seen in the partial view of Page 2 in Figure 5.21.

Text Layout on Page 3

We complete the Pages 2 through 3 spread by returning through the View menu to the Text # 17 document and selecting, then cutting, text on contraband in

China and heroin in Sweden. Through the View menu, Windows list, we return again to World Report-4 page. Here we set the View to Fit-in window (at the keyboard, Command-0) and assure the guides are showing (from the View menu). Now, after the Text Box tool is selected, a text box is drawn across into the lower two-thirds of the Page 3 within the margins. The text cursor is flashing within that box, we paste the clipboard-held text (at the keyboard, Command-V), and the text flows in.

Experimenting with view sizes and the Grabber hand (Option-drag) we arrive at a 75% view that gives a clear perspective of the text box's story. Working at the Measurements palette, we type in the **Cols:** box 2 for a consistent layout. Assuring that all the text is selected, we set it at a larger font size (14pt) from the size list and increase the leading using the **Up Arrow** until an appropriate display seems apparent. We also use the Paragraph Format dialog box to set the indents and space after the paragraphs. A Top Text Box Handle is then dragged up, enlarging the box and pulling in all the text until we reach the partial layout of Figure 5.22.

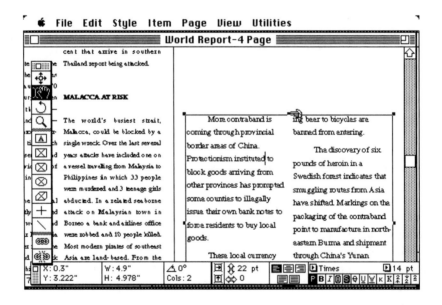

Figure 5.22 *Partial Layout of Page 3.*

Next comes creating a page 3 heading. With the Text Box tool we drag a box into place above the body text. The heading "Smuggling hot spots and responses" is typed. We deliberately key a return before the phrase "and responses" to drop it to a second line where we align it to the right.

Then **Select All** is invoked. Experimenting, we settle on Helvetica in a font size of 36pt through the drop-down lists of the Measurements palette. For an italic headline, we click the **I** button. To bring the heading lines closer together, the **Down Arrow** of leading is clicked until an agreeable 29 pt is reached.

Finally, on this page we add a comment line "New areas affected" and format this to fit as seen in Figure 5.23.

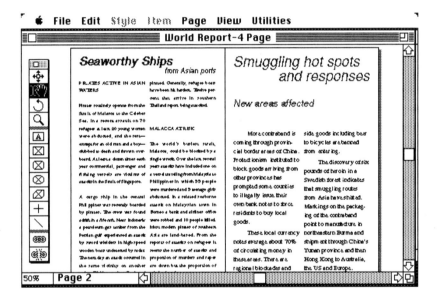

Figure 5.23   *Pages 2 and 3 with final adjustments.*

Text Layout on Page 1

Back at the Document Layout palette, we double-click on the icon to move our view to page 1. We're going to Text #17 document. Also we'll add a small table of contents for articles on the other pages. In Text #17 we drag-select and cut the articles on crossing Antarctica, the highest battleground, big game hunting, and the Greek merchant fleet, leaving only a piece on San Francisco maps behind in the text document. This we'll fit on Page 4, later.

We proceed in much the same manner as we did with Page 2, dragging out the text box, pasting in the text, setting two columns at the Measurements palette, eliminating first paragraph tabs, and creating small headlines for each piece.

Here, however, we want these in-line headings to stand out more since the articles are unrelated. Selecting the first head, we choose Helvetica, 18 pts at the Measurements palette where we also click the buttons for bold and italics.

Figure 5.24   In-line heads adjusted.

Also, to close up the vertical spacing which appears awkward at this large head size, the selection is clicked off and the text cursor clicked into place in the first line of the head. Then at the Measurements palette the **Leading Down-Arrow** is used to reduce the leading to 16, as seen in Figure 5.24. At this point we apply a shortcut to each of the other heads on Page 1 using an approach that works in almost any program that deals with text.

SHORTCUT

One shortcut to repeatedly applying type styles and other text formatting repeatedly works well for short text. For instance, headings may all require the same style and format. First set up the headline, exactly as it and its sibling heads should appear. Then select and copy it, move to the next head location and paste in that first headline. Select this pasted text and type the wording of the new head-line in its place. Using the above method for each of the remaining three heads on Page 1, we paste the first heading at each heading location, carrying along all of its formatting. Then we select the newly pasted head and rewrite it for that location. The formatting stays while the words change. In this way, all the heads are adjusted within a minute or so.

N O T E

The other way to apply recurring styles to a series of paragraphs involves the creation and use of style sheets, a subject explored in detail in Chapter 8. These are the tried and true way to preserve style and format selections to reapply. However, for merely three or so uses as we did here, it proves no faster or necessary than the shortcut above.

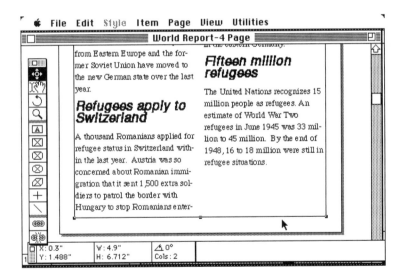

Figure 5.25   *Copy fit too tight for contents box.*

In adjusting the Page One heads all goes well, except one small feature. As shown in Figure 5.25, the text fits within the box, leaving insufficient room in the lower-right corner for the table of contents we'll be

In this case, we apply a simple solution. We enlarge the text box slightly to lengthen columns enough to open space at the bottom of the right column. This is accomplished easily by pulling upward ever so slightly on the middle box handle into the ample space below the title rule (as shown in Figure 5.26).

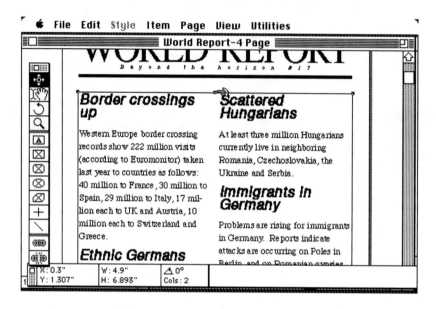

Figure 5.26   *Enlarging the text box vertically using the handle.*

A Table of Contents

Now we set up a table of contents. Our plan is that a small listing in the lower-right corner may entice readers on to the other articles. We first choose the Rule tool and draw a line across the right column to help separate copy above it from the contents below it. Then after a click on the **Text Box Tool** button, a small text box is drawn within the available space of the corner as in Figure 5.27. (Note that the **Text Runaround** function, which will be described in detail later, is not a factor here since the new text box is well clear of any text.)

All the material is now in place except the remainder, which we've destined for Page 4. So we can set up a list headed, Also in this issue, describing the contents of Pages 2, 3, and 4. Using the Measurements palette we apply Helvetica, italic, and 16 pt size to the contents heading, 14 to the list. And we adjust tracking in each, positive tracking to spread out the heading, and negative tracking to tighten the listed lines. As these final adjustments are completed, so is Page 1, shown in Figure 5.28.

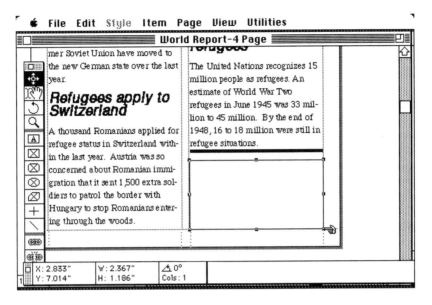

Figure 5.27 *Contents text box drawn over the body text box.*

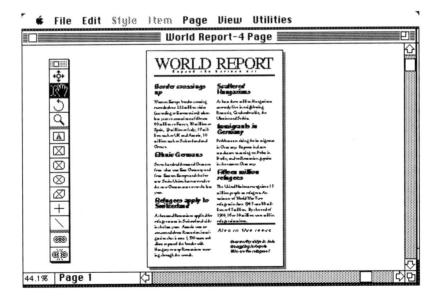

Figure 5.28 *Page 1 completed.*

Text Layout on Page 4

Now our attention shifts to Page 4 and to placing the last story of the newsletter. We bring the Document Layout palette onto the screen through the View menu, double-click on the icon for Page 4 and then use the Grabber hand (from Option-Drag) to slide the page to the center of the window. At the tool palette we click on the **Text Box Tool Button**, then draw-drag a box within the margins of the half of the page above the rule. After checking that the text cursor is flashing there, we use the **Paste** command and see the remaining text from Text #17 of flow into place as in Figure 5.29.

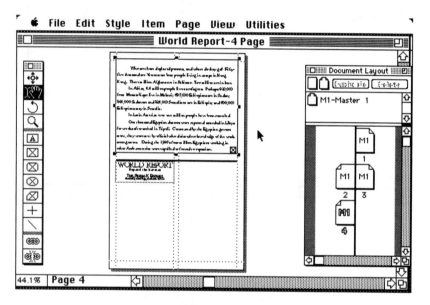

Figure 5.29 *Final text pasted.*

We specify **2** in the **Cols:** field. Next we'll have a look at the text. We select it all (Command-A) for adjusting style and format. Now what is immediately clear is that at 12pts the text will not all fit into the box we've drawn. Also clear is that we have three points that we want to call attention to. We now choose to cut out the first paragraph and make it into a heading. So, we quadruple-click to select it, and cut (Command-X). We pull-down the top of the text box by the middle handle to shorten it and make room for the heading box. Of course, this generates more text overrun, but we'll come back to that problem soon.

Now, we click on the **Text Box** button at the Tool palette and draw another text box the width of both columns above the copy already in place. The cursor appears in it, and we transfer the first paragraph text by pasting (Command-V). Once we key in changes that edit it into headline form, we select **all** (Command-A) and change font and size to Helvetica, 24pts. We then use the **Down Arrow** to reduce the leading to 22 points. And, we have a proper headline for the piece.

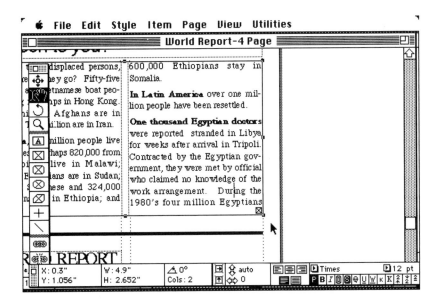

Figure 5.30 *Text overrun on Page 4.*

Next, in order to highlight each of the three points in the text we drag-select the phrase leading into each paragraph and apply bold style through the **Measurements Palette** button (**B**). As we look at our layout in Figure 5.30, the **x** in the lower-right corner of the text box indicates the overrun problem is still with us. To fit all the body text we choose to reduce the font size. (Since we're leaving the leading at auto, this will reduce the line spacing concurrently.) Experimenting with values typed into the selected size field in the palette, we arrive at the size, 11.5 points, which allows the text of the displaced persons piece to fit without being noticeably much different in size from the basic body copy in the newsletter. Figure 5.31 shows the final Page 4.

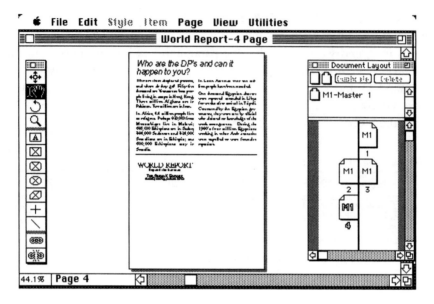

Figure 5.31   *Page 4 and the newsletter completed.*

Onward

In developing these newsletter layouts, we've applied basic text features of QuarkXPress. With these controls hundreds of well-crafted publications can be refined. However, typesetting in this program is a wide and rich field. More advanced and more powerful typographical features of the program will be explained in Chapter 8. There global document features, formatting, style sheets, linking text, and precision controls will unfold dazzling capabilities.

This grounding in the text and type functions is a strong start to creating visually expressive documents.

The next logical step is to see what QuarkXPress can do with images and the graphical features of both text and pictures. For, apart from its fonts and type-styling, text exists in boxes, which themselves possess yet more graphic features. Move on now to a grasp of the interactions among all text and graphic items.

Pictures, Boxes, and Interaction

What you will learn in this chapter:

- ❖ How to use picture boxes
- ❖ How to import graphics
- ❖ How to crop, size, and shape boxed images
- ❖ How to skew and rotate pictures
- ❖ How to reverse text
- ❖ How to align items
- ❖ How to set text runaround
- ❖ How to chain text boxes

Every element in a layout is really a graphic, even text. Drawings, photographs, rules, even the type flowing into columns creates imagery. QuarkXPress recognizes the graphic nature of every item in a page layout and works with it, whether the element is contained by a text or a picture box.

In this chapter we explore graphic aspects of both text and illustrations. We'll see what kind of images can be brought into the program's documents and how. We'll examine and use the ways to size and crop pictures, as well as the effects that any item can have on other page elements. We will begin the use of guides and rulers, and uncover the text runaround properties inherent in all items. We'll look into aligning, layering, and framing, as well as locking and rotating items and their contents.

To put all these qualities and controls into perspective, we'll start with an investigation of images that can be brought into a document. This process of importing reveals much about the graphic nature of every box and line on the page.

Pictures

QuarkXPress sees box content as either text, which we've already begun to explore, or pictures, more generally referred to as graphics or illustrations. Text and pictures, though mutually exclusive as content types, share many traits— while exhibiting some marked differences.

Unlike text, picture content cannot be generated directly inside QuarkXPress. While you can set up QuarkXPress documents that function adequately for word processing, you would be hard-pressed to do the same for generating images. On the other hand, you'll find a broad range of manipulation and enhancement tools and techniques that apply to images imported into the picture box.

Picture Forms

Let's look into how QuarkXPress provides Item boxes for images. The Tool palette is the starting point. Notice the four **Tool** buttons indicated in Figure 6.1. These are item-creating tools for pictures. They parallel the function of the Text Box tool above them. That is, while they can't produce any content themselves, they do construct Item boxes in which content—in this case picture images— reside.

The Picture Box tool you will probably use the most is the simplest. The basic rectangle Picture Box tool produces square-cornered boxes like those of the Text Box tool. It can be used to display the entire imported image, or it can serve as a matte to reveal only part of a picture. Other Picture Box tools produce boxes that function as alternatively shaped mattes through which canvases of imported graphics can be displayed. To create a rectangle picture box, you select the tool and drag out a box, as you do for a text box.

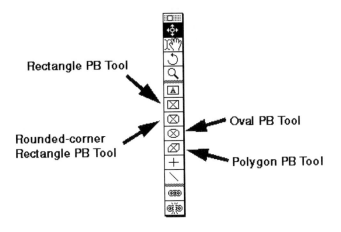

Figure 6.1   *Picture Box–generating tools.*

Your imported graphics files will almost certainly define a rectangular format. This will be true even if the image within a file appears circular or otherwise nonrectilinear. However, the display mattes through which graphics are seen in a document can be infinitely varied.

The **Palette** buttons for both the Rounded-Corner Rectangle and the Oval Picture Box tools show a likeness of the boxes they make. The rounded-corner rectangle boxes are simply variations on the rectangle box. The oval boxes are actually ellipses—that is, regular circles and circles elongated either horizontally or vertically.

Polygon picture boxes, as created with the final box tool, turn out to be much more variable. They are the odd uncles of the picture box family, being the only irregular—that is asymmetrical—shapes. Their tool, in fact, creates no particular shape at all, but facilitates the line-by-line drawing of "boxes" composed of sides in variable orientations—triangles, octagons, trapezoids, stars, and a multitude of irregular, flat-sided polygons.

Figure 6.2   *A graphic file from outside the document.*

The best way to examine what these boxes can do is to see how they contain imported illustrations. A graphic illustration can begin as a file outside of QuarkXPress, like that shown in Figure 6.2.

Such an illustration may have been produced in any Macintosh graphics program. It could also come from a PC or Windows platform program. It might have originated from software such as Adobe Illustrator, found in both software platforms. The illustration might have been generated through a screen-capture program, or it may have come through a scanner system, a digital camera, or a video-frame-capture system.

The type of file being imported can be Bitmap, TIFF, Encapsulated Postscript, PICT, and other file formats. Most will import directly into a document.

Importing into Picture Boxes

Whatever the file type, whatever the picture, the content is imported into a document in essentially the same way. The illustration in Figure 6.2 has been scanned, adjusted in a graphics program, and captured off the screen as a bitmapped image. Capable of being imported into a QuarkXPress document to various boxes, it can be masked in different forms to produce different pictures.

The method for bringing a picture into a QuarkXPress document is as follows. First, draw the box with one of the four Picture Box tools. Make sure that the box is selected and the Content tool is active, open the File menu, and choose **Get Picture**. The displayed dialog box (shown in Figure 6.3) is similar to the Get Text dialog box, and a graphics file can be selected and opened the same way—locate it and double-click. The graphic then appears within the picture box in the document.

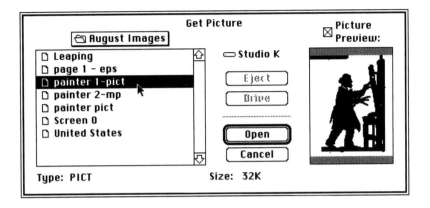

Figure 6.3 *Dialog box for importing a graphic.*

Importing a graphic

Activate a Picture Box tool and draw a box

Assure the Content tool is selected

At the File menu choose **Get Picture**

Locate the graphic file in the dialog box and double-click

Notice in the Get Picture dialog box that below the directory list is a heading, File Type. When you click to highlight a file in the list window the File type is indicated next to this heading. You can use the Get Picture dialog to search for graphics. When the **Preview** checkbox is X-ed a small thumbnail of the image appears to the right of the directory list as you highlight a file name. This is a great boon when you have the image but not the name fixed in your mind.

When a file is imported to a picture box, as shown in Figure 6.4, it is automatically seated in the upper-left corner of the rectangle that describes that box. In other words, the upper-left corner of the graphic is positioned in the upper-left corner of the box. In the case of Figure 6.4, the original image had a narrow black strip running partway across the image from the upper-left corner. This strip can be seen plainly at the upper-left portion of the picture box. Note that large white spaces extend to the right and bottom of the picture box (where you see what looks like a grabber hand). This picture box was larger than the picture being imported.

Figure 6.4   An imported image seated in the upper-left corner of a picture box.

When a picture box is smaller than the incoming graphic, some of the graphic may be obscured at the right and at the bottom. It may seem to be cropped off, but it's still accessible, as we shall soon see.

N O T E   As a file is being imported, the page-number indicator in the horizontal scroll bar becomes an indicator of the percentage of the file received, growing as the file is taken in. Often with 100K-or-smaller files, the importation process is so quick that it seems instantaneous on most computers. A large file—a scanned photograph of several megabytes, for example—is another matter. This is the time to examine your other page proofs, call the printer, or make that postponed trip to the water cooler.

Imported graphics are seated in the upper-left corner in the other types of picture boxes, but in a way that may render them obscured. In Figure 6.5 we see the results of importing the same graphic into a rounded rectangle and into an oval picture box.

Figure 6.5   *An image imported into rounded-corner and oval picture boxes.*

Noticeable in both, especially in the oval, is that the upper-left corner of the image is obscured. In fact, QuarkXPress, in using the same graphic-seating scheme, has put the upper-left portion of the graphic against the upper-left corner of the item box that would enclose the picture box mattes. You can visually define this area by noting the set of eight manipulation handles that surround each in a bounding rectangle. The oval, for instance, masks off the image in an elliptical shape, but it still contains all the graphic underneath the mask.

To create a picture box with either of these two tools, follow the same approach you used with the rectangle picture box, noting that when you drag out a diagonal you are defining the item-area bounding box, which is not quite the same as the oval or rounded rectangle box.

How rectangular is a rectangle? The rounded-corner box is really just a square-cornered box with an adjustment. That adjustment can be found in the Measurements palette for the picture box. The value is on the item half (left side) of the palette and is indicated by a small quarter-circle with a radial arrow pointing toward it. Look at the value for a rectangle picture box; you'll see it's zero. By keying in a new value you can adjust the corners of either of these box types. This adjustment is also found in the Picture Box Specifications dialog box (Item menu to **Modify**) as **Corner Radius**.

The final Picture Box tool to consider creates not one kind of form, but countless kinds. The Polygon Picture Box tool might take a little getting accustomed to. Its operation is simple, though. Imagine a shape you wish to form out of straight sides (a star, a lopsided triangle, and so forth). Select the tool and click at one of the corners of the shape. Drag the mouse to an adjacent angle point (noticing that a side stretches into place as you do so) and click there. Continue until you've come full circuit back to the first point, and double-click. This creates a polygon—that is, a many-sided figure. The simplest polygon picture box you can make is a triangle.

Making a polygon picture box

Using the Polygon tool, click at each angle in turn
Return to the first click point and double-click

Figure 6.6 shows a polygon picture box made this way in the form of a jagged-sided box. The image file was imported into it directly. Notice that, once selected, the box's manipulation handles are displayed in a rectangular boundary around the polygon shape, and that the image as we know it would fit into the upper-left of that boundary.

Figure 6.6 *One result of using the polygon picture box tool.*

SHORTCUT

A shortcut for closing the polygon is to double-click at the last angle point. The final side will automatically be drawn back to the first point, completing the picture box .

The contents of a picture box bear the same relation to the box as text to a text box. Similarly, a new image can be imported into a picture box that is selected and filled, replacing existing contents. Contents can likewise be cut, copied, and pasted from one box to another, replacing the images already there.

Picture Cropping, Picture Sizing

Few images are accepted "as is" in page design. Choosing the form of a box to contain the image is one of your first layout decisions. Precisely selecting which portion of the image should appear in the layout is another. Like a photographer in the darkroom, we can mask away all that is extraneous, and enlarge or reduce where necessary. (Modifying the image in contrast, color, and so forth, is also possible. The methods for achieving these modifications will be explained later.)

Sizing and shaping the picture box are two basic functions we'll need to master to achieve graphic success. Likewise necessary are positioning the content image within the picture box, and sizing and shaping the image.

Shaping the Picture Box

A picture box is like a document window and also like a text box. For instance, you can size the picture box by dragging any of the eight manipulation handles that bound it, just as you can with text boxes. With pictures, enlarging the picture "window" sometimes reveals whole images, or portions that may have been hidden through being imported—as shown in Figure 6.7, where a small picture box on the left is seen to reveal only part of a much larger image made visible when the box is enlarged on the right. If the area visible in a small picture box is just white space, you might be tricked into thinking the image wasn't successfully imported. Figure 6.8 shows just such a situation. None of the image visible in the enlarged box on the right side was apparent when the file was first imported into the box on the left.

Figure 6.7   *Effect of enlarging one particular picture box.*

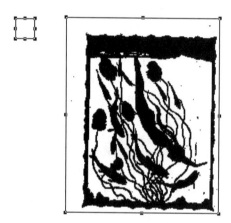

Figure 6.8   *An apparently empty picture box enlarged.*

If your page design calls for a specific area to be displayed, you could use the box handles to resize the picture box to conceal all but that area. In this case you could drag the upper-left corner handle diagonally toward the lower right until it bounded only the portion of interest, as Figure 6.9 shows only one corner of a world map.

Be advised that the above method can sometimes lead to enormous document files. Keep in mind that we have imported a representation of the entire image file in order to use a small portion of it. The document will grow by a size determined by the entire image file, not just the part displayed. Individually displaying—in different text boxes—a tenth of one entire image file would result in a document file with ten times the kilobytes (or megabytes) devoted to graphics in it. If the original image file is large—a scanned gray-scale or color photograph of several megabytes, for example—the resulting document file could threaten to overwhelm some already burdened hard-disk drives. It would also drastically increase processing time during printing.

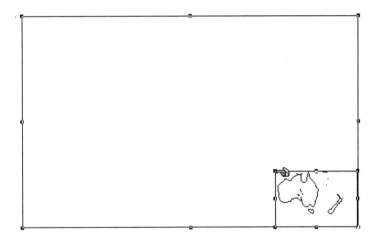

Figure 6.9   *Shaping the window around a part of the image.*

When document size must be kept within certain limits, you would do well to cut areas out of the original image file in a graphics-manipulation program and save each area as a separate image file. These sectioned files can then be imported to the QuarkXPress document where specifically called for. This takes more time, of course, so it is appropriate only when limiting document size is more important than saving time.

The Picture Grabber

In the preceding section we enlarged a small picture box that displayed one corner of the image to a large, all-revealing box, and then reduced it back to a small picture box over a different part of the image. Basically, we moved the underlying image through the picture box view. The same thing can be done directly by a single tool. The Picture Grabber Hand tool works within the picture box as the Grabber Hand tool works in a document window. When the Content tool is put over a selected box, the grabber hand cursor appears.

To use the Picture Grabber, position the Content tool over a selected picture box and press the mouse button. Then as the grabber hand appears, drag the picture within the box, sliding into view the image portion to be displayed. For example, the image in the rectangular graphic shown in Figure 6.10 was imported into the small oval picture box—shown below it on the left. Using the picture grabber, the image was moved within the oval until the chosen area came into view, as seen in the oval on the right.

Figure 6.10 *Cropping with the picture grabber hand.*

Using the Picture Grabber tool

Position the Content tool over the picture box

Drag the image through the window

The Picture Grabber tool is especially useful in conjunction with your ability to adjust the extent of the picture box around an image. In fitting a scanned photograph of a person, for instance, you can perform cropping by pulling down the top side of the picture box to exclude some sky in the background, and use the grabber to position the image of the person so it appears balanced in the box.

The Picture Grabber Hand tool is useful for precise positioning within a box, but it is by no means the only way to move an image there. The Measurements palette provides a handy alternative, monitoring and controlling the shift of an image from its original seating at the upper-left of the picture box's bounding box. These values are labeled there as X+ and Y+. By keying in new values you will cause the image to shift accordingly to a new position within the box.

Shaping and Sizing the Image

Important for manual control of pictures is the third major picture box feature, sizing the image within the picture box. As you know, dragging a box handle simply allows you to extend or reduce the box's window without affecting the image. Changing the image's size and shape, however, is an ability that will prove useful for innovative graphics within a document file.

Fortunately, this is as easy as reshaping the picture box. To resize an image residing inside a picture box, hold down the **Command** key while dragging one of the box handles. The image will grow as the picture box grows. Note that if you pull disproportionately in one direction, the image will be distorted, appearing squashed or stretched. The image in Figure 6.11 is shown (left to right) first as it was imported, next as it was after a **Command-drag** in the downward direction only, then as it was after a **Command-drag** in the rightward direction only.

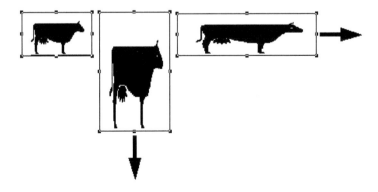

Figure 6.11 *Reshaping the image in two directions.*

Reshaping, resizing the picture image

Command-drag the picture box handles

A more numerical approach is to use the right side of the Measurements palette, which affects content. There you'll find two values, labeled **X%** and **Y%**, that monitor and control the amount of stretch and compression in the horizontal and vertical directions, respectively. Note that this will expand or reduce the image within an unchanging picture box. Using it will almost certainly require your repositioning the image within the box afterward.

It's easy to see how a series of adjustments made by dragging the image and positioning with the Picture Grabber tool, can produce a picture image that has gotten away from an experimenting designer. Two picture features, useful in their own right, are available to impose instant order on images that have grown unruly within picture boxes.

Both adjustments are automatic keyboard commands. The first resizes and reshapes the image to fit within the picture box, distorting it if necessary. It is activated by selecting the picture box with the Content tool, then holding down the **Command** and **Shift** keys while pressing **F**. The result will be an image (defined by the original imported file, not necessarily the visible image) adjusted to match precisely the dimensions on the picture box.

Instant fitting of image within picture box

Command-Shift-F

A second command resizes the image to its original proportions (height-to-width ratio) within the picture box. Engage this function by selecting as above, then holding down the **Command**, **Shift**, and **Option** keys while pressing **F**. Take note that restoring the original height-to-width ratio of the image file can lead to an unfilled picture box. For instance, a square image that has been pulled into a long, rectangular shape, will return to a square image, leaving the rest of the rectangle empty when this proportional fitting is applied.

> ## Instant fitting of image proportionally within picture box
>
> **Command-Shift-Option-F**

These functions can expedite your graphic arrangements, especially when certain picture box dimensions must be adhered to, as well as when regaining the true proportions of an image—as with photographs—is vital. Likewise, they're crucial to pulling a picture's image onto the center stage of a picture box, where it can be manipulated further.

Box Characteristics

All boxes in QuarkXPress, whether text or picture boxes, possess certain characteristics. These features greatly affect their contents. Many of these characteristics are not noticed until they're changed. Others are obvious to you. Now that you've gained some understanding of text boxes and picture boxes, let's investigate those QuarkXPress features that can most enhance the contents of both.

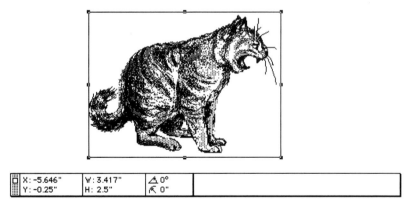

| X: -5.646" | W: 3.417" | ∠ 0° |
| Y: -0.25" | H: 2.5" | ⦨ 0" |

Figure 6.12 *The measurements palette monitoring control of box location and size.*

Two of the characteristics you've already explored; the Measurements palette will help reveal them to you. Recall how the **X** and **Y** values located the horizontal and vertical coordinates of a text box's upper-left corner on the page? These coordinate values have the same significance for boxes of either text or graphic content.

Likewise, the width and height values can apply to both text and picture boxes. The left half of the Measurements palette monitors item features, as shown in Figure 6.12. We've already seen how you can use the palette as a control device by keying in or selecting values to replace those displayed. This approach can be followed in the same way with all the box features.

Box Frames

Let's look into an altogether different feature, one common to both text and picture boxes. So far we've let the content of items in our document form their own frames. The alignment characteristics in justified text does this. The white space surrounding picture images can do so as well. But the simplest way to make text or pictures stand apart is by drawing a frame around it. QuarkXPress provides an automatic feature to do this. To adjust the frame around any item box, select the box with an Item or Content tool, then open the Item menu and choose **Frame**.

When this is done for the picture shown in Figure 6.12, we arrive at the dialog box shown in Figure 6.13. Apparently there is no frame about this picture box. However, settings in the dialog box for Frame Specifications reveal a solid frame has been applied to the box through the default setting, but the width was set at zero points. In this case it was automatically applied to the box when it was created. A look through the dialog reveals that four options are offered: Frame Type, Frame Thickness (or Width), Frame Color, and Frame Shade (or Color Density).

At the left in the dialog is a scrolling window of frame types. QuarkXPress provides 16 such types: a single-line type, three types of double-line frames, three of the triple-line variety, and nine other types. Clicking on a frame type produces a small replica frame at the top of the dialog box.

At the right is a drop-down **List** field for width, with preset choices to 12 points. You can also type in values not given in this listing, such as 4.5 points or 24 points. Below this is a drop-down list for color, set by default to black. If you plan to separate colors later, other choices could come in handy.

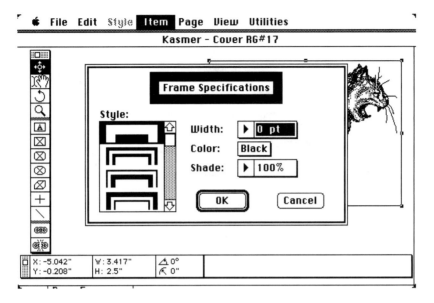

Figure 6.13 *The Frame dialog box.*

 Certain colors are made available automatically within the document. These include the RGB colors on which color monitors rely and those of the color model called CMYK. Together they provide the color choices seen on the drop-down list: blue, cyan, green, magenta, red, yellow, as well as black and white, of course. Others can be added, as you will see. (There will be more to say about color in Chapter 16.)

Third of the drop-down lists is one for shade. The percentage chosen (or typed in) for shade is applied to the color chosen in the field above, lightening or intensifying the effect of that color.

Figure 6.14 shows the result of keying in a frame width of 16 points. You'll notice that the frame was applied from the limit of the picture box inward, so that in this case it actually obscures part of the picture image. This method, inside the box, is a default setting that can be adjusted through the Edit menu's Preferences choice, by choosing **General**. We'll look more closely into preferences in the final chapter.

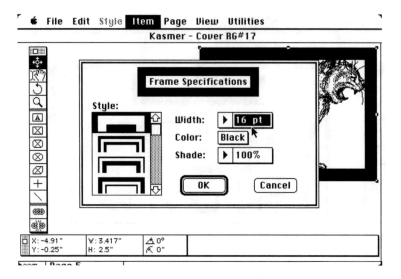

Figure 6.14 *A frame of 16 points applied to a picture box.*

Box Backgrounds

QuarkXPress boxes have another feature easily overlooked. This box feature is accessible through either the Content or Item tool and is established for each text and picture box in a document. This is the background. Each box has an adjustable background, which may vary according to color and shade.

This feature is often overlooked because the default is normally set to white, and text and images coming into boxes are most often black. However, a background need not be white. To change it, select the box by Item or Content tool, open the Item menu and choose **Modify**. A dialog box titled Text Box Specifications or Picture Box Specifications will appear, depending on the item.

N O T E

In applying backgrounds to picture boxes, you'll encounter times when a change in the background is not reflected in the picture box. What is most likely happening in this case depends on the picture image itself. If a part of the image is set to be clear in the graphics program that created it, the background of a picture box will show through. If part is set to be white, the white color will obscure the background. Since both white and clear appear identical until such moments, it's easy to mistake one for the other.

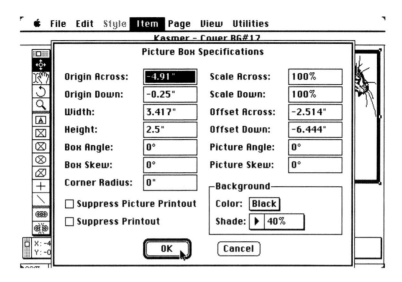

Figure 6.15   *The Picture Box Specifications dialog box.*

The **Modify** command automatically presents a distinct dialog box according to the type of item selected. Figure 6.15 shows one example of the Specifications dialog box reached through this command. Although a host of a values seems to occupy this box, you'll find at least half of them are already known to you through your use of the tool-based and Measurements palette methods described earlier. We shall return to all these values later. For now, look directly to the lower-right section of the dialog box, where the background controls are. The adjustments are simple. Color can be set to any of those available in the drop-down list. The shading of any selected color can be fixed at values between **0%** and **100%**, chosen from the drop-down list or keyed into the field. The same Background section is available in the Specifications dialog box for both text and picture boxes.

In Figure 6.16, the picture box background has been set to **Black, 30%** while the background of the text box next to it has been adjusted to **Black, 10%**, each by using the Item menu's **Modify** command.

N O T E

Working with pictures, text, and lines, you will notice that the dialog boxes and even the menu listings change according to what type of item is selected. This can be disorienting when you think you've chosen a picture item and are presented with typographical choices. Most notable is the change in the Style menu, which is really a switchable control, altering its menu listing behind the scenes as either line, text, or picture is selected. Figure 6.17 shows the three variations of the Style menu. Also significant are the sibling Specifications dialog boxes arising from the **Modify** command of the Item menu. These different dialogs are shown in Figure 6.18.

Figure 6.16   *Setting different backgrounds in adjacent boxes.*

Style	**Style**	**Style**
Font ▶	Color ▶	Line Style ▶
Size ▶	Shade ▶	Endcaps ▶
Type Style ▶	Negative ⌘⇧–	Width ▶
Color ▶		Color ▶
Shade ▶	✓Normal Contrast ⌘⇧N	Shade ▶
Horizontal/Vertical Scale…	High Contrast ⌘⇧H	
Kern…	Posterized ⌘⇧P	
Baseline Shift…	Other Contrast… ⌘⇧C	
Character… ⌘⇧D		
	✓Normal Screen	
Alignment ▶	60-Line Line Screen/0°	
Leading… ⌘⇧E	30-Line Line Screen/45°	
Formats… ⌘⇧F	20-Line Dot Screen/45°	
Rules… ⌘⇧N	Other Screen… ⌘⇧S	
Tabs… ⌘⇧T		
Style Sheets ▶	Flip Horizontal	
	Flip Vertical	
Flip Horizontal		
Flip Vertical		

Figure 6.17   *Three versions of the Style menu.*

SHORTCUT

A quick way to bring up an item's Specifications dialog box is to double-click on that item with the Item tool.

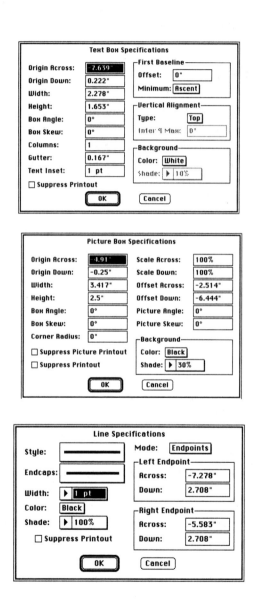

Figure 6.18 *Three variations of the Specifications dialog box.*

Backgrounds can be useful all by themselves. By creating boxes that contain nothing but gray or black backgrounds, for instance, you can include QuarkXPress-generated shadows behind text or picture boxes to make them appear to float on the page. To do this, create a box of the same size and then adjust its background to a black or grey shade.

Picture Content

Picture boxes are adjusted the same way in any type of picture. But adjustments to the image within the box can be made only to bitmapped images. As you might know, bitmapped images are composed of pixel dots arranged in a very fine mosaic, in which each square pixel is either black, white, gray, or a color. When QuarkXPress encounters bitmapped images, it is able to perform changes in color, contrast, and and other features. We'll now look at those adjustments we can perform on any imported image file. Keep in mind that a fuller range of special bitmapped adjustments will be covered in Chapter 12.

Content Colors

There are several adjustments that affect the nature of any image, text, or line. One of them is color. QuarkXPress assigns a color to every text, image, and line as it is created or imported. That color, which we take for granted, is black.

But you can assign a color of your choosing to any of the items in a document. Of course, elements in documents destined for color separations definitely require this kind of adjustment. But, as you'll notice, color is useful for indicating nonprinting features on the screen as well. Margin, rule, and grid lines are displayed in distinct colors.

Even if you're not planning on printing in color, you can use it to make certain pieces stand out for easy recognition during layout, as you might with a story that is being jumped between several pages. You can color each of several stories differently to see how they play throughout your document.

For the moment, we'll consider color variations of the black-and-white variety. The same principles will apply for all the colors available in QuarkXPress. (Chapter 16 details color use.) We'll begin with the simplest of items, the line. To demonstrate variability, three lines have been dragged across the drawing shown in Figure 6.19. The line across the top has been changed to white through the Style menu, Color list; the line at the midsection has been changed to Black on the Color list, 30% on the Shades list; the line through the bottom to Black, 65% (set through Other on the Shades list).

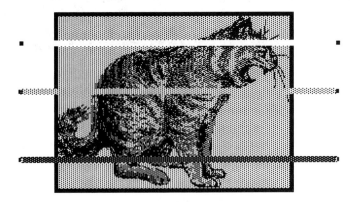

Figure 6.19   *Three lines of different color/shade settings.*

To change a color, select the item (if picture or text, use the Content tool), open the Style menu, open the Color list, and click on the color. To change a shading, do likewise, opening the Shade list and clicking, or choosing Other and keying in a value.

Shading choices are not available with White, simply because in the "print world" white is the absence of any color.

N O T E

With picture elements, changes in color and shading can have dramatic effects. Notice how changing the color of the sketch picture to white has given an etched appearance to the image on the left side of the illustration shown in Figure 6.20.

With picture elements, there is another option on the Style menu that changes the image features to the background color and shading, and vice versa. This choice is labeled *Negative*. It's effects on the image shown in Figure 6.16 are seen on the right side of the illustration shown in Figure 6.20.

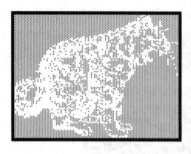 

*Figure 6.20   Effects of applying the color White, and the **Negative** command.*

Reverse Text

It is with text that color and shading adjustments are perhaps most dramatically applied. Used in coordination with the background controls, text coloring can produce the attention-getting reverse-type effect.

Achieving this sort of typographic "shout" is a two-step process. Begin by selecting the text box with the Content tool, then select the text to be reversed. Use the Item menu's **Modify** command to go to the Text Box Specifications dialog box. There, set the background to **Black, 100%**. Using the Style menu's Color list, choose **White** for the selected text. The result is white text in a black box, as shown in Figure 6.21.

> Time will reverse
> many of your
> present opinions

Figure 6.21   Reversed type.

Instead of choosing white, you could choose a faint shade of a text color, as in Black, 20%, though this tends to diminish the reversed text's impact. Note also that shading text on a white background can produce interesting headlines and subheads.

Reversing type

Select text

Open Specifications dialog box, set background to **Black, 100%**

Open Style menu, choosing **Color** as **White**

Rotating Boxes

Another feature shared by text and picture boxes is their *orientation*. Typically, we see boxes created in the upright position. For instance, all text begins in lines running horizontally across the page, imported pictures normally are brought in upright. But the box that encloses type or image need not remain horizontally fixed.

Any picture, any text box can be rotated. You can rotate items from the Measurements palette. You might have noticed a value in the Text palette not yet explained. This is the rotation value for the box, or the box angle. In Figure 6.22, two text boxes have been created, one to serve as a simulated note, the other as a caption. The Note box was rotated 15° by selecting that field above the column value in the Measurements palette and keying in the amount. Any box can be similarly rotated, simply by adjusting the box angle in its Measurements palette. Positive values indicate counterclockwise rotation; negative values indicate clockwise rotation.

Two other means of rotation exist in QuarkXPress. One is through adjusting the **Box Angle** value in the Specifications dialog boxes seen earlier. The other is through the Rotation tool, found below the Content tool in the Tools palette. This method is especially suited for those who like the live action of seeing the box and contents roll around on the screen. It's also chosen as the method most likely—from time to time—to bewilder those who use it. However, as it provides active real-time control, it might be best employed when trying to achieve a precise, visual angular fit.

Here's how to use the tool: First, imagine that you're using a lever to turn the box. The lever can be anywhere, inside or outside the box. Select the box. Then using the Rotation tool, press the mouse button down at a point that will serve as the fulcrum; a small registration-style image will be displayed. Then, still holding the button down, drag out the lever arm, and lift or pull down around the fulcrum point (with the arrowhead cursor that appears). The box will move as you do. Release the button when you've finished the rotation.

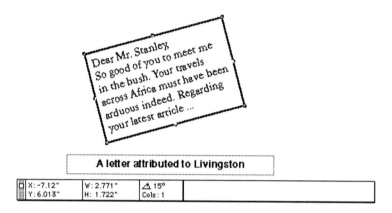

Figure 6.22   *A rotated text box over one not rotated.*

Using the Rotation tool

Select the box

Click a fulcrum point

Drag out a rotation lever

Pull the lever around the point

It's usually wisest to select a fulcrum rotation point outside the box, and to drag out a long lever arm to gain the best torque control. Otherwise, you might notice the box moving rather wildly.

In-Box Picture Rotating

In the case of picture boxes, there is another form of rotation. The other rotation moves the image within the box while the box remains unrotated. In Figure 6.23, the picture in the box on the left has been rotated 45°. The picture in the box on the right has also been rotated 45°, and the box itself has been rotated -45°. This in-box feature is labeled Picture Angle in the Picture Box Specifications dialog box, and is also located at the extreme upper-right of the Measurements palette.

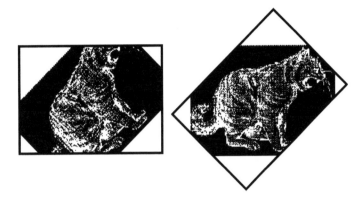

Figure 6.23   *Image rotation and combined box and image rotation.*

Picture Skewing

Another feature peculiar to pictures is *skewing*, which is somewhat like dealing with a rubber canvas. Imagine a stretched canvas in which the two side stretcher bars were installed with hinges. The bottom side of the canvas can be seen to be anchored in place while the top and the two vertical sides are unjoined at their corners, left free to move sideways. If the rest of the canvas were then flexible and the free sides were pulled left or right horizontally, you would see a distortion in one dimension only, or a skew. Figure 6.24 shows an image of the now-familiar Tool palette next to the same image skewed to 45°. Notice how the buttons are at precisely the same heights they were on the original unskewed image, though they have been drastically shifted horizontally.

To skew the image in a picture box, select the box with the Content tool and key in an angle value in the Measurements palette at the lower-right corner, or in the Picture Box Specifications dialog box. Skewing can be used more subtly to create surprising effects, or to simulate shadows, especially when black and shading are applied to the skewed image.

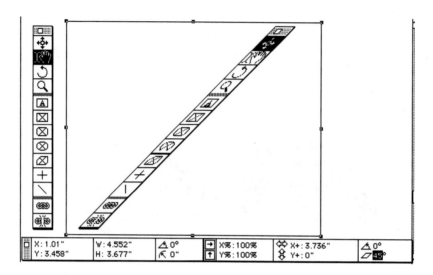

Figure 6.24 *An image and its skewed copy.*

Rulers, Guides, and Grids

It's hard to imagine laying out complex document pages without the help of rulers and guides. QuarkXPress provides every document window with a pair of rulers that can be displayed or hidden through the View menu **Show Rulers/Hide** Rulers toggle command. These are active monitors, indicating by faint dotted markers when the Item tool is dragging out a selection box, or when an item box is being created or moved. They help when you want feedback about your hand-eye coordinations on the page. You can adjust the units in which they are marked just as you can adjust the units in which measurements are displayed—by the **Preferences** commands (which are explained later).

Hidden in the usefulness of the rulers is their ability to release guidelines that show onscreen (in contrasting color) but don't print. To pull out a guide, point the cursor on the ruler and drag onto the page. A guide will come out of the ruler when you do so. You can pull out as many guidelines as you desire or move guides already in place as you create a design grid.

The display of these guides is controlled through the View menu's **Show Guides/Hide Guides** toggle command. The **Snap to Guides** feature can be set through the View menu as well.

Creating a guideline

Assure that the rulers are displayed

Point on the rule, oriented as the guideline will be, and drag out a line

---

N O T E

The **Snap to Guides** feature exerts a pull on any item being dragged near a guide. When an item approaches within a minimum distance set in Preferences, it is forced toward that guide, its nearest side stopping against the guide. This is a handy, automatic method for quick, precise alignment. You will find, though, many times you'll want to deactivate the feature and turn off its "helpfulness."

How Items Interact

On pages, ads, and other graphic designs we find that text, pictures, and lines are neighbors to each other; they overlap. Sometimes one box pushes the contents of another out of it altogether. When your layout juxtaposes elements in close proximity in a design, no item will remain unaffected by its fellows.

Next, you'll see what effects text, pictures, and lines have on each other, and how these effects can be exploited in fulfilling your design plans.

Monitoring Multiple Items

What happens when more than one item is selected? And what can we do if we've chosen a set of disparate elements like the picture boxes and text box shown in Figure 6.25?

QuarkXPress treats every set of selected items as though a great bounding box had been established around them all. This imaginary bounding box extends as far as each of the bounding boxes within it. When multiple items are selected, the program monitors and allows control of the origin point (X and Y coordinates), the item angle, and the background of the set of items. In such a case, the origin (the upper-left corner) indicates the position of the great bounding box that would contain all the items.

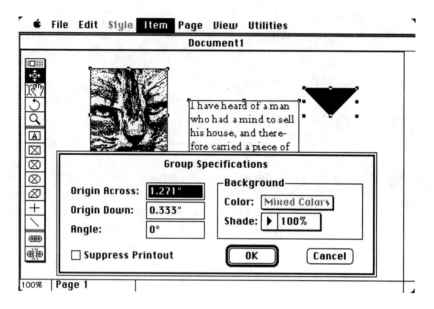

Figure 6.25   *A set of items selected together.*

Look at the Measurements palette or at the Specifications dialog box (from the **Modify** command) for a set of selected items—as shown in Figure 6.25. You'll see that options there have been limited to those few qualities that can be handled collectively. In other words, select several items at once and QuarkXPress will let you work on features they share as a set.

Aligning and Spacing

Let's consider items on a page. True, they can be positioned and ordered by manual methods. Automatic methods, however, are more precise. QuarkXPress provides a dialog box that allows you to position items in relation to one another. You can specify a vertical or horizontal alignment. You can call for a particular spacing of items on the page. This spacing can be accomplished by measurement, as in setting items so many inches apart, in the range from 0 inches to 10 inches. It can be achieved by percentage (as in moving items to, say, 50% of their previous separation, or 200%) in a range from 0% to 1,000%. You space items by setting a distance between them, one of their sides, or their centers. You can also direct the program to space the items evenly within the limits set by their farthest members.

The **Space/Align** command is found under the Item menu. To use it, first select the items, then choose the command. At the dialog box (shown in Figure 6.26) click on the checkbox for the orientation you wish to space: Horizontal, Vertical, or both. If you have a specific separation, make sure that the **Space** button is engaged before you key in your value. Next, in the Between drop-down list choose one of the four options. (Note that the **Space/Align** command considers each item as the bounding box that surrounds it.) Click **Apply** to pre-view the change, and **OK** when it's to your liking.

Alternatively, you might have the program arrange for uniform separation of the items selected. Do this by clicking the **Distribute Evenly** button. (Note that in this case at least three items must be selected.)

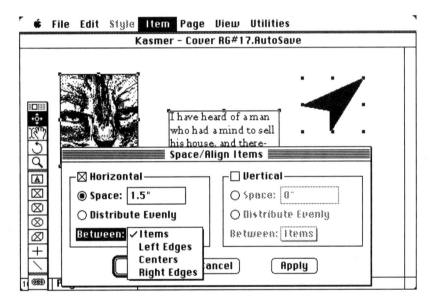

Figure 6.26   *The Space/Align dialog box.*

When aligning or spacing horizontally, the program will keep the leftmost item fixed and move the others to accomplish the spacing. In aligning or spacing vertically, the uppermost item is kept fixed as the others are moved.

To align items along a horizontal or vertical axis, activate the checkbox that represents the other direction, and key in **0**. In Figure 6.27 for instance, the three items were all aligned flush to the top by checking **Vertical**, keying in **0**, then choosing **Between Top** edges.

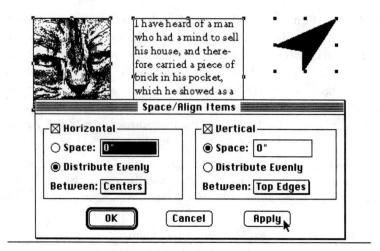

Figure 6.27 *Aligning to a horizontal.*

Depths of Layering

Items are added to a document in layers. Layering provides a way to manage images, text runaround, and visually interactive overlays. If you limit yourself to arranging items side-by-side, you'll never deal with layering, but you'll also miss the many functions it provides.

As soon as two items overlap, the effects of relative depth become significant. As an item is created, one specific layer is established that belongs to that item alone. Until it is specifically assigned to another layer, any item will remain at a certain depth on your document, no matter where it may be shifted horizontally or vertically. In other words, moving an item in the X and Y axes will not affect its position along the Z axis. The first item created on a page resides in the layer closest to the page. As other items are created, they are put on layers of their own, each above the earlier items. This is demonstrated in Figure 6.28, where first a circle was drawn, then a square, then a triangle.

Item-depth order is established as items are created. But an item may be reshuffled within the layers. Two controls exist for this in the Item menu: sending an item back to the layer closest to the page and bringing it to the topmost layer.

Note that moving an item to the top layer, for instance, does not put it at the same depth as the item already there. Rather, this action reshuffles the layers so that the item previously on top becomes second to the top.

To move an item to a different layer, select it and choose the appropriate command from the Item menu.

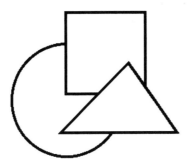

Figure 6.28   *Layering depths created when a circle, then square, then triangle are drawn.*

In Figure 6.29, the triangle is shown being sent to the backmost layer using the **Send to Back** command. In layering, background becomes especially significant. Although the backgrounds, White and None, often look identical, the former obscures items behind it, the latter reveals them.

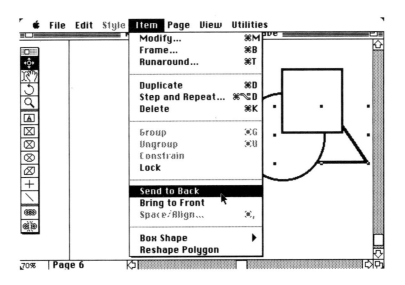

Figure 6.29   *Sending an item, the triangle, to the lowest layer.*

Text Runaround

Every item in a document bears a special relationship to text with which it comes into contact. Text reacts when it flows into space occupied by some other item. It may write over the item, flow around the item, flow around the bounding box of the item, or be otherwise redirected in its layout. This effect is known as *text runaround*.

There are two conditions that determine when text flow will be affected by another item: when the text box sits on a layer behind the item, and when the item has a runaround applied to it. Using the layer control discussed above, you can satisfy the first of these conditions. The second is adjustable through a dialog box when the item is selected. Although there are countless variations of effects, they all come from one of four settings in QuarkXPress. Figure 6.30 shows the Runaround Specifications dialog box, which is reached through the Item menu by choosing **Runaround**.

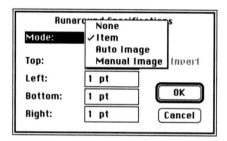

Figure 6.30 *The Runaround Specifications dialog box.*

Figure 6.31 shows two modes of text runaround. The text on the left has simply run over the picture image. In this case there was no runaround in effect; the runaround mode was specified as None. The text on the right has flowed around the rectangular bounding box of the image. Here the runaround mode was specified as Item.

In the Runaround Specifications dialog box, four fields—labeled **Top**, **Left**, **Bottom**, and **Right**—sit below the **Mode** field. Each designates the offset of text from the object in question—that is, how close text can be to the object before it breaks to the next line. Be aware that in QuarkXPress text lines will flow only to one side of the runaround object. The program is designed to make a line-by-line determination of which side provides the most horizontal space, and to place the text on that side.

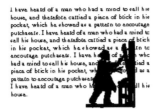

Figure 6.31   *Runaround Modes: None and Item.*

Establishing text runaround

Assure the runaround item is selected and above the text
layer

At the Item menu choose **Runaround**, select the Mode and
set the offset spacing

The program can also perform a more custom-fit text runaround. The two other
modes of runaround are shown in Figure 6.32. The left side gives an example of
Auto Image mode. Here QuarkXPress detects the extent of the image and wraps
it in a kind of unseen fence to which the text is allowed to approach each line
according to the offset value entered in the dialog box.

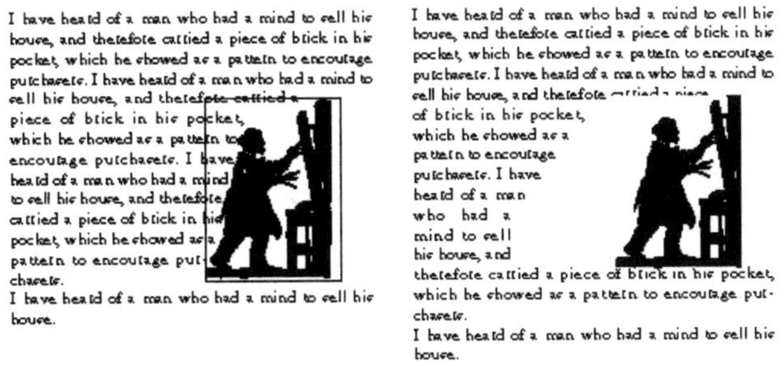

Figure 6.32   *Runaround Modes: Auto Image and Manual Image.*

The right side shows what happens with Manual Image mode—and a bit of tinkering. In Manual Image, the "fence" is displayed in the form of a runaround polygon, complete with handles connecting line segments. You can move a handle or a line by clicking on it and dragging. That's just what was done in the figure. By holding down the **Command** key and clicking you can insert new handles, or remove existing ones. You can drag the runaround polygon sides and handles anywhere, inside or outside the item bounding box.

Adjusting a manual image

Drag the side or handle into place

Add or remove handles by **Command-click**

Text Box Linking

Since we're dealing with relations among items, one special area deserves attention: the connection between one text box and another. We've seen picture boxes, lines, and text boxes interacting on the page, most often as a result of proximity. A different sort of association arises between some text boxes, one that is independent of proximity or visual connection: *text chaining*.

We've already seen that QuarkXPress's automatic text box feature generates a flow of text through boxes on different pages. In fact, you can direct the flow of text through any set of boxes in a document, as you choose. Should the boxes be moved, resized, made to runaround, or otherwise modified, the linkage established will stay intact unless you break it. You can break the linkage at any point of a chain and establish it through some new text chain.

Here then is the means for jumping stories from Page 1 to Page 23—or for fragmenting text to create an ad that jogs the reader's eyes through a design, or for trying page layout possibilities when your text exceeds the limits of a single text box. In the last chapter we let QuarkXPress establish this link automatically in the letterhead version of the newsletter. Now we're doing it manually. You can link boxes that contain text or ones that don't. (Text can also be added after linking.) We'll use the Linking tool. Second from the bottom on the Tools palette, this tool resembles three joined chain links.

To link text boxes, choose the Linking tool at the palette, and click on the text box in which the text flow originates, or will originate. A dashed-line bounding box will appear around it. Then click on the box that is to be second in the text link. A gray arrow will appear, tailfeather in the first box, arrowhead in the second. If there are more boxes to be added to the chain, simply click on them in succession. An arrow will appear between each pair of linked boxes. The text will be chained to flow through the boxes successively in the order that the links were established.

Establishing a text chain

Using the Linking tool click on the first box in the chain
Click on every other box in order

Any time the Linking tool is chosen after a box is selected by Content or Item tool, the arrows indicating links between all the boxes will appear, and the chain of text flow will become visible, as shown in Figure 6.33. If the boxes are empty of text and you click content in any box in the chain, all the boxes in the chain will display as though active, but the cursor will appear in the first box.

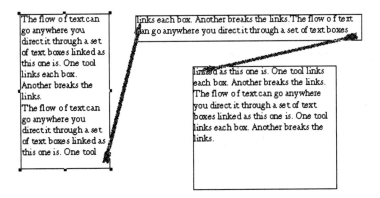

Figure 6.33   *Linked text boxes forming a text chain.*

Once you've established a text chain, you can include another text box within that chain, even in the middle of it. You do this by using the Link tool. First click on the box already linked (box A, let's say), then click on the box you wish to include in the chain (box B, let's call it). The result will be a linkage through the new box (showing arrows from box A to box B to the box that previously fol-lowed box A in the chain).

Linking a text box in an existing text chain

Using the Linking tool click on the box before the insertion point
Click on the new text box

Text Box Unlinking

Breaking up a text chain can be done surprisingly quickly. Choose the Unlink tool from the palette, and click on the arrowhead or tailfeathers pointing to the box at which you'd like to sever the link. Be sure to aim carefully. That box and all that follow will then be disconnected from the chain. All text that may have run through them in a story will be consigned to the boxes upstream that remain in the chain.

Breaking a text chain

Select the Unlinking tool
Click on an arrowhead or tailfeather

You might want to remove only one box from the chain, while keeping boxes downstream still in the text flow. Holding the **Shift** key, use the Unlinking tool and click on the unwanted box. It will empty, and the arrows will bypass it as they point onward through the downstream part of the text chain.

Removing one box from a text chain

Select the Unlinking tool
Shift-click on the unwanted box

Flipping Box Contents

One of the most startling controls in QuarkXPress provides the ability to flip the contents of any item box. This enables you to make reversed images of the sort seen in lettering painted on the inside of a window showing out. You can use this feature to flip images or text in either the horizontal or the vertical position. Figure 6.34 shows both types of adjustments for text, and Figure 6.35 shows these adjustments for an image.

Figure 6.34   *A nameplate text box flipped horizontally and vertically.*

You can readily engage this control when the box is selected and the Content tool is active. Clicking at the Measurements palette at either of the two boxes containing arrows found at the middle of the palette will perform the flip; so will choosing either of the commands from the Style menu. If your work involves preparing film reversed in this fashion, you can save a mechanical step by commanding the software to perform the flip onscreen.

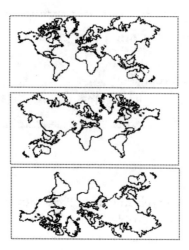

Figure 6.35 *A map picture box flipped horizontally and vertically.*

Onward

Text, pictures, boxes, and lines—their adjustments and interactivity make for rich and visually rewarding layouts. Whether text chains or a picture rotation, boxes form the foundation of QuarkXPress documents. Master them, apply the techniques we've just covered, and you will find virtually everything else you learn about the program will come much more easily.

These methods can conquer an amazing variety of layout challenges. In Chapter 7 you can observe and prepare two documents, putting to work skills with items, pictures, and interactions in that most practical of volumes, the guidebook.

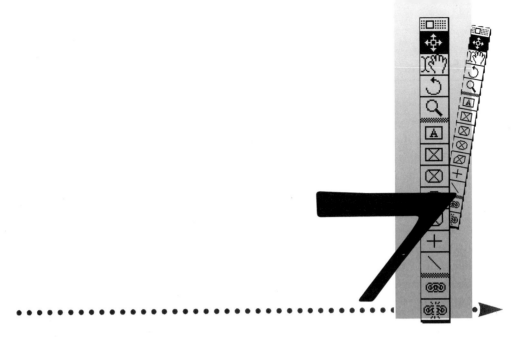

Guides on the Job

What you will learn in this chapter:

- ❖ Controlling the interaction of page items
- ❖ How to lay out pictures with text
- ❖ How to apply picture adjustments in a spread
- ❖ How to align borders
- ❖ How to key text to a picture

Graphics, text, and the other page elements can be made to play off each other smartly in the great dance, which occurs within QuarkXPress layouts. Carefully handled, the interactivity of these live elements can strengthen the unity and heighten the movement of any document.

Here we will follow the development of two guides. The first document is a piece designed as part of a brochure. Its purpose is to generate interest in the newly opened wing of a museum by summarizing the exhibits there. The second document employs the same source files of text and graphics to a different effect. It is a section of a walking guide to be used by exhibit-goers. As each of these documents are assembled, notice how the techniques of previous chapters are coming together to adjust and juxtapose picture and text elements.

Underlying each of these two documents is the intent to lead their readers by coordinating visual and text cues. Our task will include applying QuarkXPress to achieve this coordination successfully.

The Brochure Guide

Imagine someone saying to you, "Here are several bitmapped images and a text file. Now make a two-page spread that will be the interior of a brochure to promote our new exhibition." That's the task put to us in this first document.

We decide to make a largely graphic display, since the pieces are what interest these museum-goers the most. We're going to include a border that bleeds to the edge of the page, but we want the main elements in the design to be contained at least 0.75 inch from the edges.

We start by opening the File menu and choosing **New**, then **Document**. Clicking on the **Facing Pages** checkbox and setting the margin guides at 0.75 inch for the **Top**, **Bottom**, and **Outside** fields, and at 0 for the **Inside** field, we complete the New dialog box. With Page 1 in front of us, we open the Pages menu, choosing **Insert**, and type **2** (leaving the master page selection created for Page 1). Next we move to the Pages 2 and 3 spread with the scroll bars. Figure 7.1 shows the New dialog box that established the page spread behind it.

Now we'll concentrate on setting up our spread design. This simple one sets the text in columns along the lower fifth of the page, distributes pictures in the upper area, and allows for a border to run within the margins. We'll want that border to be offset from the rest of the design by 0.75 inch. To allocate our spaces and provide for alignment, we pull out guides from the rulers to all these limits. From the Vertical ruler we pull two guides, one to the 0.5-inch and another to the 8-inch mark on the Horizontal ruler.

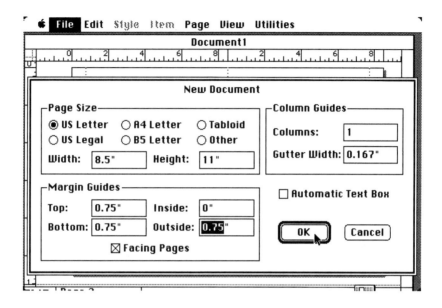

Figure 7.1 *The New dialog box from which a page spread is established.*

Normally, pulling from the ruler produces a guide that extends across just one page. From the horizontal ruler we'll use a trick that pulls out guides across the whole spread and into the pasteboard. The technique is to pull the guide into a space off the page, into the pasteboard. In this case a guide extends across our spread as we pull it into an area of pasteboard showing at the right of the spread.

Pulling a guide that extends across a spread

Point the cursor in the horizontal ruler above the pasteboard

Pull directly down

The first item added to the spread will be the text box at the bottom. We want it at the bottom, but not all across the bottom, because we're planning on putting a title at the lower right. We want to put a text box that will fit into a six-column grid across the spread. Since we want to use some of the space for the title, we'll fit in five columns, leaving what amounts to the sixth column empty. The text box will then occupy three columns on Page 2 and two columns on Page 3.

We first create a small text box, then set the number of columns at 5 through the Measurements palette. By dragging out this text box within the bottom space, but limiting it to part way across the right side of Page 3, we create the test space. The centerfold will be our guide as we adjust the box. We pull out to the right by a box handle so that the column gutter falls centered over the break, as indicated in Figure 7.2.

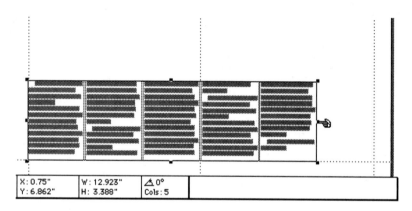

| X: 0.75" | W: 12.923" | △ 0° |
| Y: 6.862" | H: 3.388" | Cols: 5 |

Figure 7.2   Positioning a five-column box in a six-column grid.

Text is next imported through the Get Text dialog box. (This text is partly dummied and will serve as a place-holder for the final file.)

Next, we put the title in place by drawing out a text box and typing **The Junior Exhibit**. After some experimenting, we use the Measurements palette to adjust the text to Helvetica, 36 point. We open the Frame dialog box choice under Item, and there apply a 1 point plain frame. Then we call up the Text Box Specifications dialog box. To do so quickly we hold down the **Command** key, which gives us temporary Item tool functionality. Then we use the double-click method to open the Specifications dialog box.

At the Specifications dialog box we key in a value of **8 pt.** in the **Text Inset**: field to bring our text away from the frame. This inset value, as shown in Figure 7.3, pushes our title text, The Junior Exhibit, to the right slightly. We leave the text area for the moment to bring the graphics files onto the spread.

Momentarily switching to the Item tool

With any but the Zoom tool engaged, hold down the
Command key

Instant opening of the Specifications dialog box

Using the Item tool, select, and double-click on the item

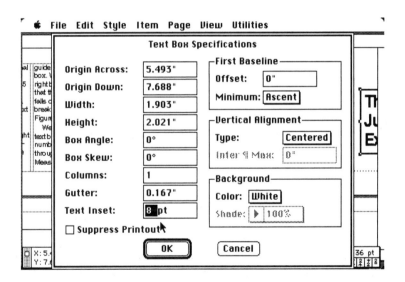

Figure 7.3 *Adjusting text inset in the layout.*

Using the Rectangle Picture Box tool, we draw out all the boxes we'll need, then use the **Get Picture** command for the first three files. We can see that the images coming in are so large that our spread could never accommodate the whole lot at that scale. We thus drag the boxes smaller, using the **Command-Shift-Option-F** keyboard command to force-fit each image proportionally into each box in turn.

Now we have all the picture boxes (with images centered within them) positioned roughly around the spread, as shown in Figure 7.4.

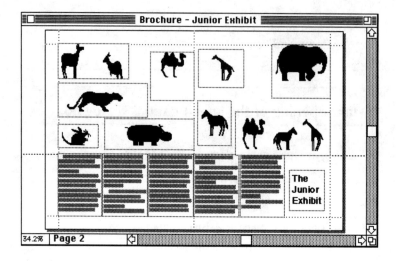

Figure 7.4   Roughly positioned, sized picture boxes.

 What QuarkXPress interprets as an image might not coincide exactly with what we see at first glance. When useful images are surrounded by stray pixels or large white space, individual adjustments **N O T E** will be required at each box.

We turn first to the picture box in the upper-left corner. To enlarge the image proportionately, we select the picture box with the Content tool, then change the **X%** and **Y%** values to **60%** each. Then we drag on the box handles until the box encloses the image tightly, and use the Grabber Hand tool for finely positioning the image within the box. The result is shown in Figure 7.5. The importance of pulling the box in to a tight fit will become apparent when we apply the **Space/Align** command. (Recall that alignment and spacing are relative to the picture box, not necessarily to the image inside it.)

Following the same approach, we resize and prepare all the remaining picture boxes. Our object is to achieve a pleasing fit and proportion within the space remaining on the spread.

As we turn to the second box, we find, as we size it, that the box next to it obscures our view, so we apply the Item Menu command, **Bring to Front**, which raises the picture box to the uppermost layer and reveals all of the image within. But now we notice that in trying to size the box, we experience it being forced toward the centerfold line. This problem is the result of the Snap to Guides feature. We open the View menu and highlight this toggle feature to switch it off. Now we proceed to adjust the bounding box of this second image into a tight image fit of appropriate size.

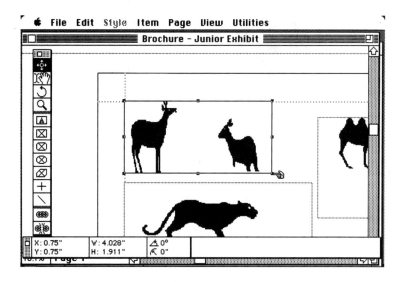

Figure 7.5 *Cropping to the useful image.*

In making up the page spread, we see that there is a preponderance of similarly proportioned images. To break up this uniformity, we enlarge some images, using the method shown in Figure 7.6. The image is cropped using the box handles to pull the box narrower. Then, to enlarge proportionately, we use the old trick of drawing along a diagonal line through opposite corners. To get this diagonal we make use of the Show Guides feature and position an empty picture box behind the one we're about to enlarge, and with upper-left corners matched. The empty box will show both diagonals as a large X through the box. We next hold down the **Command** key (to pull the image as we pull the box) while dragging the lower-right corner of the box along that line to the size we want. Then we delete the extra, empty picture box.

Notice that the original images were all black on white. This tends to make the page seem uniform. To counteract for this effect, we do two things. First we select each box and individually apply color to some of the images through the Style menu. (This, of course, does not show in the figures here. You can imagine the use of the Color list to set one to Blue, another to Red, and so on.) Remember that the image is the aggregate of black pixels on the screen, not the figures that are represented in white here. We also change some of the images to shadings of less than 100%, using the Style menu's Shade listing.

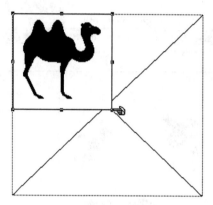

Figure 7.6 *Cropping and enlarging proportionately using a diagonal.*

Scaling a box proportionately by sight

Draw a line through and beyond the opposite corners of the box

Or create and position an empty picture box with diagonals showing through Show Guides

Resize the box by dragging one corner along the line

Second, we take a bit of liberty with the two montage images. We attempt to reverse the images through the **Negative** command under the Style menu. However, these images were not saved in a format (such as TIFF), which responds to this command. So we work around this by using two commands to accomplish the same effect. As shown in Figure 7.7, by applying the **Color** command from the Style menu, then setting the background to Black in the

Specifications dialog (Item menu, **Modify** choice), we are able to reverse their Black on White to White on Black, creating more variety on the page.

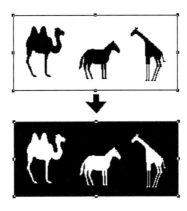

***Figure* 7.7**   *Reversing the image.*

Our final task in laying out the pictorial part of the spread involves positioning the picture boxes. For this we will use the top and outside margin guides, in conjunction with the Space/Align dialog box. Recalling that this command anchors the item in the upper-left area of a set of items, we first move that item into the upper-left margin corner. To help with this, the Snap to Guides feature is reactivated in the View menu. Then, at a Fit in Window view we drag the item enough to let it snap into place. Now, since we want even spacing of picture items across the top from the left-to-right margin, the rightmost item is dragged until it too snaps into place against the right guide line. (Its vertical positioning is unimportant for the moment.)

By dragging an enclosing box with the Item tool, we select all the picture boxes at the top of the spread and, opening the Item menu, choose **Space/Align**. Figure 7.8 shows the dialog box with this arrangement. We've used the **Apply** button to make sure that the spacing is just what we want. Since we seek to have all the boxes flush with the top margin, the **Vertical** checkbox is clicked and a space value of **zero** is left in the field. From the Between: list, **Top Edges** is selected. Because we want the pictures evenly spaced across the spread, the **Horizontal** checkbox is clicked and the **Distribute Evenly** button is engaged with the **Between** setting at **Items**.

We select the three picture boxes along the left margin next. Using the same command, we arrange similarly the picture boxes along the left margin with the same top-left picture box acting as an anchor, with the Vertical Distribute Evenly feature chosen this time. The dialog box and its result are shown in Figure 7.9. Notice that horizontal spacing was set for zero along the left edges.

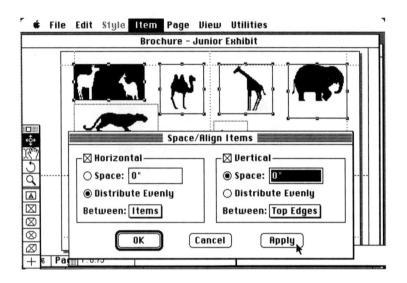

Figure 7.8   Using **Space/Align** to distribute along an uppermost horizontal.

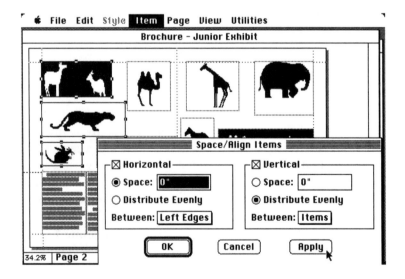

Figure 7.9   Using **Space/Align** to distribute along a leftmost vertical.

The last phase of positioning requires working with those remaining picture boxes along the bottom. Dragging the rightmost picture box to the right margin guide, we prepare for another spacing change. We drag a selection box around those bottom items, then use the **Space/Align** command to set up the dialog box shown in Figure 7.10. Here the **Apply** button has aligned the items. This time we've designated a vertical zero space along the bottom edges and an even distribution between items in the horizontal. Now all the picture boxes are in place.

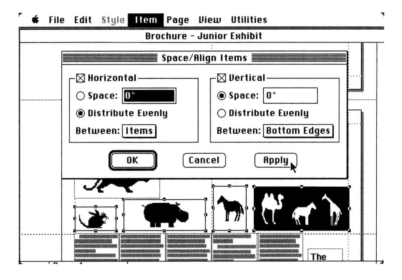

Figure 7.10   *Using **Space/Align** to distribute along a bottommost horizontal.*

The border is all that remains. For this project we've chosen to use text in the form of all the animal names in the exhibit. This border will be a band of reverse type running around the spread.

Using the Text Box tool, we create a text box, type in the names (with spaces between them), then select all the text (keystroke **Command-A**), copy it to the clipboard (keystroke **Command-C**), and paste it (**Command-V**) several times to provide plenty of text for our border. Next we draw out three more text boxes. Using the Linking tool we click on the first (the one with all the text), then click on the second. An arrow forms to show the text chain. Next we click on the second, then the third, and repeat this process until the fourth box is clicked on. This establishes the text chain shown in Figure 7.11.

Coming very close to completion now, we have to rotate, size, and position the text-chain boxes. But first, we reverse the text. (Recall that this is done by setting the color of the text to white and the background of the text box to black.) We select all the boxes as a set of items, then, opening the Item menu, we choose **Modify**. In this dialog box we set the background to **Black, 100%**. Next we use the Content tool to select all the text. Opening the Style menu, we choose **White** from the Color list.

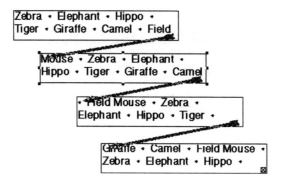

Figure 7.11   A text chain established for four linked bordering boxes.

Now we rotate the text boxes through the Measurements palette with an eye to where we will put them in the margin spaces, keeping the order clear. The first box at the top is horizontal, so there's no change; the second box, at the right, will be rotated -90°; the third box, at the bottom, will be rotated -180°; the fourth box, at the left, will be rotated 90° (-270° would do as well).

This leaves us with the text boxes shown in Figure 7.12. Putting each in its own margin around both the main text and the picture boxes, and stretching each border text box to fit as we do so, we complete the document.

A Museum Guidebook

Now let's turn to a somewhat different document. Guidebooks as used in museums are intended to lead visitors through exhibits. We're going to create one section of a museum guidebook. These pages will guide exhibit-goers through the hall described in the preceding brochure. In this two-page spread our task is to provide clear visual links between the floor plan of the hall through which visitors will be passing and the exhibits they will encounter.

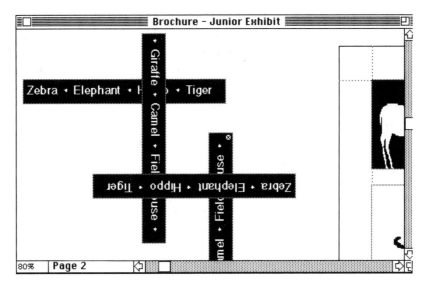

Figure 7.12   *Linked, reversed, rotated text boxes.*

We begin by using the **New** command to set up a document 5.25 inches wide by 7.25 inches high. And because we want to work with a spread, we add two pages through the Pages menu and move directly to those facing pages.

There will be text on each page in three columns separated by 0.25 inch. We use the Text Box tool, draw out a box to fit within the margin guides of Page 2, then select **Modify** at the Item menu. In the Text Box Specifications, we key in **3** after Columns, and **0.25** after Gutter.

Now we turn to the graphics that will grace this spread. One of them is crucial, a floor plan of the exhibit hall. We draw a box with the Picture Box tool and use the Get Picture dialog box to bring in the floor plan. We move this picture box to the upper-right corner, where it will be prominent enough to be noticed. Soon we will overlay numbered boxes on it, corresponding to similar boxes cited in the text.

It's time to bring in the other graphics now. For each one, we draw out a box for the next image with the Picture Box tool, then use **Get Picture**. Following the procedures we've used before, we size the images to their approximate final proportions. This includes using the **Command-Shift-Option-F** keystroke to scale the image to the box, dragging on the handles to crop the box, using the Grabber Hand tool to position the significant image within the box, and so on.

We're almost ready to set up text runaround for the pictures. In order to proceed, though, we want to see how the runaround is interacting with our text. So we click the Content tool in the text box on Page 2, and use the **Get Text** command to import the copy. We select all the text (**Command-A**) and use the Measurements palette to set the text to Times, 10 point. In a short time the layout shown in Figure 7.13 is before us.

All the pictures are in the runaround default mode, which is Item. This "boxy" runaround works for some of the images within the columns. But we decide that custom text runaround is called for the group image and in the floor plan. We select the floor plan picture first and, opening the Item menu, choose **Runaround**. At the dialog box we select the manual mode, and set in 8 point offset. The manual choice actually creates an automatic runaround with the option to adjust. We use that one because, if the program does an adequate job, we can leave the runaround as it turns out. On the other hand, we can adjust it easily if we have to.

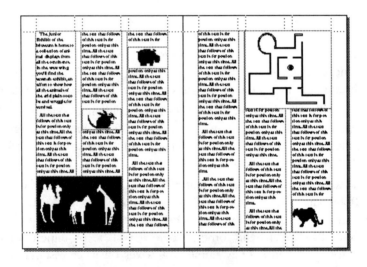

Figure 7.13   *Preliminary layout with item runaround.*

In the case of the image of the floor plan, the automatic runaround is fine except for the bit of text that's slipped into the third column. We adjust this by pulling a side of the runaround fence to the right, as shown in Figure 7.14.

At the large image on the lower left, however, we have some custom box reshaping and cropping to do. In order to create a tapered image, we are going to convert the rectangular picture box to an adjustable polygon picture box. To do so, we select the picture box, then at the Item menu choose **Picture Box Shape**. A pictorial list of boxes appears (as shown in Figure 7.15). These are alternative box shapes. Choosing one redefines the apparent matte around the picture, within the same bounding box. We choose the bottom figure, the polygon shape, because we wish to customize the picture box around this image.

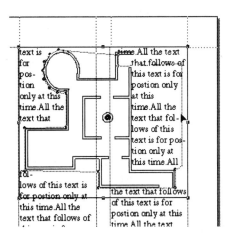

Figure 7.14   *Pushing out text by moving a runaround boundary.*

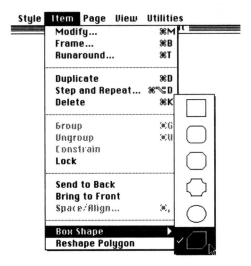

Figure 7.15   *Choosing a new picture box shape.*

Next we choose the last command on the Item list, **Reshape Polygon**. This gives our cursor tool the abilities to add and remove handle points and to pull sides into new positions, the same abilities available when the polygon picture box tool is active. The difference here is that we can now work on revising an existing box form.

Positioning the mouse on a box side, we see the tool change to a small arrow head. By holding down the **Command key**, we call up a tool shaped like a little rounded box. Clicking, we add a handle where we want the box to angle. We add similar handles around the corner of the box we want to adjust and remove other handles until the box appears as shown in Figure 7.16. (Over an existing handle, the Command key cursor changes to an "X-ed" circle.) The arrowhead allows us to move entire sides, and the familiar pointing hand allows us to move handle points.

Figure 7.16   *Reshaping a picture box.*

Converting a picture box shape

Select the box

Open the Item menu, then the **Box Shape** submenu, and
select the replacement shape from the list of shapes

Adjusting a polygon picture box

To change the shape of the box, drag an angle point or side

To add an angle point, point along a side and **Command-click**

To remove an angle point, point over an existing point and **Command-click**

NOTE

An advantage to using the Reshape Polygon feature is that we adjust the text runaround at the same time we precisely crop the image. This occurs when the runaround is set to **Item**.

Our next task involves reversing text, the approach we've chosen to connect the floor plan map visually with the rest of the layout elements. First, to set the section apart, we'll manually insert a large reversed "out" drop-cap at the start of the page. We do this by creating a Text Box with the text box tool, setting the box background to **Black**, **100%**, in the Specifications dialog box (from the Item menu's **Modify** command) and choosing White from the Color list in the Style menu. The typeface chosen is Helvetica, set at 48 points in the Measurements palette. Keying in the first letter of the body copy, we then delete that letter from the copy itself. In the Measurements palette the formatting is set to center, and in the Specifications dialog box the text offset to 6 points (to position the letter more centrally within the box). We assure that the Runaround is set to **Item**, and move this text box to the extreme upper-left of the spread. It pushes down and over on the body text, which reflows around it. (This is the manual method. We'll soon see in an upcoming chapter how to generate standard drop caps automatically through paragraph formatting.)

Now we set about making label captions for the pictures. The choice is a reversed-out text box with bolded Helvetica typeface of text taken from the copy. We set this up for one of the illustrations first. Then, to save effort, we'll copy this text box and modify the duplication. After formatting the first, we use the keyboard copy command (**Command-C**), then a few paste commands (**Command-V**) that produce a stack of identical text boxes. For each of the other illustrations we select the text in each (**Command-A**) and key in the text appropriate to it.

To point body copy to the floor plan, we use the same text box clone from above, drag it to be narrower, and key in **1**. At the pasteboard, we use the Item tool to select it. Then we copy (**Command-C**) and paste (**Command-V**) several boxes, and using the Content tool we select the text in each (**Command-A**) and key in subsequent numbers. The appropriate number will then visually point each animal paragraph to a location on the map. Figure 7.17 shows labels—captions and number boxes—in the process of being positioned.

Each of those numbers will be needed to label locations on the floor plan. So we also select and copy the whole set of numbered boxes to use as markers there. Moving to the pasteboard adjacent to the map, we paste them near it. To complete the visual linking of the map to the text and pictures, we drag each of the duplicate numbers to its appropriate location on the map, as shown in Figure 7.18.

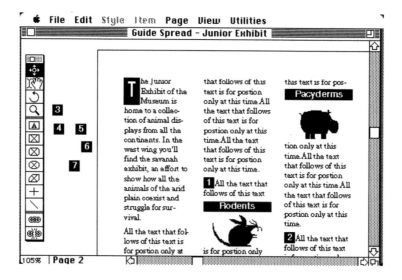

Figure 7.17 *Positioning reversed labels.*

To guide visitors to the hall, we add arrows leading in through the entrance at the top of the map and out through the exit below. After one final minor adjustment to the map runaround boundary, the section completes the spread (as shown in Figure 7.19).

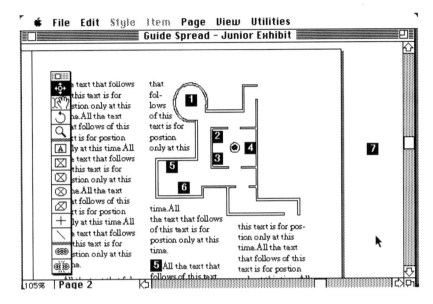

Figure 7.18   *Positioning number keys.*

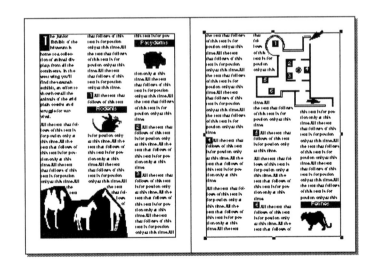

Figure 7.19   *The completed section.*

Onward

Nowhere can you accomplish greater union of page elements than in controlling the interactions of text with text, text with graphics, or with items in general. The graphic and content natures of items provide countless opportunities for unifying your layouts. Adjusting picture displays through box sizing, cropping, and runarounds is one of the surest ways to make the clearest visual statements with your graphic files.

Yet even finer control over page design is possible. The precise formatting of stories and paragraphs is the classic art of the typesetter and one of the major strengths of QuarkXPress. In Chapter 8 we'll see how spacing, hyphenation, paragraph alignments, scaling, and justification can be controlled for the benefit of any text layout.

Paragraphs, Stories, and Typographic Controls

What you will learn in this chapter:

- ❖ How to format paragraphs
- ❖ How to control indents and create hanging indents
- ❖ How to specify hyphenation and justification
- ❖ Revealing and using the baseline grid
- ❖ Widow and orphan control
- ❖ How to control horizontal and vertical scaling
- ❖ Applying the three types of vertical alignment
- ❖ How to create drop caps

Prepare to Enter Deep into the Realm of the Typesetter

Few publishing programs approach the powerful broad strokes and intricate subtleties offered in the typographic controls of QuarkXPress. This chapter will show you just how these controls work at the paragraph and story levels, how to regulate hyphenation and justification, and how to accomplish special effects with type.

You'll discover how to uncover the hidden typographic characters that define every paragraph and line of text. Also revealed is the powerful baseline grid, which can pull disparate lines of type into precise line agreement. Shown also are the several ways to adjust paragraph indentation, vertical alignments, and automatic drop caps.

Every serious publication producer and page designer must pay close attention to type. Whether or not you have extensive experience with typography, the techniques described in this chapter will lend your documents the highest caliber appearance.

Formatting

At the crossroads of text control is the Paragraph Formats dialog box. It manages paragraphs and groups of paragraphs. QuarkXPress treats any text separated by a single tap of the **Return** or **Enter** key, as a paragraph.

Paragraph markers, however, can be difficult to find in unformatted text. One way to identify paragraphs is through a toggle command in the View menu called **Show Invisibles** and **Hide Invisibles**, shown in Figure 8.1 with text in which the paragraphs might be otherwise overlooked. The invisibles referred to here include tabs, spaces, new line codes, special indent codes, and paragraph markers. All are treated as nonprinting characters by QuarkXPress, which identifies the paragraph by the standard ¶. While these symbols can be distracting during layout, it's good to know how to bring them forward when you need them.

> ### Locating nonprinting character codes in text
>
> Open the View menu and choose **Show Invisibles**

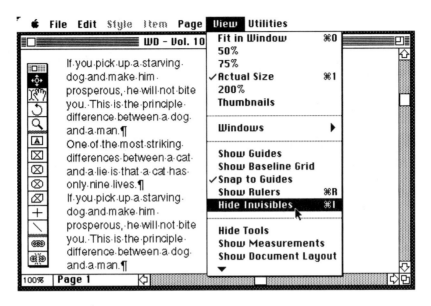

Figure 8.1 *Showing nonprinting markers.*

Once you start to format a paragraph—for instance, by adding an indent at the first line, or an extra space after the paragraph—you will be able to discern paragraphs without the **Show Invisibles** function.

Adding paragraph definition and otherwise modifying formatting is what the Paragraph Formats dialog box is all about. The first step to making this feature accessible lies in using the content tool to make a selection within a text box. To reach the dialog box, open the Style menu and choose **Formats**. A dialog box such as the one shown in Figure 8.2 will be displayed. Figure 8.2 depicts a Default dialog box that specifies relatively unformatted paragraphs.

Here is the perfect opportunity to apply some of the attributes that make typeset paragraphs look like, well, typeset paragraphs. Note that the Paragraph Formats dialog box makes changes to whichever paragraph the text cursor is in, wherever the text selection exists. If a group of paragraphs has been selected and highlighted, each paragraph in that group will be reformatted according to the dialog box entries. If a selection extends into two paragraphs, for example, both paragraphs will be formatted by your dialog box entries.

In the example shown in Figure 8.3, the cursor sits in the first paragraph of the text box at the right. Changes have been made in the Formats dialog box next to it. It is not strictly accurate to say that the paragraph began with no formatting. Even the zero values shown in Figure 8.2 indicate a state to which the paragraph could be returned by using the Formats dialog box to key in and select those undistinguishing attributes. The text, for example, was initially set in 14 point Helvetica typeface with automatic leading (here 120%, or about 16.8 point leading); it's left-aligned, with no indentations and no extra space before or after the paragraphs.

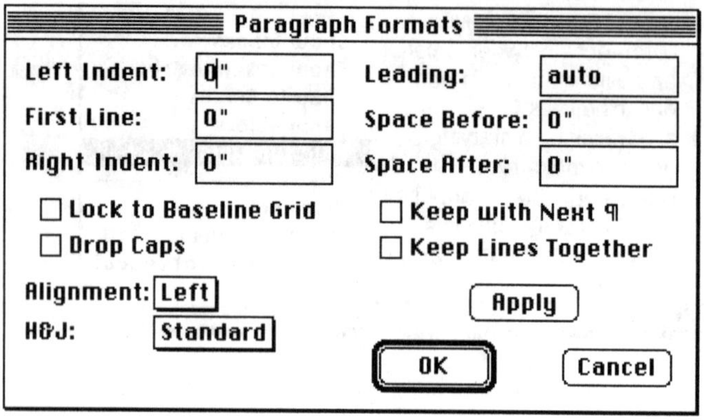

Figure 8.2   *The Paragraph Formats dialog box.*

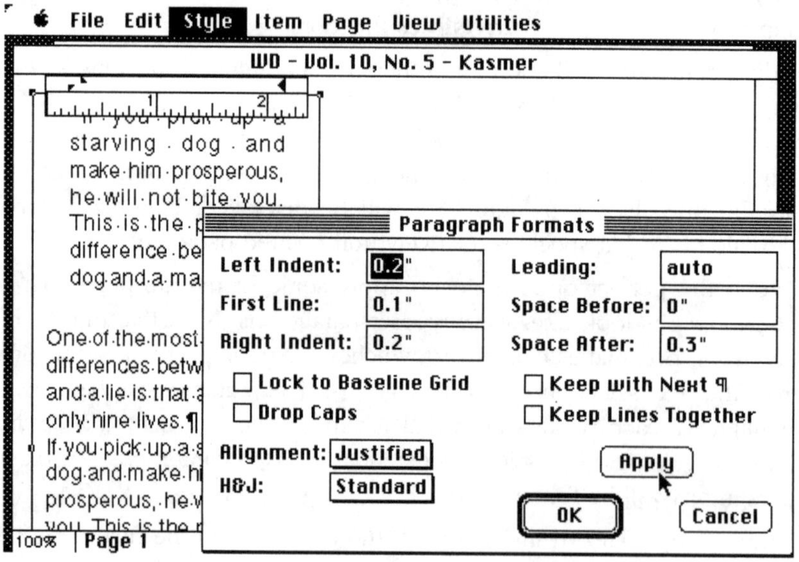

Figure 8.3   *A Formats dialog box for an altered paragraph.*

Now let's examine the dialog box to see just how format changes affected that first paragraph shown in Figure 8.3. Just above the selected paragraph in the text box you'll see a ruler. Notice that the two small black triangular marks at the left have slid over rightward of the zero mark, and that the large triangle on the right has been moved leftward. These three triangles indicate values in the first three fields of the dialog box, labeled **Left Indent**, **First Line**, and **Right Indent**. They also serve as an alternate means of indent adjustment. Indentation of the entire paragraph from the left edge can be controlled on the format ruler by the lower of the two small triangles as well as by the **First Numerical** field. In this case, the value entered was **.2 inch**. The same effect would have been achieved by pointing the cursor on the triangle and dragging it rightward to the .2-inch mark on the dialog box ruler. Incidentally, as any of these marks is dragged, the location on the ruler is tracked in the dialog field boxes and indicated numerically there.

The **First Line** field sets indentation at the paragraph's first line, where a typist normally presses the typewriter's tab key. This feature is alternatively controlled by the small triangle in the upper portion of the dialog box ruler. We've chosen the value, **.1 inch**. Notice that this first-line indentation is added to the left indent applied to all the lines of the paragraph.

The **Right Indent** field sets the extent to which text lines can run across the text column. This control can likewise be set by dragging the large triangle from the right.

Adjusting indents

Select the paragraph(s)

Call up the Paragraph Formats dialog box, locating the ruler above the paragraph)(s)

Slide the triangular markers into place as follows: first-line indent, small top marker; left-indent, small bottom marker; right-indent, large marker

Or, key values into corresponding fields

NOTE

As you fashion a paragraph selection through Paragraph Formats, QuarkXPress provides for step-by-step changes. That is, you need not decide on all your changes at once. Rather, you can try changing some particular attribute, click the **Apply** button, observe the change, and then decide whether you wish to make your change definite. If you decide yes, you can click **OK**. Or you can continue adding formatting instructions to the dialog box, and trying them with the **Apply** button. When you reach a satisfying format, click **OK** to fix your changes to the selection.

Another obvious change in the text of Figure 8.3 is the reduced spacing between the lines of the first paragraph. The rest of the text carries an automatic leading, which for 14 point type is 16.8 point spacing. However, in the dialog box we keyed in a value of **14 point**, to bring the lines closer to each other. This is the same leading control available through the Measurements palette, as well as through the Style menu.

The first paragraph has also been separated from its successor by added spacing. Note the **Space After** field, and its entry of **.3 inches**. In similar fashion, the Space Before field can be altered for all paragraphs—except the first.

One final change that distinguishes this paragraph from its neighbors is alignment. We've seen that flush left, flush right, centered, and justified features can be set from both the Measurements palette and the Style menu. In this case we've used the drop-down list near the bottom of the dialog box to justify the text of the first paragraph.

There are countless variations that can be achieved with these controls in the Formats dialog box. Figure 8.4 shows examples of five different paragraph formats brought about by different adjustments to indents, leading, alignment, and spacing.

One special format that you'll find causes paragraphs to stand out is *hanging indents*. In these paragraphs, the bulk of the text appears to be indented from the left, while the first line is not. The effect is that text appears to be "hanging" from the first line. Figure 8.5 shows a series of paragraphs to which the hanging indent feature has been applied.

The technique for achieving hanging indents relies on the ability of QuarkXPress to set the first line to a negative value. Note that the first line's indent value is relative to the left indent. So a zero first-line indent results in the first line being flush left with the rest of the lines of the paragraph. A first-line indent with a positive value results in an apparent tab-over. A negative first-line indent pulls the line to the left. So, in Figure 8.5 the **First Line –0.5"** signifies .5 inch to the left of the **Left Indent of +0.5"**. In other words, the first line is set at zero. The left triangular markers in the Formats ruler make this more apparent.

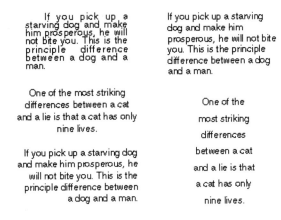

Figure 8.4   *Paragraph formatting variations.*

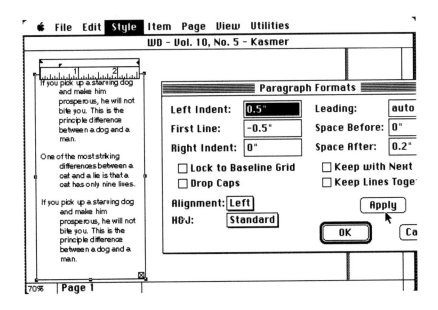

Figure 8.5   *Creating hanging indents.*

Creating hanging indents

In the Paragraph Formats dialog box ruler, drag the left
    indent over
Drag the first line indent back leftward of the left indent

N O T E

As you work with paragraph formatting, you'll need to see what happens with each new formatting change. Admittedly, the Paragraph Formats dialog box takes up a large amount of space, especially on smaller monitors. And even with the benefit of the **Apply** button to try out formatting changes, you might feel it's necessary to quit the dialog box just to see what you've done. A better way is to recall that, like every window and dialog box, this one can be moved. Therefore, in order to see your paragraph changes, you would do better to move the Formats dialog box by clicking on its title bar to grab and drag it temporarily to another location. As long as you can see part of the title bar, you can always drag the whole dialog box on screen.

N O T E

When you choose the Formats dialog box, the cursor or the selection in the text seems to disappear. This is only a temporary display lapse. QuarkXPress keeps track of which paragraphs you've designated for formatting. When you leave the dialog box, the paragraph selection will be returned just as you left it, and the *formatting changes* will have been made.

Hyphenation and Justification

Other adjustments can be made from the Formats dialog box, including hyphenation and justification control, labeled in the dialog box as **H&J**. Hyphenation and justification methods are actually set up elsewhere. The Formats dialog box offers a means of choosing from among those available methods. We now turn to the dialog box that establishes these methods to see about controlling **H&J** features.

Within the QuarkXPress document, standard specifications exist that control how each line will fit within a column, given the various indents in effect. These specifications determine when to break words with hyphens—hyphenation. Specifications also determine how to increase or diminish space between words and characters in order to align paragraphs in justified mode—justification.

Gaining Access to Hyphenation and Justification Specs

When you start to work with QuarkXPress, you may find no lines ending with hyphenated words. The reason can be found in the Formats dialog box under the heading, H&J, **Standard**. In this specification, automatic hyphenation is normally switched off for a new document. You can modify the Standard specifications, create new ones, delete them, copy them, or transfer them from other QuarkXPress documents.

To gain access to the H&J specifications, open the Edit menu and choose H&J. You'll see the dialog box shown in Figure 8.6. To get at the specifications, click on the **Edit** button, and the dialog box shown in Figure 8.7 will be displayed. In it you'll see all the preset values and choices automatically applied, by default, to new documents.

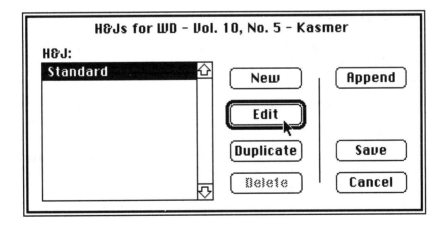

Figure 8.6 *Access to hyphenation and justification settings.*

One way to switch hyphenation on is simply to click the **Auto Hyphenation** checkbox. All the paragraphs in the document will then automatically be hyphenated according to the specifications in this dialog box, the preset

Standard Specifications. This on-or-off approach is just one way to handle hyphenation.

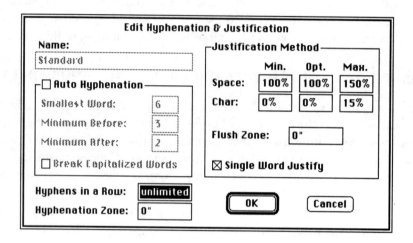

Figure 8.7 *Specifications for hyphenation and justification.*

Changing Hyphenation Specifications

Another way to apply hyphenation is to create another set of H&J specifications. Click the **Cancel** button from the Edit Hyphenation and Justification dialog box, and you'll be at the H&Js dialog box shown in Figure 8.6.

Now click the **New** button and you'll return to an Edit Hyphenation and Justification dialog box that resembles the one shown in Figure 8.7, except that the name will be blank. If all you want to do is switch on hyphenation, click the checkbox to put an x in **Auto Hyphenation**. Key in a name, such as **Hyphen On**. Then click the **OK** button, and you will be returned to the H&Js dialog box. The next step is important to make the new specifications available. Click the **Save** button so that when you next call up the Formats dialog box, you'll be able to choose **Hyphen On** from the drop-down list under H&Js, as shown in Figure 8.8, and apply hyphenation selectively to paragraphs.

This is one of the simplest H&J specification changes. You can do much more to detail the methods for applying both hyphenation and justification to your text. Let's suppose we wanted to elaborate the methods to be applied from the Hyphen On specifications. To do so, we again open the Edit menu, choose

H&Js, then select one of the Specifications, say **Hyphen On**, from the H&Js list. Click the **Edit** button, and you'll see a dialog box like the one shown in Figure 8.7 again.

Let's consider those features appearing under the Auto Hyphenation heading first. In that box, three fields indicate how and where words may be broken. **Smallest Word** indicates the minimum number of characters a word must have before Auto Hyphenation affects it. The default is six characters. The possible range runs from three to twenty characters. **Minimum Before** sets the lower limit on the number of characters that must be present before an automatic hyphen is inserted. The default is three characters; the range runs from two to eight. **Minimum After** sets a lower limit on the number of characters that are made to follow an automatic hyphen. The default is two characters; the range runs from two to eight.

The defaults indicate that five-letter words will not be hyphenated. They cause even the word, "before", to be passed over for hyphenation, because the *be-* syllable is too short to qualify, while a word like "yesterday" could be hyphenated at the first syllable, *yes-.*

Moving to the bottom of the dialog box, at the field labeled, Hyphens in a Row, you can restrict the number of consecutive lines that will end in a hyphenated word. The default, Unlimited, means "anything goes." For work that is more artistic than practical—where you don't want hyphens stabbing the right indent willy-nilly—you might want to limit this value to 1.

Next we encounter the *Hyphenation Zone*, an imposing term that requires a bit of explanation. Here's what QuarkXPress does with it. Applied to nonjustified text, the Zone is measured from the right indent of the text. It sets up conditions for hyphenating. If a word that does not require hyphenation falls into the Zone, the word after it will not be hyphenated. On the other hand, if the hyphenation fragment of a potentially hyphenatable word falls inside the Zone, the word will be hyphenated there.

These are the hyphenation specifications. With them, you can limit word splits to very large words, to occasional words, to words of many syllables, and so on, to affect the way text appears in columns.

Changing Justification Specifications

Adjacent to the hyphenation specifications in the dialog box are specifications for justification. The first six fields in the Justification Method box can have profound effects on how tight or loose the lines in your justified text appear. In particular, the tighter the text, the less chance that dreaded rivers of white space can flow through your paragraphs, leading the reader's eye astray.

Consider the fonts you use. Each typeface has implicit in its design a predetermined *optimum spacing value*. QuarkXPress interprets optimum values for both word and letter spacing, which it designates as 100%. We can see this designation applied to the default values for specifications, the set of values at work until you change them. The first row of the Justification Method box, Space, indicates manipulation of the spacing of words. In order for justification to work, an optimum value (default is 100%) is specified between maximum and minimum spacing variations. Similarly, the second row, **Char.** (for character), manipulates spacing variations among adjacent letters and other characters, from the optimum spacing (default is 0%). Taken together the values shown in Figure 8.7 specify the default method for justification.

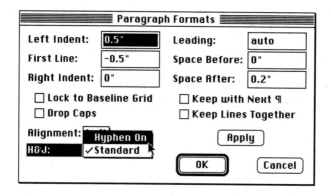

Figure 8.8   *A new H&J specification made available in the formats dialog box.*

N O T E

There are two distinct schools of thought regarding justification methods. One holds that the minimum letter and word spacing must not drop below the optimum value. In this approach, the minimums are set to the optimum and the maximum values are given a wide range. The second school believes that it is best to reduce the range of variation but make the minimum lower than the optimum level. In this second scheme, the values might run Minimum at 85% and Maximum at 110%. Figures 8.9 and 8.10 illustrate the two approaches respectively, on the section of text shown above each dialog box.

Training is everything. The peach was once a bitter almond; cauliflower is nothing but cabbage with an education. Training is everything. The peach was once a bitter almond; cauliflower is nothing but cabbage with an education. Training is everything. The peach was once a bitter almond; cauliflower is nothing but cabbage with an education.

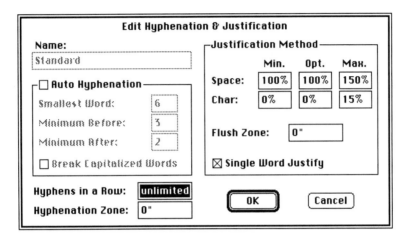

Figure 8.9 *Effect of the mi nimum equals optimum spacing.*

As shown in Figure 8.10, you can adjust the justification spacing values to alter the setting of your justified type. You can also adjust other factors in justification. You can determine, for instance, the circumstances under which a paragraph's last line of justified text will be extended across the indents. QuarkXPress handles this control through a feature known as the *Flush Zone.* When the last line enters the Flush Zone (measured from the right indent), space is added between words and characters to make the line fill the entire space from left margin to right margin. At the default of zero inches, of course, this will never happen.

The **Single Word Justify** checkbox is intended to extend the last word of a paragraph across the column. It sometimes proves useful for special type effects, such as stretching an unusual headline across a wide space.

Remember that the H&Js edit function can only create or modify these options. It's through the Style menu's Formats dialog box that you actually apply any particular specification set to text. But if you apply an H&J model to text and then edit that H&J, the text will reflect the change without being reformatted. This occurs once the **Save** button on the Edit H&J dialog box is clicked.

Training is everything. The peach was once a bitter almond; cauliflower is nothing but cabbage with an education. Training is everything. The peach was once a bitter almond; cauliflower is nothing but cabbage with an education. Training is everything. The peach was once a bitter almond; cauliflower is nothing but cabbage with an education.

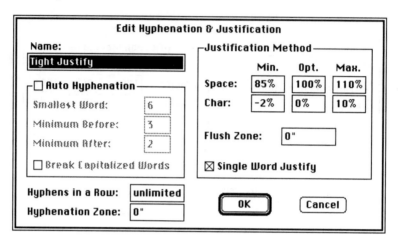

Figure 8.10   *Effect of tight spacing.*

Vertical Alignment

Another feature that can determine the formatting of text is a powerful control tucked away in the Text Box Specifications dialog box. Paragraph alignment works on text in the horizontal; this function works in the vertical. With it you can accomplish broad-stroke vertical positioning and spacing within a text box. The Vertical Alignment drop-down list provides four choices. The first three—**Top**, **Centered**, and **Bottom**—are shown in Figure 8.11 and correspond roughly to the positioning within the text box. More specifically, they work between the first baseline and the text inset at the bottom of the box.

Another option, more drastic, is the **Justified** choice in this same drop-down list. With **Justified**, you can automatically spread out lines of text to fit the text box you're working with. Leaving the **Interparagraph Spacing** field at zero, choosing the Vertical Alignment of **Justified**, and clicking **OK** produces the text box at the left in Figure 8.12. By entering a value into that Inter-¶ Max. spacing field and clicking **OK**, you'll force the paragraphs apart by that value—and line spacing will adjust to accommodate, as shown in the text box on the right.

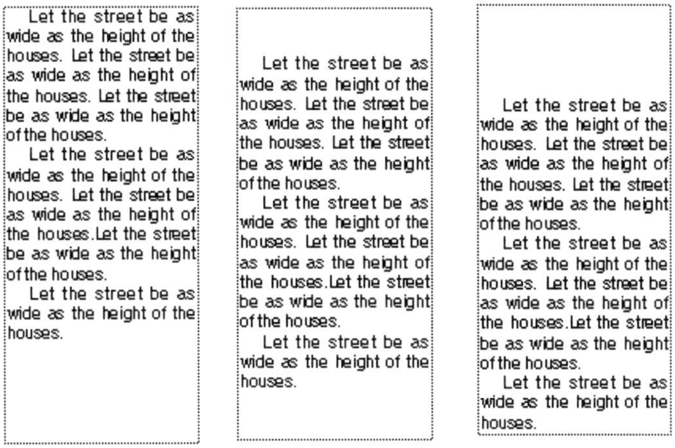

Figure 8.11   *Vertical text alignments—top, centered, and bottom.*

Vertical justifications occur from top to bottom in a single-column text box. In a multicolumn text box, however, they're effective only on the final (rightmost) column.

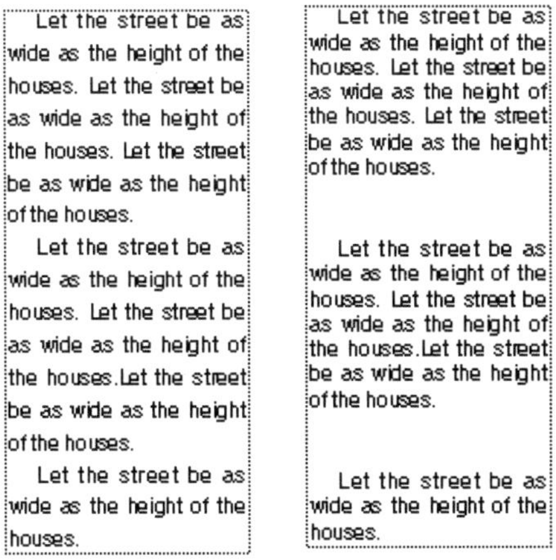

Figure 8.12 *Vertically justified text, with and without interparagraph spacing.*

The Baseline Grid

Leading and vertical justification might seem to be as far as we can go with line-spacing control. There is, however, another means by which lines of type in a paragraph can be set. It's available throughout a document, but invisible unless you switch it on. This additional method involves the *baseline grid*. This grid is a set of guidelines that provides the ability to set every line of text in a document to the same spacing. To gain full control over this method requires adjustments in three different commands. We'll start at ground level and work up to full control.

The first step in using the baseline grid is to make it visible through the View menu's **Show Baseline Grid** command. What you see is a set of horizontal lines running through the page and across into the pasteboard, as shown in Figure 8.13.

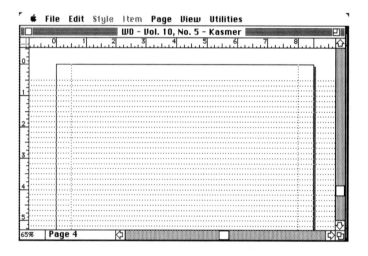

Figure 8.13   *The Baseline Grid displayed.*

N O T E   Note the General Preferences (under the Edit menu to **Preferences**, then **General**) determine whether all guides, including the baseline grid are show in front or behind items on the page. If the setting is **Behind**, a text box will be above the grid, obscuring the baselines. Choose In Front to allow the non-printing grid lines to show over the text and other page items.

In this case, the lines begin at the .5-inch mark on the vertical ruler and repeat every 12 pts downward, the default setting in the Typographic Preferences dialog box.

The value of baseline grids is that every paragraph of every page of an entire document can be locked to the same line spacing. This is accomplished in a per-paragraph control determined by the Paragraph Formats dialog box. You can choose to display or hide the baselines, but the control remains engaged either way.

To lock lines of text to a baseline grid, first select the paragraphs involved (as you would for any formatting change), then, in the Paragraph Formats dialog box, click the **Lock to Baseline** checkbox.

Notice the difference in leading between the left text box and the right text box shown in Figure 8.14. Both have corresponding paragraphs set to the same point sizes, and to auto-leading. However, in the right-hand box all of the text was selected, and the Formats dialog's **Lock to Baseline** checkbox was clicked. This command is a powerful one, overriding all local leading and providing a quick method to achieve leading consistency, so that text in adjacent columns lines up, for example.

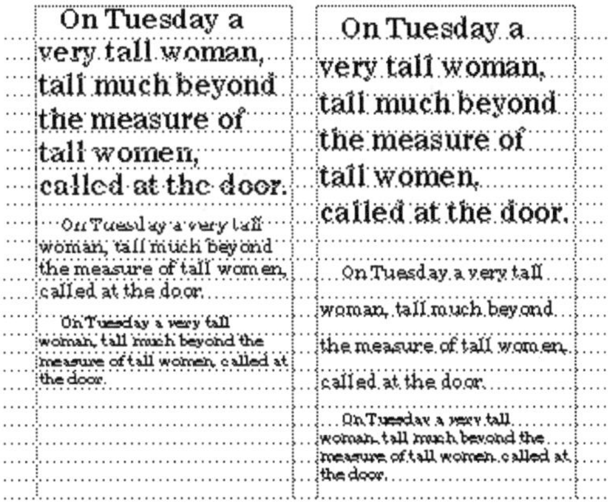

Figure 8.14 *Fixed leading versus text locking to baseline.*

Look at the text of the last paragraph in the right-hand box, and you'll see that it has lined up precisely with every baseline running through it, while the other two paragraphs have lined up with every other baseline. The **Lock** feature works out the nearest match in baseline multiples. Notice also that the first line of text is placed on the first baseline at the top of the box that will accommodate it fully within the box (allowing for text inset, if any).

You can specify how far down in the text box you'd like your text to begin. To do so, in the Text Box Specifications dialog box (Item menu to **Modify**) type any distance into the First Baseline box in the field marked **Offset**. QuarkXPress will then locate the first line of text on the first baseline encountered only past that distance downward in the text box.

Widows and Orphans

Now we come to some typographical surprises that are the scourge of typesetters everywhere. *Widows* and *orphans* are no welcome visitors when they deflate a precisely set story or book layout. Widows are solitary lines of paragraphs which settle themselves alone at the top of a column or page. Orphans are small words that often fall on the last line of a paragraph, as well as those first lines of paragraphs to be stranded alone at the bottom of a column or page. In Figure 8.15 you can see an invasion of widows and orphans in one box of hapless text.

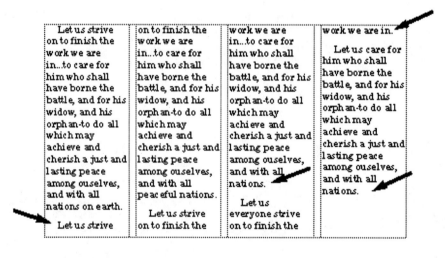

Figure 8.15 *Text replete with widows and orphans.*

QuarkXPress deals with widows and orphans through the Paragraph Formats dialog box. The approach behind this command is to hold the paragraphs together as much as is specified, entirely or in pieces.

The primary widow and orphan eliminator is the Keep Lines Together box. To engage it, click an **x** into the checkbox you see there. When you do, the dialog box will expand to include options for paragraph line control, as shown in Figure 8.16. If you are adamant that a paragraph not be broken up in any way, then assure that the **All Lines in Paragraph** button is engaged. To keep single lines from appearing in isolated locations, click the button below it. The default value for the **Start** field requires that at least two lines are needed to start a paragraph at a given location. This is the widow-killer. The **default** value for the **End** field allows a paragraph to break only when at least two lines from it appear in the next column. This is the orphan-killer. You can apply this feature to a single paragraph, or to all the paragraphs in a story. Figure 8.17 shows the results of applying it to all the text in the previous text box.

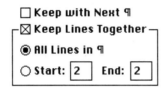

Figure 8.16   *The widow and orphan controls of the Format dialog box.*

| Let us strive on to finish the work we are in...to care for him who shall have borne the battle, and for his widow, and his orphan-to do all which may achieve and cherish a just and lasting peace among ouselves, and with all nations on earth. | Let us strive on to finish the work we are in...to care for him who shall have borne the battle, and for his widow, and his orphan-to do all which may achieve and cherish a just and lasting peace among ouselves, and with all peaceful nations. | Let us strive on to finish the work we are in...to care for him who shall have borne the battle, and for his widow, and his orphan-to do all which may achieve and cherish a just and lasting peace among ouselves, and with all nations. | Let us everyone strive on to finish the work we are in. Let us care for him who shall have borne the battle, and for his widow, and his orphan-to do all which may achieve and cherish a just and lasting peace among ouselves, and with all nations. ⊠ |

Figure 8.17   *The story of Figure 8.15 cleared of widows and line orphans.*

All of the single lines, top and bottom, are gone. But notice that single-word lines still linger. One way to fix this is to adjust tracking, or horizontal scaling.

Horizontal Scaling

Let's face it, some typesetting controls are more fun than others. Horizontal scaling is my nomination for one of typesetting's most pleasing controls. This feature is easy to use and powerful. It affects individual type characters and is highly visual. *Horizontal scaling* is a simply a way of stretching or compressing characters. Purists might be inclined to scorn its use. After all, it distorts the design of the typeface. But it can be so useful in subtle ways, and can produce heavy-handed effects with such ease that you can't afford to overlook it when you face typesetting challenges.

To compress or expand any selected text characters, open the Style menu, then choose the **Horizontal/Vertical Scale** command. the dialog will be set to receive a horizontal scaling value which you can key in directly. The range is from 25% to 400%, in tenth-of-a-percent increments. As shown in Figure 8.18, the original text of the upper box was selected and scaled to 90% of the original character width to produce the fit in the lower text box, by using the dialog box shown. Some might even argue that the compressed appearance is an improvement. Clearly, this feature is of great value in subtly reducing the space required for a given body of text. A 95% scaling, for instance, would go unnoticed by almost all readers.

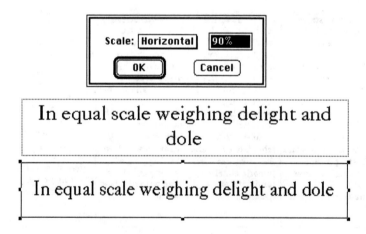

Figure 8.18   *Effects of horizontal scaling to 90%.*

You can, of course, go to an extreme with this feature. Figure 8.19 shows the upper box text expanded to produce the text in the lower box.

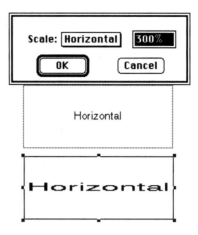

Figure 8.19 *Expanding text 300%.*

Vertical Scaling

Text scaling advances to its next logical step in QuarkXPress—vertical scaling. *Vertical scaling*, which compresses or expands text in height while leaving its width unchanged, is controlled the same way as horizontal scaling—selecting the text, then opening the Style menu to the **Horizontal/Vertical Scaling** command's dialog box. There, clicking on the field box which shows Horizontal reveals the **Vertical** selection. Choosing Vertical provides the same range and increments as **Horizontal**.

But there is a significant difference between the two types of scaling. With vertical scaling, in changing the height of the characters you are toying with the line spacing. For instance, expanding a word 200% in a line of text can create extra space above the line under automatic leading. Of course, using vertical scaling in single line headlines avoids this problem.

N O T E

In terms of letter form, a word expanded through vertical scaling can take on the same shape as one compressed with horizontal scaling. The difference will be the size of the resulting word.

Drop Caps

It's safe to say that *drop caps* will become one of your favorite features. *Drop caps*, the large initial capital letters that often lead off in stories and sections of newspapers, magazines, and books, are popular because they can signal the beginning of a section of text while adding visual spice to a text-heavy document. QuarkXPress has a highly effective method for producing drop caps.

If you've used desktop publishing programs before, you might have had to create a large capital, send it out to the clipboard or another program, then import it back as a graphic to use with text runaround features.

The method in this program is quite direct. To make an initial drop cap, first insert the cursor anywhere in the paragraph to receive the capital, then open the Paragraph Formats dialog box and click an **x** in the **Drop Caps** checkbox. When you do, the dialog box will expand to include two specifications for drop caps. The first of these is a box for the number of characters to be part of the drop cap. You can have just the initial letter set as a drop cap, or an entire word or more according to the value put here. The second specification for drop caps is the number of lines into which the capital will be dropped.

Figure 8.20 shows a standard drop cap set in the first paragraph of a text box. The default for the number of characters rendered as drop caps is **1**, and the number of lines in which to fit the drop cap is **3**. These defaults are quite serviceable, but changing them and experimenting is quite a simple matter.

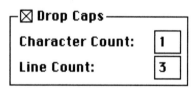

Figure 8.20 *A drop cap applied using the expanded Formats dialog box.*

Tabs

Tabs, those markers that send text over to a certain position within a line, were simple, (though limited and tedious things) in the days of typewriter text. Now the choices have grown. The typewriter was suited for tabs measured over from the left. If you wanted to center your tabs, or align on a decimal as for a column of prices, you had to count spaces or rely on an unwavering eye.

We've already made use of the preset tabs provided in Documents (left tabs at half-inch intervals). With QuarkXPress you can precisely align tabs to the left, center, and right, to a decimal, to a comma, or to any other character you designate. Access to tab adjustments is gained through a dialog box in which you can position new tabs, adjust, or remove existing tabs. This dialog box is opened through the Style menu when the Content tool is active. Tabs apply to paragraphs. By its location, the cursor will designate one paragraph, or more may be selected. There is also limited adjustment of left tabs through the Column ruler appearing when the Paragraph Formats dialog box is active.

Each time you press the **Tab** key in a line while working in text, the program will move the cursor over as though a wide invisible character had been keyed in. The width of this character is determined by the positioning of the tab markers. You can see the tab characters represented in the text by switching on **Show Invisibles**. In Figure 8.21 this has been done for a text box in which the **Tab** key was pressed several times to engage the preset default half-inch left tabs.

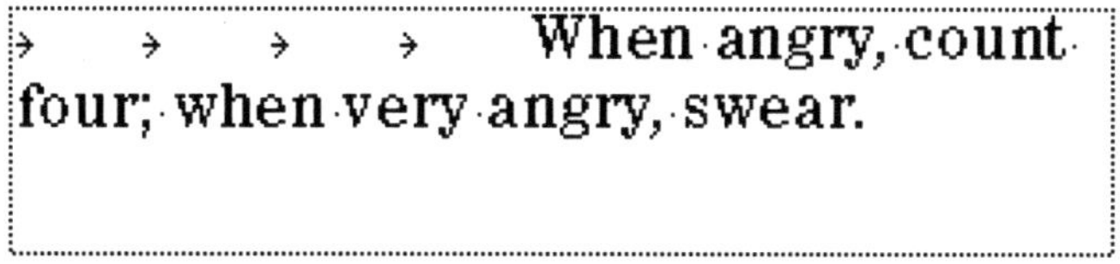

Figure 8.21 *Tabs revealed through Show Invisibles.*

To adjust tabs, open the Style menu and choose Tabs. A dialog box will be displayed and a ruler will appear above the column in question. Initially, there will be a drop-down list and three fields for entering specifications. Figure 8.22 shows the dialog box with the drop-down list opened to reveal the types of tabs available.

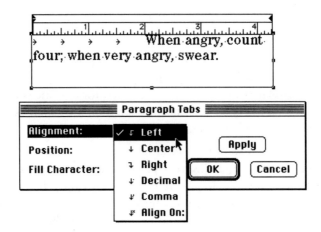

Figure 8.22 *Tab choices.*

There are two methods for inserting tabs. In each you first select one of the tab types in the drop-down list. In one method, you then simply click in the Dialog Ruler. A marker corresponding to the tab chosen in the list will appear.

For a more precise approach, do the following: key in the position measured from the left origin of the text area in the Position box. A tab marker will likewise appear.

Each time you click in a tab, its location will be indicated in the Position field. If you change the position value here, rather than move the tab, the dialog box will create a new tab marker when you press the **Apply** or **OK** button. You can insert two, three, up to twenty tab markers per paragraph.

To remove a tab, drag it out of the ruler space. To reposition a tab, drag it along the ruler to the new location. To modify tab features, drag out the old tab and insert a new one according to the above procedure.

Normally, each tab will be preceded by blank space. You can, however, modify this so that the space will be filled with a character typed at the keyboard. To do so, click on the tab in question, key in the character you wish to precede that position—that is, the character to fill that tab space—then click the **Apply** or **OK** button. You can modify tabs already present in the text, or set up tab markers to be applied to text tabs yet to be keyed.

The moment you click the **Apply** button after clicking a tab into the ruler, or after entering a value into the **Position** field, you'll insert a tab that overrides the default tabs. In Figure 8.23 a period has been entered as the tab leader, here called **Fill Character** and a tab has been clicked into place at one-and-a-quarter inches. You can visually correlate tab markers with the actual tabs that will be displayed in text. Note in the figure how the periods have filled the tab space in the paragraph.

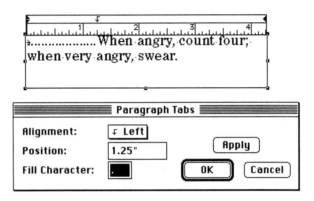

Figure 8.23   *Aligning the Tabs dialog with selected text box.*

Choosing **Right Tabs** gives a justified appearance to tabular text; choosing **Center Tabs** produces very orderly columns. Choosing **Decimal Tabs** will cause items in each line to align on the decimal point. Similarly, you can choose some other character, such as an apostrophe, to align a list of possessive names. When you choose **Align On** from the Alignment list, a field will be displayed next to it—which is where you key in the alignment character you wish to use.

Paragraph Rules

Rules, those sharp delineators, can be drawn out with the line tools, as we have seen. But you can also specify them through commands that apply them automatically to text. Like formatting features, they will be applied to the paragraphs selected.

To initiate the command that does this, first select the text with the Content tool. Then open the Style menu and choose **Rules**. You'll see the dialog box shown in Figure 8.24. Click an **x** into one or both of the checkboxes, **Rule Above** and **Rule Below**, and the dialog box will expand into one like that shown in Figure 8.25. The controls here are consistent with others we have encountered thus far, and you can install rules that will follow the paragraph, wherever it may appear in the text box. Available rules can be adjusted to run across the column or across the width of text, can be of various forms and shadings, and can be set close to or farther from your paragraph.

Paragraph Rules

☐ Rule Above
☐ Rule Below

[OK]   [Cancel]   [Apply]

Figure 8.24 *The Paragraph Rules dialog box.*

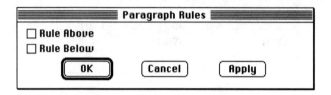

Paragraph Rules

☒ Rule Above
Length: [Indents]   Style: ▬▬▬▬▬
From Left: [0"]   Width: ▶ [2 pt]
From Right: [0"]   Color: [Black]
Offset: [0%]   Shade: ▶ [100%]

☒ Rule Below
Length: [Text]   Style: ▬ ▬ ▬ ▬ ▬
From Left: [.5"]   Width: ▶ [Hairline]
From Right: [.5]   Color: [Black]
Offset: [50%]   Shade: ▶ [60%]

[OK]   [Cancel]   [Apply]

Figure 8.25 *The Expanded Rules dialog box specifications.*

Preferred Ways to Work

Let's turn to the subject of measurement. Surely no typesetter would feel at home if nothing but the English system of inches were available. For the specialized world of type and page layout, measurement by pica is easier and quicker to integrate with type sizes. Picas provide flexibility and compatibility that correlates directly to type, rules, measuring, and positioning. A *pica* is defined by QuarkXPress as one-sixth of an inch, the equivalent of twelve points.

You can easily switch between measuring systems within the document, using whichever measurement is appropriate to the circumstance. The default, as we've seen, is inches. To switch to picas, open the Edit menu and choose **Preferences**. Another menu will be displayed, as shown in Figure 8.26. From this menu, choose **General** to open the dialog box shown in Figure 8.27. Notice the **Horizontal Measure** and **Vertical Measure** fields. By opening their dropdown lists, you can select **Picas** and convert the rulers, all the dialog boxes, and the Measurements palette to that system. You can just as easily convert back to inches, or to one of the other systems offered.

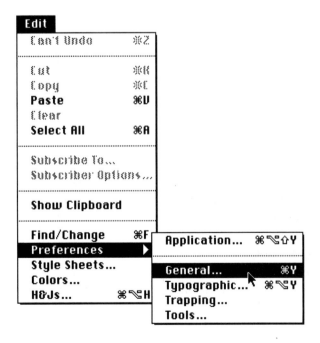

Figure 8.26 *The Preferences juncture submenu.*

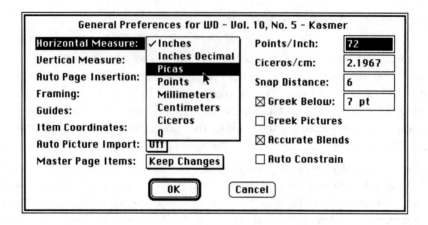

Figure 8.27 *General Preferences.*

You might also notice some of the other functions here. You can change the value for greeking text. The default is 7 pt. Replace this value with 2 pt and you'll see a truer representation of text at reduced views—at the cost, however, of slower screen redraw. Also note as mentioned earlier, that you can move the guides between the uppermost (**In front**) level and the deepest (**Behind**) level, which makes picking up objects on them easier. And the framing method for all boxes can be adjusted between framing inside (the default) to framing outside (which will not obscure box contents). More on other preferences later.

Onward

Typography is the soul of publishing. Controlling the appearance of paragraphs and stories can influence the way readers react to content. Typography speaks to the heart of QuarkXPress, for which it has few rivals. To master the page, the publication producer must master typography through methods of the sort we've seen in this chapter.

When these features are put to work, the page can come alive. Can there be a nobler cause among page craftspersons than using type to create a moving and honest display of content? How do these features come together? The answer can be found in one of the most typographically demanding media to enter our daily lives, the newspaper. The next chapter looks at typography at work in one such example.

On the Job:
Newspaper Pages

What you will learn in this chapter:

- ❖ How to set up a newspaper page layout
- ❖ Adjusting guides and preferences during design
- ❖ How to apply hyphenation and justification
- ❖ How to use centered and right-aligned tabs to best effect
- ❖ Using formatting to fit text
- ❖ Adjusting text runaround in body copy

Newspapers begin the day for millions around the world. On a full news day, Page One might expose readers to a dozen stories. It could direct them to a dozen others. Word-heavy by nature, most newspapers are designed to lure a scanning, screening, discriminating audience to every story it can. Daily journalism, wrestling with the chaos of each day's events, demands typography that is lucid, provoking, and orderly.

In this chapter we'll work with the front page of a newspaper to put into practice techniques introduced in Chapter 8 and earlier. We'll establish the optimum spacing between headlines, subheads, and body text, set up hyphenation and justification, adjust indents and rules, and apply other typographical adjustments that bring order to the daily tumult of news stories. We'll see how to set up a table of contents and produce entry alignments through tabs. We'll also see how to make use of the graphic placeholder and to apply text runaround features to make everything fit precisely.

The Front Page

This page one requires a banner title, articles with headlines, and lead-ins to inside stories. We're working in a large format here, a 23 by 13.75-inch document. It folds across in the middle for display in a stack or a rack. Our layout needs to take this into account, as well as the fact that large headlines are needed to catch the eye of the casual glancer.

First we'll set up the document by creating the file, changing the measuring system, and setting margin guides in place. Then we'll be ready to handle the top matter as we convert this publication to electronic format.

Setting Up the Newspaper Document

We begin as with any document. Turning to the File menu, we choose **New**, sliding over in the menu to select **Document**. In the New dialog box for width, we key in **13.75**, and for height, **23**. Setting up a strong grid is vital for a newspaper, and we opt for six columns to keep our stories tightly in line. Conveniently, the gutter width is already set for **.167**, which is 1 pica, the separation we're looking for. And we leave the default half-inch margin all around, while clicking an **x** to activate facing pages.

We click off the Automatic Text box because the many stories on each page will each require their own varying boxes. As a result, the six columns, which are laid out, will serve strictly as guides. But important guides they will be, unifying the look of a variety of stories. Clicking **OK**, we create a large-format newspaper document.

Next, we change to the measurement system we prefer, and make some other document-wide display changes. Opening the Edit menu, we choose **Preferences**, and at the submenu that is displayed we choose **General**. In the **General** Preferences dialog box (shown in Figure 9.1) we use drop-down lists to convert the horizontal measure and vertical measure to picas.

This type-heavy newspaper will be an all-text document as far as our work is concerned. As we move along, we will add placeholder picture boxes for photos for position only. Being able to see text at different views is important. So, we click off the checkmark in the **Greek Below** checkbox. We click **OK** to activate these preference adjustments.

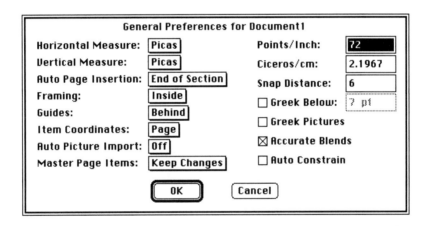

Figure 9.1   *Changing measures and display features for the document.*

N   O   T   E

Your choice of whether to greek text (and if so, at what font size) will depend on the speed with which your computer system can redraw the screen and the demands made on it by the formatting of the text. There is a trade-off here between speed of response and precision of display. The sometime sluggishness of slower machines with limited memory in the video graphics card would encourage users to leave greeking on at the default, while the responsiveness of faster, higher-end machine with ample video memory would suggest no greeking, or setting the greeking at a low pixel value for greater screen-display text clarity.

Now as we proceed with Page One we experience a change of mind: we'll use a different approach to adjust the margin guides. The margins can be set in two places: at the New dialog box when you first create a document, and afterwards once the document exists at the master pages. We reach the master pages by opening the Page menu and choosing **Display**. A submenu appears, as shown in Figure 9.2. Here, as in all newly created documents, there is only one master page. It's designated M1-Master1. Sliding the pointer over to select it brings us to the facing master pages.

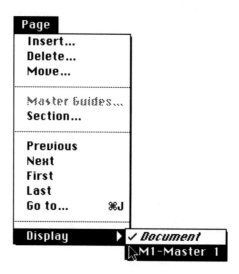

Figure 9.2   *Displaying a master page.*

At the master page we have just one task to do—readjust the margin guides. To do this we open the Page menu and choose **Master Guides**. When the dialog box is displayed, we key in new values for the margins. We're now using picas, in this case **3p** all around except for the inside margin, for which **2p** is typed (shown in Figure 9.3). Now all margins are properly set for our paper.

When using the pica measuring system in QuarkXPress, it's wise to type pica values as **1p**, **2p**, and so on. If the letter **p** does not follow the value, QuarkXPress assumes the value is in points (which are one-twelfth of a pica). Keying in **3** in a pica field would result in 3 points being assigned to that field; on examining the field later you would see it appear as p3. The convention, then, is picas—*p*—points. A pica and a half (1 pica, 6 points) would be displayed as **1p6**, 10 would be interpreted as **p10** or 10 points, while **10p** would be interpreted as 10 picas.

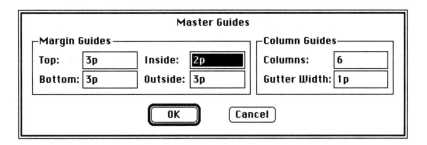

Figure 9.3   *Readjusting margin guides.*

We return to Page 1 by opening the Page menu and choosing **Display**, then, at the submenu **Document**. First we pull a guide across at midheight on the page by clicking in the horizontal ruler and dragging down. Now our layout can take into account what will show when the paper is folded. The page is 138 picas long, so we know that the midpoint is 69 picas from the top. We check this location by using the Picture Box Rectangle tool to draw a box the length of the page over the page. When the box is selected, its side handles will mark the midpoint.

Finding the midpoint

Drag a box between two extremes
The item handles at the sides will fall at the midpoint

Top Matter

We're going to establish the head of this page first, including the banner and accompanying information. First, we use the Text Box tool to draw a box at the top for the banner title. With the Content tool selected, we choose the appropriate display font, type a size of 110 points at the Measurements palette and click on the **Centering** button there. At the Text Box Specifications dialog box (Item menu, **Modify**) we set the vertical alignment at **Center**. Then, back at the text box we key in the name, Morning Chronicle, as shown in Figure 9.4. This begins the typesetting of Page 1.

To improve banner appearance we adjust the tracking –3 on the selected text by keying in that value at the **Tracking** field of the Measurements palette. This improves the appearance except for crowding the r against the n in Morning. Inserting the cursor between them we then adjust the kerning between these two letters to –3 again through the Measurements palette, which balances the banner title. Note that the rulers indicate picas, and the Measurements palette likewise displays values in pica units.

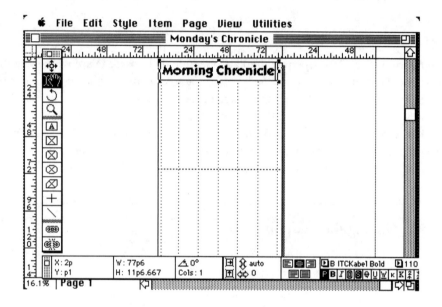

Figure 9.4 *Establishing the banner title.*

To separate the banner from the material below it, we use the Rule tool and drag out a line from margin to margin. Two picas below this, we drag another line. We select the upper line, and turning to the Measurements palette, we key in **.5** in the **W:** field to make it half a point thick. Selecting the lower line, we key in **4** at the palette to make this line 4 points thick, and use the drop-down list to select the double-line attribute with a thin line over a thick one. The result is a set of enclosing lines.

Between these bounding lines we use the Text Box tool to drag a box across margin to margin. This box will carry three phrases, Final edition, the date, and the price. The date and price are set off by two special tabs.

N O T E Many symbols and characters not apparent on the keyboard can be derived through special characters produced with the help of the **Option** key. For instance, to type a cents symbol, hold the **Option** key while pressing the number 4. A ¢ character will be displayed. More about special characters in Chapter 18.

We adjust the text style and format in this line. Selecting it all (Command-A) with the cursor in the text box, we use the Measurements palette to set the type to a darker bold. Then with a Command-double-click in the box we bring up the Text Specifications dialog where vertical alignment is set to **Centered**.

It's next time to adjust those tabs. We want to position the phrase Final edition, flush left; the date, centered; and the price, flush right. With the cursor still in the text box, we open the Style menu and choose **Tabs**, thereby opening the Paragraph Tabs dialog box.

The first phrase is already in position, because the text is left aligned. The date, however, is one **Default** tab stop over. We want this stop to be at the center of the text box. So, we'll numerically figure the center from the width of the text box, shown in the Measurements palette as nearly 78 picas. We therefore want the date centered about 39 picas, with our wide, single-column text box. At the Paragraph Tabs dialog box, we open the **Alignment** drop-down list and choose **Center**. Using the scrolling arrows to locate 39 points in the Dialog Box ruler, we click there; a center tab is inserted. At second glance we determined the center precisely by selecting the text box with the Pointer tool and noting the center box handles that appear sliding the center tab above the handles puts the it at 38 picas and 6 points (shown in Figure 9.5).

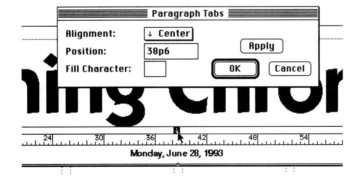

Figure 9.5 *Inserting a center tab.*

Last to be positioned is the price. We want it aligned to the right limit of the text box. This is the second tab stop in the box. Returning to the Paragraph Tabs dialog box, we open the **Alignment** drop-down list and choose **Right**. In the position box we type in the approximate position of the right end of the box, 78 picas. But a dialog notice appears indicating the value must be between **0** and **77p4**, the precise width of the box. We then key this value into the **Position** field and click the **Apply** button. The price, 50¢, is aligned flush right, as shown in Figure 9.6.

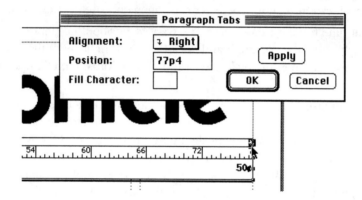

Figure 9.6   *Adjusting a right tab.*

This completes the top matter of page 1.

The Stories

Most newspapers follow a Page One layout format that varies only in minor points from day to day. One popular layout approach designates one story each issue to run as a regular feature in a single column down the left of the page. We follow that plan here with a section labeled, ON LOCATION. Using the Text Box tool at Fit-in Window view, a long column box is dragged downward into the leftmost column. We rely on the **Snap to Guides** feature to make the box fit across the column exactly.

To create the column head, we type in the label, triple-click to select the line, then open the Style menu and choose **Character**. In the resulting dialog box we select a sans serif font, a size, all caps, and bolding.

To emphasize this label, we open the Style menu again and choose **Rules**. At the Paragraph Rules dialog box, we click on the checkbox marked **Rule Below**. After the box expands, we choose **Text** from the **Length** drop-down list. The rule will now run under our label like an offset underline. We key in a Width of **1** for thickness in points and an offset of 25% for positioning the rule under the section heading. The resulting section head label is shown in Figure 9.7. Selecting **OK**, we turn next to the story headline.

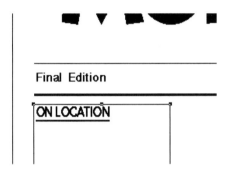

Final Edition

ON LOCATION

Figure 9.7   *Character and rule formatting applied to a section head.*

In this design the body and headlines are all set in the same typeface, the ever-hardy Times Roman style. We key in a headline and a lead-in. Then, at the Measurements palette we make the following adjustments. The head is set at 24 points, the lead-in at 14. Both paragraphs are selected together and the tracking is reduced –5%.

Now the label, head, and lead-in are selected together in order to add paragraph spacing. At the Paragraph Formats dialog box (through Style menu to **Formats**) a value of p8 eight points) is keyed into the **Space After** to separate the three paragraphs. Once we click **OK**, we see the three paragraphs spaced as shown in Figure 9.8.

N O T E

Sometimes it's tempting to separate a paragraph from its neighbors by adding both **Space Before** and **Space After** through the Formats dialog box. Beware, this can become a trap. Because the spacing format doesn't stop with the paragraph in question, it continues to be applied as new paragraphs are successively generated. After this kind of formatting, separation of paragraphs is compounded. The space after paragraph one, for instance, will be combined with the space before paragraph two. The result can be an archipelago of paragraph islands in a sea of white space. You might want to consider using only **Space After** for successive paragraphs—making sure that paragraph spacing is reset following the stand-out paragraph.

Final Edition

ON LOCATION

A Spectacle in
London

Bull-baiting records reveal
happenings townspeople
are trying to forget

Figure 9.8   Uniform spacing applied between three paragraphs.

In this layout we have a byline to include. Our design calls for an all caps name set off by a thin rule from the headline and lead-in we've just completed. We begin by selecting 10 points, bold, at the Measurements palette and typing By and the reporter's name, Bret Burton, on a new line. Next, we drag to select just the name and open the Style menu. We choose **Character** and, in the Character Attributes dialog box, click **All Caps**. We leave the bolding setting and the other attributes as they are shown in Figure 9.9 and click **OK**. We're also accepting the paragraph spacing, so we leave the Formats dialog box unchanged.

This byline should have a rule running above it across the column. The Style menu is opened and **Rules** is chosen. We click on the **Rule Above** checkbox and, at the expanded dialog box of Figure 9.10, choose **Indents** from the **Length** drop-down list. We also key in an offset of 20% (to lift the rule 20 percent of the line spacing from the line) and change the width to 0.5 points before clicking the **Apply** button. One look confirms this is the appearance we want, so we click the **OK** button.

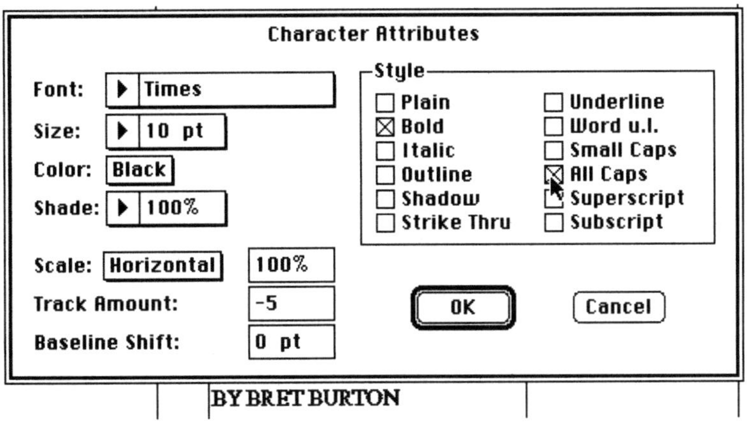

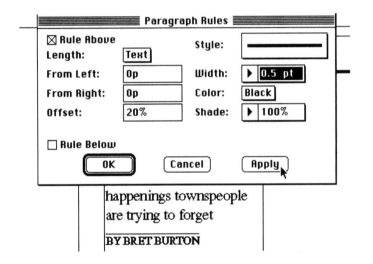

Figure 9.9   *Formatting a byline.*

Figure 9.10   *Applying a rule across the column above the byline.*

Now it's time to add body copy into our story box. We're going to prepare for this text by adjusting the character and paragraph attributes. When the story is imported, we want its formatting to resemble the desired appearance of the final product. Here's what we do. Tapping the **Enter** key puts the cursor one line below the byline, where the story file will begin. Using the controls of the Measurements palette, we select plain text, Times Roman, 10 points, justified, with tracking set at zero. At the Paragraph Rules dialog box, the **Rule Above** checkbox is clicked to be blank, removing the rule established in the previous paragraph. Then at the Paragraph Formats dialog box (Style menu to **Formats**), the **Space After** value is set to zero since we want no interparagraph spacing in the body text. Also, the **First Line** indent is set to 8 points—typed as **p8**—so that each paragraph will be indented about three characters. And finally the checkbox, **Lock to Baseline Grid**, is clicked to **x**, engaging this function. The default baseline spacing of 12 points will work fine with the 10-pt. body type we'll be using.

With the text cursor placed where the body copy will begin, we open the File menu, choose **Get Text**, and double-click on the file, London Spectacle. The story flows into the text box. Figure 9.11 shows the text with the Baseline Grid turned on.

![A Spectacle in London - newspaper layout shown with baseline grid]

A Spectacle in London

Bull-baiting records reveal happenings townspeople are trying to forget

BY BRET BURTON

London—On the morning of the day the bull, or any other creature that is to e baited is led round. It takes place in a large open space or courtyard, on two sides of which high benches have been made for the spectators.

First a young ox or bull was led in and fastened by a long rope to an iron ring in the middle of the yard;

Figure 9.11   *Body copy locked to baseline grid.*

Looking at the result, we see that a feature vital to the narrow column layout of a newspaper is not applied here. The **Hyphenation** function is switched off. **Hyphenation Off** is the default for a new QuarkXPress document. We'll have to adjust the H&J specifications. Here we choose to generate a new specifications set that will be applied to body copy.

NOTE

Sometimes you will want to change hyphenation or justification specifications once some text has been formatted satisfactorily in document columns. Changing an existing set of specifications, however, might also change those paragraphs already in place. All text to which another set of specifications is not applied automatically is assigned an H&J of Standard. So, in general, if you are pleased with the text already in the document, create a new set of H&J specifications.

Opening the Edit menu, we choose **H&Js**. At the H&Js dialog box that is displayed, we click the **New** button. This presents the specifications for Standard in the Edit Hyphenation and Justification dialog box. We key in a name, **Standard2**, and then click an **x** into the Auto Hyphenation dialog box. At this dialog box we make some other adjustments in order to avoid the looseness of the default settings. These modifications include setting the **Smallest Word** value to hyphenate on a 5-character instead of a 6-character word, changing the **Minimum Before** to two instead of three characters, adjusting the word spacing minimum and maximums to 90% and 130% (from 100% and 150%), and the letter spacing equivalents to –3% and 5% (from zero and 15%). The **Single Word Justify** feature is also deactivated before clicking **OK**.

Having made this new set of specifications, we then select the body copy and apply the new standard. This we do through the Paragraph Formats dialog box by locating **Standard2** in the **H&J** drop-down list. Figure 9.12 shows the new specifications for adjusting the body copy.

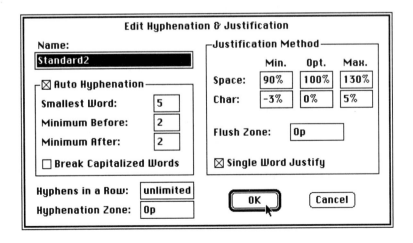

Figure 9.12   *Adjusting hyphenation and justification for body copy.*

N O T E

In taking care of the body copy, we've established a Hyphenation/Justification standard, the specifications set **Standard2**, which can be used for any or all body copy in the paper. Developing standards for character and other formatting is performed similarly. These other standards can be saved in sets of specifications known as *style sheets*. In Chapter 10, style sheets will be explored in detail.

One small item remains to be fixed in the first paragraph. The dateline, London, should be capitalized. To do this we select the word by double-clicking, open the Style menu, choose **Character**, then click **All Caps** and **OK**. Now the body of this story on Page 1 has been set. All that remains on this page is to signal the reader that the story has been jumped to the inside. We'll do this by adding a small continuation notice at the lower extent of the text box. Since our design calls for other stories to begin at 106 picas from the top, we produce a guide by clicking and dragging from the horizontal ruler down to that point, as indicated on the vertical ruler. Then we pull the Spectacle in London text box up above the guide.

We create another small text box for the jump notice—using the Text Box tool to drag one into place below the Story text box. In the Runaround Specifications dialog box (in the Item menu) we select **None** from the **Mode** drop-down list. At the text box, using the Content tool we key in the jump information, choosing the same text style as the body but reducing the size to 9 points and adding bolding at the Measurements palette. The result is shown in Figure 9.13.

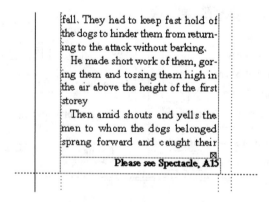

Figure 9.13 *A jump notice installed.*

Now we can fit in other stories across multiple columns at the top two-thirds of Page 1. The headline text boxes are drawn separately across the columns and left as single column boxes. The multiple column body text boxes are set through the Measurements palette to the number of columns matching their width on the grid guides. By applying the already established **Standard2** hyphenation and justification specifications, using similar styles, formats, and rules, we incorporate the other stories of Page 1 into the design. A horizontal rule of 3 points is drawn to separate the two stories stacked in the rightmost columns. And because a photograph will be supplied to our specified proportions and pasted in, we use the Rectangle Picture Box tool to drag out a picture box across three columns at the top of the layout, as shown in Figure 9.14. This serves as a placeholder for the halftone picture to be provided later.

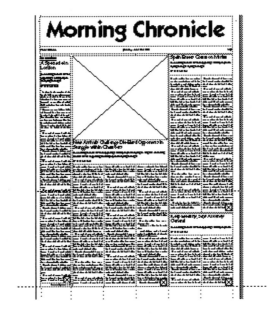

Figure 9.14   *A blank picture box as placeholder among text.*

The Inside Box

No Page One of a contemporary newspaper would be complete without a small table of contents built on blurbs extracted from the stories inside. In our design, that inside section is set in the two middle columns of the grid. It will be flanked by stories on either side, below a guide that we placed at 106 picas down. We'll include several short paragraphs based on articles located deeper within the paper.

We'll want a heading for the table of contents in one box and the actual contents in another. We'll position them so they appear integrated. First we use the Text Box tool to draw two boxes across the two center columns, one above the other. The one on top is a short box, to hold the heading of the inside section, which fills out the space of the two columns below it. Both of these boxes will have frames. We will align them so they appear to be one box.

We draw the large box with the Text Box tool, from column guide to column guide, letting the **Snap to Guides** function pull the sides in line. Then we draw the smaller heading box the same way, placing the heading box one layer in front of the large box. We select both boxes with the Item tool, open the Item menu, then choose **Frames**. At the dialog box we key in 1pt and click **OK**. Next we open the Item menu, choosing **Space/Align**. At the dialog box we click the **Vertical Alignment** checkbox, click the **Space** button, leaving the value at **0p**, and at the **Between** drop-down list select **Top Edges**. Clicking **OK** returns us to the layout with the small box positioned over the large one and appearing like a division of that larger box.

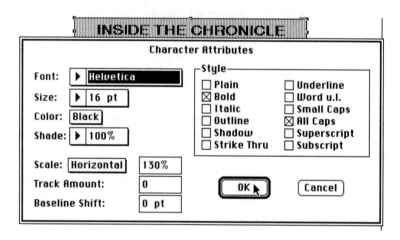

Figure 9.15   Style formatting of the box heading.

Choosing the Content tool, we click within the heading box and type, inside the chronicle. Command-A selects all the text. At the Character Attributes dialog box

(Style menu to Character) shown in Figure 9.15 we format by clicking the **All Caps** and **Bold** checkboxes, make the font and size choices, and key in a 130% horizontal scale for wider characters.

Next, we click below the heading in the larger box and type in the blurbs to appear there. Selecting **All** (Command-A), we open the Character Attributes dialog box and change the font and size. Then we open the Paragraph Formats dialog box (Style menu to Formats) and adjust the left and right indents to three picas. The indent for the first line of each paragraph is pulled in 1 pica (–1p in the dialog). We also make sure to suppress the formation of widows and orphans with the **Keep Lines Together** checkbox. Space after each paragraph is keyed in as 1 pica. Figure 9.16 shows the text and the dialog box.

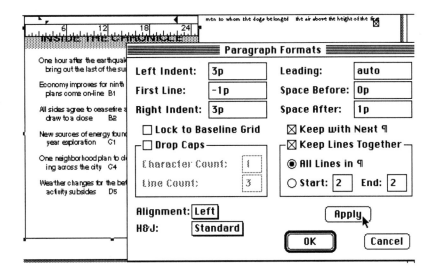

Figure 9.16   *Formatting the paragraphs.*

We've added a tab before each page reference at the end of every paragraph. We want to adjust these tabs to be right tabs to the end of the column, so we select all (Command-A). The Paragraph Tabs dialog box is opened (through the Style menu), and we make the adjustments there, as shown in Figure 9.17.

There is another adjustment required to make sure the text shifts downward within the text box. We've accomplished this by clicking on the heading box to select it and opening the Item menu, and choosing **Runaround**. In the Specifications dialog box as shown in Figure 9.18, we've used the **Mode, Item,**

and set its bottom offset to 24 points to push down the text in the box below a full 2 picas as shown.

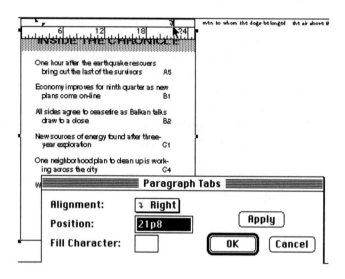

Figure 9.17   *Aligning page numbers to the right with tab adjustment.*

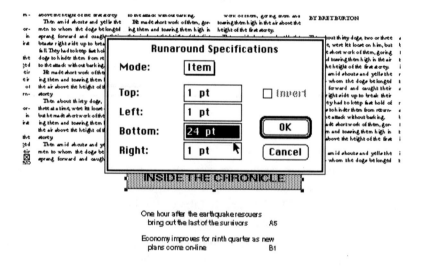

Figure 9.18   *Pushing down text through **Runaround** of the heading box.*

Finally, adding a story on either side of the Inside box completes the typesetting of Page One.

Onward

Typography controls can surely distinguish text matter. At the same time they forge a unified look for disparate stories on a single page as in the Page One we've worked with in this chapter. As you've seen, adjusting the nuances of paragraphs, text, and typography can instantly produce significant visual results. Still more typographical controls are to be found in QuarkXPress. They affect text on the document wide level, connect to the master pages, and provide special effects.

In the next chapter we will explore a wider range, examining typography and other features across the document, using style sheets, and controlling document flow. These functions are vitally important and highly useful as you turn to longer documents and multipage spreads.

Document Flow

What you will learn in this chapter:

- ❖ How to create and use master pages
- ❖ How to create and import style sheets
- ❖ How to group items
- ❖ How to anchor inline graphics and text
- ❖ How to manage multi-page spreads
- ❖ How to set up sections
- ❖ How to number pages automatically and create jump lines

As documents grow, pages multiply and stories are jumped. Designs expand while they carry along formatting from story to story, page to page. In this avalanche of change one concern begins to override all others: how to organize and unify the material.

In this chapter we look at unifying QuarkXPress documents. We also examine features that help integrate text, picture, and line items in versatile and visually compelling ways.

Two features of QuarkXPress will prove especially important for producing complex documents: master pages and style sheets. They let you apply your best formatting and layout efforts to all parts of a publication, and to change them quickly and universally if you wish. We will examine them in detail along with other page and item capabilities that make for the well-integrated document.

Master Pages

Every page is different. In some cases the difference is minor, as in novels, where the only difference in appearance may be the positions of page numbers on verso and recto pages. In other cases, the difference is so great that readers may forget which publication they are reading. Haven't you ever been momentarily waylaid by a full-page ad, and before leaving it forgotten what magazine you were holding?

Almost always, pages in a publication are related graphically to each other. It may be only by a rule positioned at the top, or by page numbering. Or there may be similarity in the number and location of columns, in section headings, in graphic emblems, or in dozens of other layout features.

Using Master Pages

Much time and effort can be saved by preserving and automatically transferring those elements and layouts repeated page after page. This is the essential function of a master page. Every page in a new QuarkXPress document is automatically built on one. Called *M1-Master 1*, it is established through the **New** command with certain dimensions, certain guides, margins, and perhaps a text box. It is but one of countless possible master pages.

Additional master pages can be produced and used as the basis for either new or existing pages at any stage of document development. Special linking through text boxes on a master page can trigger the program to automatically generate hundreds of typeset pages as needed by the quantity of text. Master pages can be applied to certain pages, dissociated from others, or even removed from the document altogether.

In every single-sided document the master pages themselves are of one format, from a Blank Single Master. In every facing-pages document the master pages can be of such single-sided format or of a double-sided variety, this from a Blank Facing Master. These master page types provide the bases for creating new master pages or modifying document pages.

Master Page Designation and the Document Layout Palette

The Document Layout palette is a useful window overlooking the activity of pages and master pages. It normally appears on the screen when QuarkXPress is started. Recall that it can be called up through the View menu by choosing **Show Document Layout**. As shown in Figure 10.1, it's divided into three parts. The topmost section is a narrow strip showing two page icons—one representing single-sided pages, the other with dog-eared corners representing facing pages. Next to these are two buttons for duplicating and deleting pages; they work on the middle and lowest sections.

Figure 10.1 *The Document Layout palette of a new document.*

Page icons also appear in the middle section. There is always at least one, the M1-Master 1 icon, representing the default master page. If other master pages have been created they will be represented by icons in this middle section as well.

The lowest section holds icons representing document pages, arranged just as the pages are in the document window. The number below each is the page number, the designation on each indicates the master page on which it is based.

By selecting and using the buttons of the uppermost section or dragging icons from either of the two upper sections, changes can be made to individual pages, such as inserting pages, removing pages, or changing the master on which a document page is based. The collection of master pages can be selectively altered through the two buttons of the upper section.

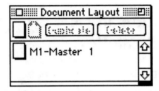

Figure 10.2 *Applicable master pages.*

In Figure 10.2 we see the simplest of master page situations. Three different master pages are represented. Each of the two icons in the upper section, the Blank Single and Blank Facing Masters, represents a master page choice that can be applied to pages. Each provides a format that can be applied to any new or existing master pages, answering the question, Should this master page be formed as a single-sided page or part of a facing-pages spread? Note that in this case only the Blank Single Master and M1-Master 1 choices are in dark outline, and therefore accessible. That is because this document was set up through the New dialog box as a single-sided publication with the **Facing-Pages** checkbox unchecked.

Figure 10.3 shows the Layout palette of a document with more diversity. Here you can see that the blank masters of both single and facing pages have been applied as indicated by blank page icons on pages 1, 6, and 7.

Recall that dog-eared page icons indicate a facing-page master has been applied. Here, facing-page masters have been applied to Pages 2 and 3 and Pages 6 and 7 (indicated by **M1**, **M3**, and **M4** within the page icons). Notice in particular that though they are facing pages of the same spread, Pages 2 and 3 are based on different master pages, **M1** and **M3**, respectively.

The Blank Single Master and Blank Facing Master of the upper section always remain devoid of all content, items, or guides (except that they reflect choices in the New dialog box regarding page dimensions and margins). The other master pages, designated M1-Master 1, M2-Master 2, and so on, can contain anything a document page is capable of holding, and more.

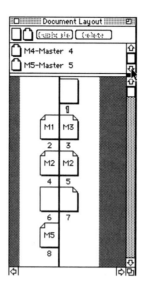

Figure 10.3   A Document Layout showing a variety of master pages applied.

Access to the Master Pages

Of course, the moment you make a new document, you create a master page with it, M1-Master 1. How can you work with this?

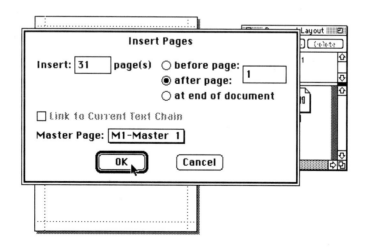

*Figure 10.4   Master page, **M1**, applied automatically in Insert Pages dialog.*

Let's consider a simple case. When a new document of facing pages is created with the **New** command, we find ourselves at a page like Page 1. If this document is expanded to a 32-page document, by adding pages through the Page menu's Insert Command dialog box, the **Default** master page, **M1**, will be automatically applied to the added pages as shown Figure 10.4. Or, by using the drop-down list (labeled **Master Page:**), you can choose to apply one of the other available masters (blank single and blank facing pages) to your pages, either through the Insert Pages dialog box or the Document Layout palette.

Applying a master page through the Document Layout palette

At the Document Layout palette, select the page or pages

Press **Option** while clicking on the master page

You can easily move a master page (not counting the blanks, which are untouchables) into the document window, by opening the Page menu and choosing **Display**. A submenu pops up, as shown in Figure 10.5.

Figure 10.5 *Moving to a master page through the Page menu.*

After sliding the mouse pointer over to the name of the master page (M1-Master 1, for example), you'll see the master page layout displayed. Alternatively, using the Document Layout palette, just point and double-click on the master page of interest.

Moving to a master page

Open the Page menu and choose **Display**

At the submenu, choose the master page

or

At the Document Layout, double-click on the master page icon

Notice that the master page spread looks much like any document-page layout. It reflects the choices made in the New dialog box (or the Document Setup dialog box) for the document. If you chose **Facing Pages** through the checkbox when you created the document, you'll find that **M1** will be displayed as two facing pages. Margin and column guides will also be displayed, just as on a document page.

N O T E

What is called a master page can be just one page, or it can be a spread of two. In cases where it is a spread, the master page can also be applied to a single document page. QuarkXPress will assign the corresponding left- or right-page master page.

On the master page, you will also notice an icon in the upper-left corner. This is a text chain icon and refers to the **Text-Linking** checkbox—recall the **Automatic Text Box** checkbox—you engaged when the document was created. If you chose to activate automatic text boxes through the checkbox in the **New** command, the icon will appear as a set of connected links, like the Text-Linking tool. Every page inserted into the document will have a text box linked to the next page's text box. This was the approach we used in creating a word processing document file. It's also the approach that would be used to typeset a book.

If you choose not to engage the **Automatic Text Box** checkbox in the New dialog box, the master page's corner icon will appear as the Unlinking tool, a set of links broken in the middle, as shown in Figure 10.6. In this case you'll see no text boxes. And automatic text box linking will be inactive.

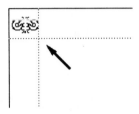

Figure 10.6   Master page indicating automatic text box linking is inactive.

Working in Master Pages

Working on a master page is just like doing layout or typesetting on a document page. For instance, if you want to put a rule across the top of the document page, you select the Rule tool and drag out a line there. You can make all the same adjustments, such as choosing a thicker width at the Measurements palette. Of course, you'll normally lay down fewer items on a master page than you might on a document page. But remember, these items will be on every page to which the master has been applied.

Figure 10.7   The left member of a master page spread.

Figure 10.7 shows the left page of a two-page master spread, **M1**, in one document. Several items, including lines, text, and picture boxes, have been laid out and positioned just as they might be on a document page. A different but similar layout has been used on the right page of the same master. Together both pages represent the M1-Master 1 page spread, as indicated in Figure 10.8.

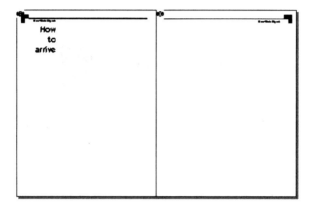

Figure 10.8   *A master page spread.*

Adjustments of Master Items on Document Pages

All document pages with master page designation will have all the items in place exactly as on the master page. But they can normally be modified, moved, and deleted just like those created on the document page.

For instance, you can use the Content tool to change the document-page text of a text box created in the master page. In Figure 10.9, a heading on a document page has been changed by modifying the text box the original master page text box as it appears on that page. You can also move items by selecting and dragging as usual.

However, there may be times when, because of very precise positioning requirements, you won't want master page items moved or deleted under any circumstance. For these cases, QuarkXPress provides a useful option. On the master page, you can lock items in place, just as on a document page, so that they can't be moved or resized using a tool. Just select the item or items, open the Item menu, and choose **Lock**. Conversely, choosing **Unlock** frees the items to be relocated.

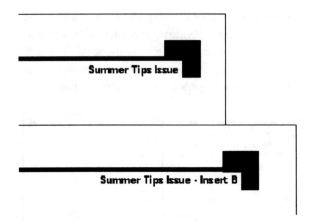

Figure 10.9   *Editing a master page item on the document page.*

Locking items

Select the items

Open Item menu and choose **Lock**

Locking an item fixes its position and size, but only in relation to the tools. If you try to use the Content tool or the Item tool to pull a locked box or rule to a different size or to move it, you'll see the tool change to a small padlock cursor, indicating that the action is locked out, as shown in Figure 10.10. However, the item can still be repositioned or sized. Do this through entering new values in the Measurements palette or the Specifications Box (Item menu to **Modify**). The contents and attributes of the locked item are subject to change as always.

Adjusting position or size of a locked item

Select the item

Enter new values in the Measurements palette

N O T E

An item locked on the master page can be selectively unlocked page by page. If you are working on a document page and unlock such an item, you'll see that on subsequent pages based on that same master page, the item will be locked. Of course, unlocking the item at the master page unlocks it at all document pages.

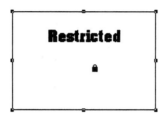

Figure 10.10   *A locked item changing the Tool icon.*

A text box originating on a master page may be modified in all the usual ways on a document page. Even if the box is locked, its text may be edited as usual. You can create a blank text box on the master page and fill in the blank on each document page as it comes up. This is one way to generate title pages or section front pages that must have a unity of design while varying in content. Lines and boxes originating on a master page may also be modified on a document page.

N O T E

An item modification on a document page will not affect the original item on the master page. Nor will it affect similar items on other document pages.

Generating Master Pages

Aside from the automatically generated master page, M1-Master 1, and the blank master page formats that wipe off master page features when applied to a document page, numerous other master pages can be produced for any document. Master pages can be based on blank pages or on existing master pages.

The method for producing new master pages involves the Document Layout palette. It is a two-step process. First the format is chosen: single or facing page or an existing master. Then the new master is inserted into the list of existing master pages.

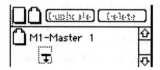

Figure 10.11   *Preparing to add a new master page.*

To create a new master page from scratch, select one of the blank masters in the top section of the palette. Now drag it down into the middle section where the other master pages are listed. A cursor like that shown in Figure 10.11 will appear. Release the mouse button in the list and a new master icon will appear instantly, inserted at that point as in Figure 10.12. It will be automatically named following the sequence of master pages that already exists in the document, M1-Master 1, M2-Master 2, and so on.

N O T E
As more masters are created, the middle section will permit scrolling among them through the scroll bar at the right. Also note that between the master page scroll bar and the document page scroll bar is a split window adjustment in the form of a small black bar that can be pulled downward to make more of the master icons visible.

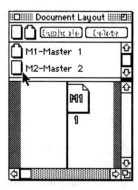

Figure 10.12   *Inserting a new master page.*

You can also derive a new master page from an existing master page. Doing so will create a new master page based on that existing master, with all its items. To carry this out, select the existing master page from the middle section in the Document Layout palette, then click the **Duplicate** button in the upper section. A new master icon will appear following the nomenclature system as before.

Adding a master page

At the Document Layout palette, drag a Plain Master Page icon down into the Master Page list

Move the arrow cursor into position on the list and release button

Deleting a master page is simple and quick, so be careful and sure of your intentions. Select the icon from the palette's list by clicking. Then click the **Delete** button in the upper section. The master page will be removed without confirmation.

Removing a master page

At the Document Layout palette, click to select the **master page icon**

Click the **Delete** button

Changing the page type on which a master page is based takes just two steps. Select the master page first. Then press the **Option** key while clicking on the blank or the master, which will take the place of the selected master page. After a confirmation dialog box, the master page will be changed. Proceed with caution here, because this action is not reversible through the Edit menu's **Undo** command.

Changing the format of a master page

At the Document Layout palette, click to select the master page

Option-click the replacement master format

You can change the name of a master page, but not its prefix code (the M1, M2, and so on). For instance, M3-Master 3 can be renamed M3-Reviews Section, but not as just Reviews Section.

To rename a master page, click on its name next to the icon in the Document Layout palette. Then type in the new name. QuarkXPress will automatically reinsert the prefix that was applied to the original name. The prefix stays with the master page until it is deleted.

Renaming a master page

At the Document Layout palette, click on the name next to
the master page
Key in the new name

To reach a master page directly from the Document palette, simply double-click on its icon. The master page will appear in the document window. You can quickly move between master pages this way. An alternative is to open the document's Page menu, choose **Display**, and locate the appropriate master page in the submenu.

Automatic Page Numbers

There is one special way a master page can function interactively with the pages in the document. It can function as a vehicle for automatic page numbering. On nearly all publications this is helpful, and on long ones, especially so.

QuarkXPress handles page numbering through a placeholder inserted in a text box on the master page. The program can automatically number all the pages in a document of any length. Anywhere a placeholder is put on any master page, a corresponding page number will appear on the document page .

To set up automatic page numbering, first create a text box. Then, with the text cursor active, type **Command-3** within the box. This is the code for the page-number placeholder. You might note that the **3** key is home of the pound sign (**#**). In fact when you type in the placeholder keystroke you will see a pound sign inside angled brackets (**<#>**). This character code can be adjusted and formatted within the text box, just as any other text can. You can also mix text with it (for example, **Page <#>** or **-<#>-**). Figure 10.13 shows the page-number placeholder on the master page and next to it the page numbering on a corresponding document page.

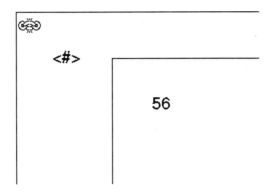

Figure 10.13 *Master page number placeholder and resulting document page number.*

Establishing automatic page numbering

At the master page, prepare a text box
Press **Command-3**

Note that you will need to put the placeholder on both left and right master pages in a facing-pages document. One quick way to do this is to copy the text box used on one page of a facing pair and paste the duplicate on the other page of the pair. The **<#>** code will stand in for even or odd numbers.

Style Sheets

As you work in QuarkXPress, formatting and applying style to text, you will inevitably develop a need for greater control. You'll find you've fashioned paragraph formats and type styles that would work perfectly applied to different portions of text in the document. Therefore, the question arises: How can we re-use style and formatting specifications already laboriously set in text?

In QuarkXPress, as in other desktop publishing programs and word processors, this need is answered by one of the most powerful methods known to electronic publishing. This method relies on format and style models that are known as *style sheets*. Style sheets are to text what master pages are to document pages.

The principle of style sheets is simple. You set up style and format for text paragraphs in the text itself and save the typesetting specifications in a kind of subdocument, the style sheet. Or, you can establish the style sheet and set up specifications within it directly.

Remember how H&J specifications were established? Style sheets are likewise specifications, but of all the text and paragraph attributes for a paragraph. Each style sheet can be applied selectively to any text within a document. Any style sheet can be made accessible in a variety of ways.

You can create a style sheet from scratch, or format text just the way you like and then designate a style sheet based on that text. You can import style sheets from other sources, such as other QuarkXPress documents or word processors. And you can export them as well.

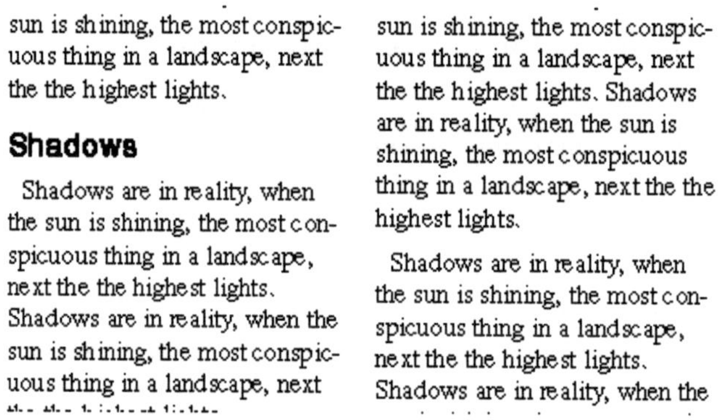

sun is shining, the most conspicuous thing in a landscape, next the the highest lights.

Shadows

Shadows are in reality, when the sun is shining, the most conspicuous thing in a landscape, next the the highest lights. Shadows are in reality, when the sun is shining, the most conspicuous thing in a landscape, next the the highest lights.

sun is shining, the most conspicuous thing in a landscape, next the the highest lights. Shadows are in reality, when the sun is shining, the most conspicuous thing in a landscape, next the the highest lights.

Shadows are in reality, when the sun is shining, the most conspicuous thing in a landscape, next the the highest lights. Shadows are in reality, when the

Figure 10.14   A subheading within body text.

More than any other feature, style sheets provide for unified typography within a design document. Consider the case of subheads in an article as shown in Figure 10.14. Here you find style differences between the one-line paragraph (the subhead) and the ocean of body text that surrounds it. Each time another subhead is to be typeset, the same set of formatting and type specs will be called for. With style sheets available, the typesetting desktop publisher simply selects the paragraph and designates it a subhead through the style sheet. Without them, the typesetter must reformat each paragraph into subhead form using a list of typographical settings.

Applying Style Sheets

There are two ways to associate a style with a paragraph or a selection of paragraphs. In each case, the first step is to select the paragraph or paragraphs with the Content tool. Placing the cursor within it is sufficient for a single paragraph. For a range of text, select all or part of each paragraph.

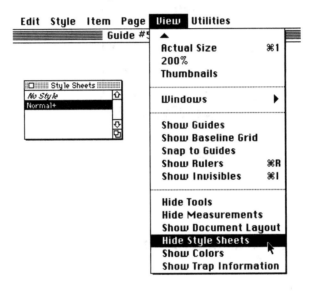

Figure 10.15   *Displaying a Style Sheets palette.*

One method of applying style to the selected text requires displaying a palette that lists all the style sheets available in a document. The command to do this is a **Show/Hide** palette command, like those we've used for the Tools, Measurements, and Document Layout palettes. To display the Style palette, open the View menu and choose **Show Style Sheets**. In Figure 10.15, you can see both the **Show/Hide** command and the palette it puts on the screen. Next, to apply a style sheet to the text, click on the name in the palette listing. All selected paragraphs will be reformatted and restyled.

The other method of applying style is through a submenu. Open the Style menu and choose **Style Sheets**. A submenu will appear, as shown in Figure

10.16. To apply the style, slide the pointer over the listing to the style sheet preferred and release the mouse button.

Figure 10.16   *Applying style sheets using the Style menu.*

Applying a style sheet to text

Select the paragraph(s) with the Content tool, or insert cursor

At the Style Sheets palette, click on the style sheet

or

At the Style menu choose **Style Sheets**, then select the desired style sheet

What It Means to Have No Style

In new documents, QuarkXPress provides at least two style sheet choices, as illustrated in Figures 10.15 and 10.16. One of these, **Normal**, is a default style sheet automatically applied to any new text box. It specifies, as all style sheets do, the font, leading, indents, tabs, and so on in the paragraphs to which it's applied. We'll look more at this in a moment.

The other choice is **No Style**, which allows current style sheet formatting to remain on a paragraph regardless of subsequent changes to the style sheet itself. When you apply **No Style** to a paragraph, there is no change in its appearance. If you later reformat the style sheet that was previously applied to the paragraph, other paragraphs will take on the new formatting, but the **No Style** paragraph will retain the original formatting.

Figure 10.17 shows text in which all the paragraphs received a Normal style sheet formatting when Normal was defined as Times Roman, Plain. Then just one paragraph, in the center, received the **No Style** formatting. Next, the Normal style sheet specifications were changed to Helvetica Bold. Of all the text, only the **No Style** paragraph in the center retained the original formatting.

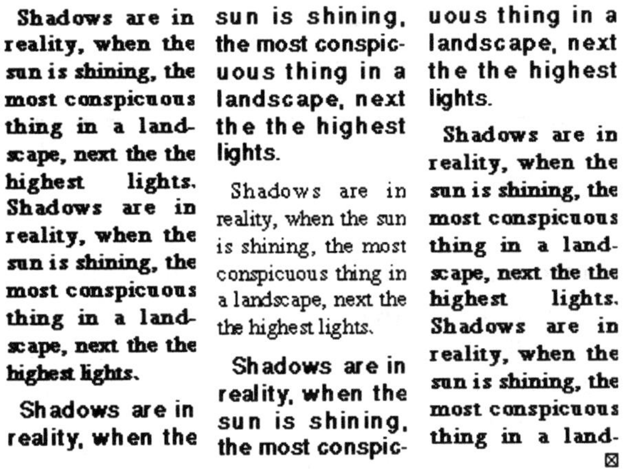

Shadows are in reality, when the sun is shining, the most conspicuous thing in a landscape, next the the highest lights. Shadows are in reality, when the sun is shining, the most conspicuous thing in a landscape, next the the highest lights.

Shadows are in reality, when the

sun is shining, the most conspicuous thing in a landscape, next the the highest lights.

Shadows are in reality, when the sun is shining, the most conspicuous thing in a landscape, next the the highest lights.

Shadows are in reality, when the sun is shining, the most conspic-

uous thing in a landscape, next the the highest lights.

Shadows are in reality, when the sun is shining, the most conspicuous thing in a landscape, next the the highest lights. Shadows are in reality, when the sun is shining, the most conspicuous thing in a land-

Figure 10.17 **No Style** *preserves formatting for one paragraph when the style sheet is modified.*

Creating and Adjusting Style Sheets

How, then, do we create the various style sheets that a full-length publication demands: headlines, subheads, captions, body text, pull quotes, teasers, page-jump notices, section titles, bylines, and so on? The answer lies in the style sheet controls and in a dialog box that stores specifications of paragraph formatting, paragraph rules, tabs, and character type attributes.

To reach the style sheet controls, open the Edit menu and choose **Style Sheets**. The dialog box shown in Figure 10.18 will appear. Along the bottom, a running description is displayed of all the attributes and formats of the style sheet selected.

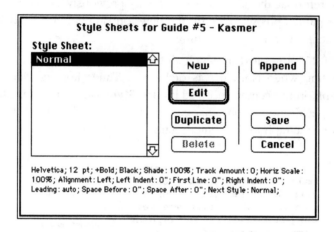

Figure 10.18 *The Style Sheets dialog box.*

The four buttons in the center of the dialog box represent basic controls. At the right in the dialog box is the **Append** button, which sends QuarkXPress to a dialog box for access to the disk. Its function is to import into the document various style sheets that have been created elsewhere. For instance, you can locate another QuarkXPress document with dozens of style sheets or a Microsoft Word file (when the Word filter is present in the QuarkXPress directory folder), and import all the style sheets to the current document. Excepted are style sheets with names the same as those already existing in the document. Under such circumstances QuarkXPress will not overwrite existing style sheets.

At the basic controls, the **New** button leads to the dialog box shown Figure 10.19, titled Edit Style Sheet. Specifications are set through it, and another style sheet can be created. To use selected text in the document as a basis for a new style sheet, click on **New** and then key in a name at the Edit Style Sheets dialog box. Click **OK**. Back at the Style Sheets dialog box, you'll see the name of the new style sheet displayed in the list and the specification summarized at the bottom. Click on the **Save** button, and the new style will be available in the document.

Importing style sheets

Open the Edit menu and choose **Style Sheets**

At the Style Sheets dialog box, click the **Append** button

In the dialog that appears, locate the document containing desired style sheets and double-click

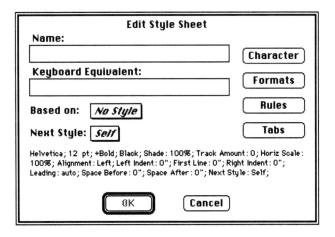

Figure 10.19 *The Edit Style Sheet dialog box.*

Creating a style from a text selection

Select the model text

Open the Style Sheets dialog box and choose **New**

At the Edit Style Sheets dialog box, key in a name, and click the **OK** button

At the Style Sheets dialog box, click **Save**

Each button on the right in Figure 10.19 leads to the dialog box corresponding to commands on the Style menu for text: **Character Attributes, Paragraph Format, Paragraph Rules, Paragraph Tabs**. Using these, adjustments can be made to all the attributes and formatting that will be applied through a style sheet, in the same way adjustments are made to text directly. Here again, you'll see the description of attributes and formats that have been specified in the dialog box.

In the **First** field of the dialog box, you can type in the name you wish to assign this style sheet, and you can invent and key in a keyboard shortcut that will select and apply this style sheet to text. **Function** keys are particularly well suited to serve as style sheet shortcuts.

The **Edit** button leads to the same dialog box and the same functionality as the **New** button, with one exception: The name is locked in place and can't be modified. Aside from that, you can change any existing style sheet through this command.

The **Duplicate** button creates a copy of the style sheet selected and leads to the Edit Style Sheet dialog box again, with the name "Copy of (whatever was selected)" in the first field. The copy will have all the text attributes and formatting from the original style sheet. You can leave this name, if you like. More likely, you'll want to key in something descriptive of the style sheet. For instance, you could design a style sheet for large headlines, then duplicate it, change the size of type and the tracking, and rename it as a subhead.

Removing a style sheet is simple. Select it in the list and click the **Delete** button. Note that the Normal style cannot be removed from a document.

When you find that the style sheets in the dialog box are suited to your uses, you can install them (new or edited) into the document all at once. Just click the **Save** button. This will add the changes and the new style sheets to listings in the palette and Style Sheets submenu.

It's important to remember to use the **Save** button. Otherwise, you'll find that changes to the style sheets will not be implemented by QuarkXPress.

NOTE

Basing Styles Sheets on Other Style Sheets

More often than not, much of the typography within a document is derived from other typography. For instance, subheadings frequently resemble headlines. Or second-level subheads may resemble primary subheads. Or a caption may simply be a smaller italicized version of the body text. Or headlines may be large, tightly tracked versions of the body text. Many times the difference between these elements is little more than one of size.

It's not unusual to put a lot of care into formatting a collection of interrelated headlines, subheads, or other text styles and formats, even while the design of your publication is still in development and subject to change. At some point you may find that you want to change just one or two aspects of the styles you've created—perhaps just the typeface or the horizontal width. If you had simply derived each related style sheet from another by using the **Duplicate** button and then renaming in the Edit dialog box, you would need to edit each style sheet separately to make changes consistent across all of them.

Fortunately, an option available within the Edit Style Sheet dialog box permits us to retain the relationships between an original style sheet and its offspring. This control works by maintaining the link to the parent style sheet, keeping track of which style sheet a later style sheet was based on. It can be engaged through the drop-down list of the **Based On** field. Figure 10.20 shows a style sheet named Subhead Two based on an existing style sheet named Subhead One.

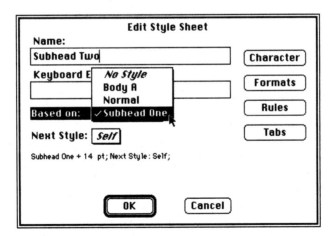

Figure 10.20 *Basing a style sheet, Subhead Two, on Subhead One.*

In this case, a change of style or format within the first style sheet will be reflected in the second. For instance, there are two levels of subheads shown in

Figure 10.21. The larger, 18-point bolded subhead, labeled Subhead One, can be seen applied to the phrases "Shadows" and "Sun's effects." The smaller, 14-point subhead is labeled Subhead Two and has been applied to the phrases "In landscapes" and "Highlights." It was based on Subhead One through the Edit Style Sheet dialog box, as shown in Figure 10.20 and varies from it only in font size.

Basing one style sheet on another

Proceed as usual, creating a new style sheet or editing an existing one

In the Edit Style Sheets dialog box, open the **Based On** drop-down list and choose an existing style sheet

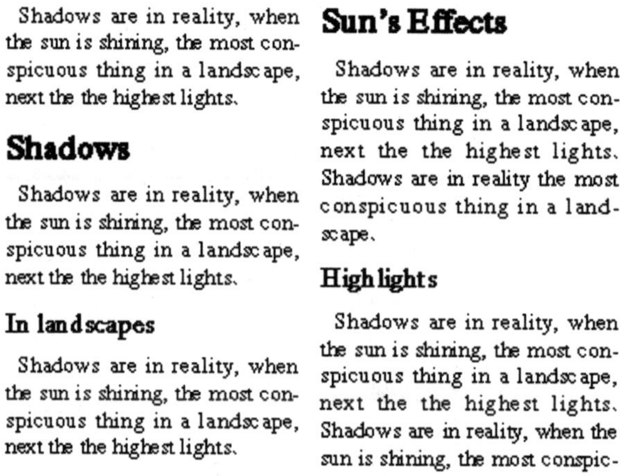

Shadows are in reality, when the sun is shining, the most conspicuous thing in a landscape, next the the highest lights.

Shadows

Shadows are in reality, when the sun is shining, the most conspicuous thing in a landscape, next the the highest lights.

In landscapes

Shadows are in reality, when the sun is shining, the most conspicuous thing in a landscape, next the the highest lights.

Sun's Effects

Shadows are in reality, when the sun is shining, the most conspicuous thing in a landscape, next the the highest lights. Shadows are in reality the most conspicuous thing in a landscape.

Highlights

Shadows are in reality, when the sun is shining, the most conspicuous thing in a landscape, next the the highest lights. Shadows are in reality, when the sun is shining, the most conspic-

Figure 10.21   Two levels of subheads, one based on the other.

The font set in the specifications for Subhead One was Times, bolded. To change all the subheads, an edit was made to the Subhead One style sheet only. In the Edit Style Sheet dialog box, the font was changed to Kabel Bold, and the extra bolding removed by clicking off the checkbox. Figure 10.22 shows the result. Not only have the first-level subheads (to which Subhead One style sheet was applied) changed, but the second-level subheads reflect the different typeface and font style as well, since Subhead Two is based on Subhead One.

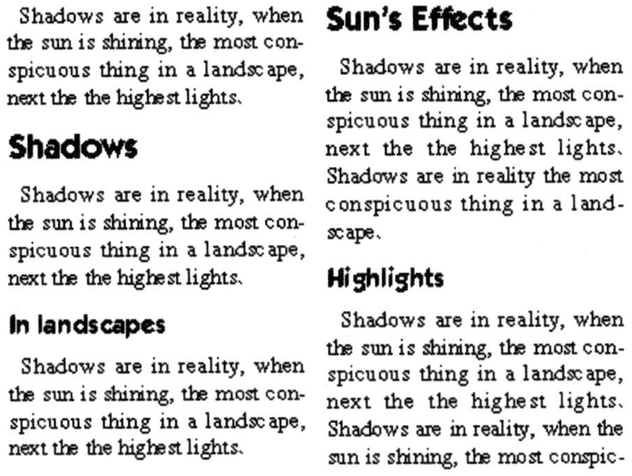

Shadows are in reality, when the sun is shining, the most conspicuous thing in a landscape, next the the highest lights.

Shadows

Shadows are in reality, when the sun is shining, the most conspicuous thing in a landscape, next the the highest lights.

In landscapes

Shadows are in reality, when the sun is shining, the most conspicuous thing in a landscape, next the the highest lights.

Sun's Effects

Shadows are in reality, when the sun is shining, the most conspicuous thing in a landscape, next the the highest lights. Shadows are in reality the most conspicuous thing in a landscape.

Highlights

Shadows are in reality, when the sun is shining, the most conspicuous thing in a landscape, next the the highest lights. Shadows are in reality, when the sun is shining, the most conspic-

Figure 10.22   The result of changing just the primary subhead.

The same kinds of effects can ripple throughout a QuarkXPress document of any length. Basing one style sheet on another is not limited; you could base a caption on a subhead, which was in turn based on a headline, which was based on body copy, and so on.

Special Item Connections

Page elements appearing as part of the document flow are generally unrestricted by other elements. Of course, text may need to run around certain items, but it does continue its flow onward. Items may be locked in place, but other items can be placed within the document freely.

However, bringing order and beauty to a layout means we must often restrict items. Perhaps we'd like certain picture and text boxes to appear together even if they flow on to other as yet unseen pages. Or we see the need for certain pictures and lines to stay together wherever the flow of text takes them. In a QuarkXPress document, there are two methods that provide ready control over such things: *grouping* and *anchoring*.

Grouping

If you've worked much with graphics software, you've no doubt already made regular use of grouping. It is a simple procedure, much like locking, except that instead of fixing an item to the page, you fix it to another item. You can group nearly any number of items—any that you can select simultaneously. This means, of course, that all the items to be grouped must be on the same page or same spread and surrounding pasteboard.

Grouping items

To group items, select them all.

Then open the Item menu and choose **Group**.

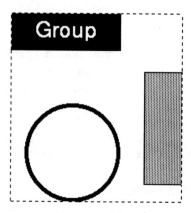

Figure 10.23   Three items grouped and their common bounding box.

When you group items, a new, dotted bounding box forms around the group, as shown in Figure 10.23. The group will now move as a single item. If you try to drag it partly across a spread boundary, as to share the items between page spreads, the entire group will reside on either one page or the other, jumping as a group when dragged halfway across.

To select the group, you need to click on one of the items, not simply the space that is enclosed by the bounding box. You can still modify the attributes that the group members hold in common. In fact, if you open the Item menu and choose **Modify**, you'll be presented with a special Group Specifications dialog box, as shown in Figure 10.24.

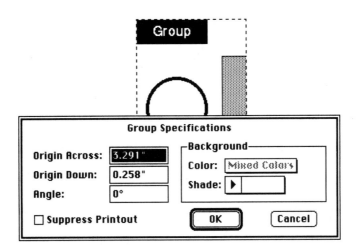

Figure 10.24 *The dialog box for modifying elements of a group.*

You can even group existing sets of grouped items. But in this case, you lose the ability to modify the resulting conglomeration.

Disassociating a group is easy. To break it up, select the group, open the Item menu and choose **Ungroup**.

With the **Group** and **Ungroup** controls, you can affix items to each other as needed, then remove the connection or reattach as your work requires. This is especially useful when you're doing precise positioning of multiple items.

Anchoring Inline Items

While grouping can associate text, pictures, and lines together, in doing so it treats them strictly as items. There is another method that combines text with other text or with pictures in a curious way that crosses the item/content separation usually characteristic of QuarkXPress. This method is called *anchoring*, and it is the principal way of inserting pictures directly into text. Often referred to as an inline graphic, the anchored picture or text box follows in the movement of text lines as though it were a single character in those lines.

The procedure goes against what we've come to expect from QuarkXPress, but it is reliable and effective.

Inserting a graphic (or text box) in line involves a peculiar twist on the usual convention of tool use. You cut with one tool and paste with another.

To place a picture (or text box) in line within text, first select the picture box with the Item tool. Next, cut or copy it (Edit menu). Then select the Content tool. Click a cursor insertion point within the text where the picture box will be located. Finally, paste (Edit menu). The picture box and its contents will appear within the text.

Anchoring a graphic or text box in line with text

Select the item with the Item tool

Copy or cut it

Use the Content tool to click an active cursor in the text line

Paste it

You'll find that you can still select and modify the picture box and contents. But the test and picture will now appear as a unified whole, as though the picture box were a character in the text. For instance, the Item tool will be unable to select both the picture box and the text box in which it resides simultaneously. Also, if you select the picture box, only three of the usual eight handles will become active. In this way you can resize or proportion the picture box, but it remains anchored in place.

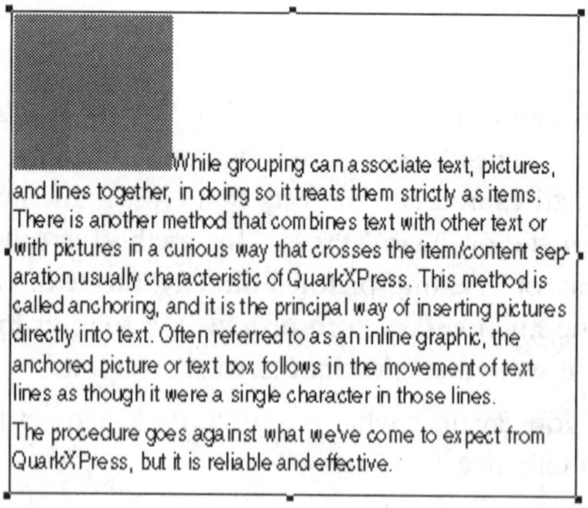

While grouping can associate text, pictures, and lines together, in doing so it treats them strictly as items. There is another method that combines text with other text or with pictures in a curious way that crosses the item/content separation usually characteristic of QuarkXPress. This method is called anchoring, and it is the principal way of inserting pictures directly into text. Often referred to as an inline graphic, the anchored picture or text box follows in the movement of text lines as though it were a single character in those lines.

The procedure goes against what we've come to expect from QuarkXPress, but it is reliable and effective.

Figure 10.25 *A picture anchored to the baseline as first character.*

The picture box now has a dual nature. It is still a picture box. But it is also a character within the text, so it can be selected as a single character with the cursor (which may elongate to match the new character if it is large). Figure 10.25 shows a picture box anchored as the first character of text within a selected box. It could as easily have been inserted as a character in the middle of a paragraph, as shown in Figure 10.26.

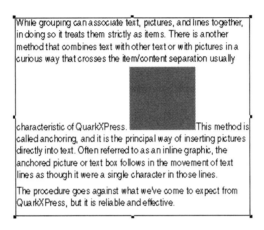

Figure 10.26 *A picture anchored to the baseline within a paragraph.*

Notice that in both cases the bottom of the character is aligned with the rest of the line. This is alignment along the baseline. And notice that because the picture is the largest character on the line, in each case it forces down the baseline for the entire line. Remember that you can still resize the inline graphic using the three handles.

Aligning Inline Graphic with Text

There is another way to position a picture box anchored inline. If you select the picture box with the Item tool, open the Item menu, and choose **Modify**. You will be presented with an Anchored Picture Box Specifications dialog box, as shown in Figure 10.27.

Notice two new controls in the upper-left corner of the box, in the **Align with Text** section. The **Baseline** pushbutton was engaged by default for the boxes of Figures 10.25 and 10.26. Clicking the **Ascent** pushbutton produces the anchoring of Figure 10.28. Here the picture box is set flush with the highest ascender of a character on that line, and then pushed down into the text, much as in runaround.

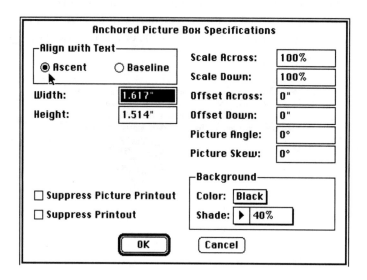

Figure 10.27   Setting picture box inline anchor.

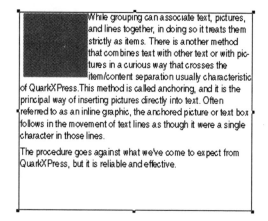

Figure 10.28   A picture box anchored to the highest ascender.

You might note that these controls could readily be used to make custom drop caps from both graphics and text boxes. All that we've seen about anchored picture boxes applies to anchored text boxes as well. Figure 10.29 illustrates a three-line text box set inline (through the same cut-and-paste method as above) with the ascender of the first line of the larger text box. In all cases, the contents of an anchored box remain accessible; they can be modified and revised within the hosting text box. Text within an inline text box can be edited and reformatted, for instance. Similarly, picture contents can be adjusted for shading, background, and so forth.

Creating special drop caps and graphic inserts

Anchor the item as usual and select it with the Item tool

Open the Item menu and choose **Modify**

At **Align with Text**, click on **Ascent**

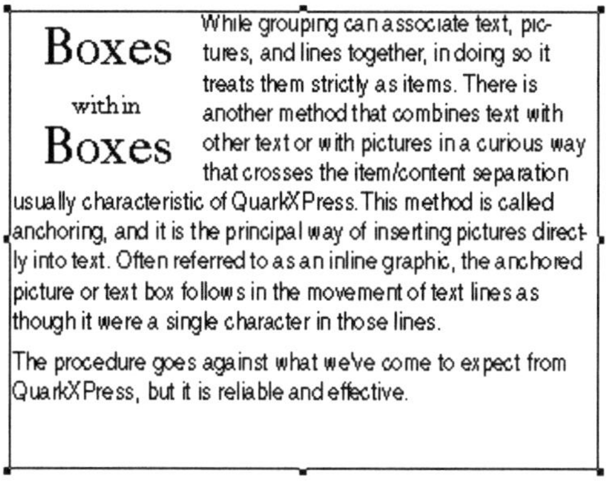

Boxes
within
Boxes

While grouping can associate text, pictures, and lines together, in doing so it treats them strictly as items. There is another method that combines text with other text or with pictures in a curious way that crosses the item/content separation usually characteristic of QuarkXPress. This method is called anchoring, and it is the principal way of inserting pictures directly into text. Often referred to as an inline graphic, the anchored picture or text box follows in the movement of text lines as though it were a single character in those lines.

The procedure goes against what we've come to expect from QuarkXPress, but it is reliable and effective.

Figure 10.29   A text box anchored to the first line of another text box.

Special Page Flows

Becoming mesmerized by the sweet dream of predictability can happen in any field. In publication design and layout, this dream rises out of the seeming conformity of facing-page after facing-page spread, numbered sequentially from beginning to end. But at any time a new project that doesn't follow this simple plan can rouse us into attentiveness.

Not all publications restrict their pages to simple verso-recto rhythms or running Arabic numbering. Controlling the flow of text and graphics in these exceptional circumstances is made possible by the sectioning and multiple page-spread capabilities in QuarkXPress.

One type of page flow, which requires such frequent readjustment, cries to be automated. Constant readjustments can threaten to consume inordinate amounts of layout time in multiple-story publications. This area is that of jump lines. Clearly, they are vital to keeping the reader's attention, but they are also easy to overlook, even in final page proofs. Luckily, there is an easy way to let QuarkXPress keep track of them.

Multiple-Page Spreads

We need to only look on the nearest magazine rack to note significant exceptions to the two-page spread. Not every publication is so limited, and QuarkXPress addresses these with the ability to expand to as many pages as will fit in the 48-inch document limit.

To find this capability look to the Document Layout palette. In laying out a publication completely with two-page spreads, you might normally add a page by selecting a page master, and dragging to position the **Insert** arrow at or between pages on a spread. The new page obediently pushes pages aside to assume its position among them. The pushed pages realign themselves in new page spreads if necessary, and the effect ripples downstream through the document.

However, you can use the same approach to extend the spread out an additional page, or, as in those full-page glossy ads that fall out across your lap, to three, four, or more pages.

To add a page to expand a spread, select a master page as before, but now locate the **Insert** arrow to one side of the spread, and it will change into an icon of the type of master you've chosen, as shown in Figure 10.30 (single blank). Release the mouse button, and the spread will automatically widen as a new page falls into place. You can use this approach to intoxicating lengths, as shown in Figure 10.31, where a five-page spread (Pages 4 through 8) has been unfurled.

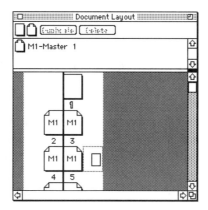

Figure 10.30 *Adding a third page to a spread.*

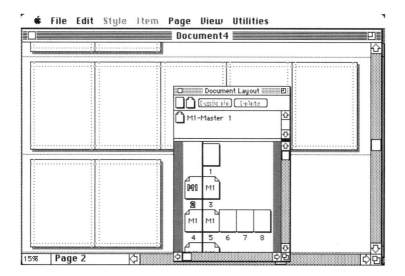

Figure 10.31 *A five-page spread.*

Expanding a page spread

At the Document Layout palette, select a master page

Drag the cursor to the outside of the spread icons and click

Sectioning

If your layout and design work involves newspapers, manuals, proposals, or various other sectioned documents, you know that every publication does not begin at Page 1 and run numerically uninterrupted to its end.

Clustering pages into sets of numbered sections is a matter of telling QuarkXPress which page will begin the section and how the numbering (or lettering) will proceed. QuarkXPress will keep track of the conventional, absolute page numbers (Arabic 1 through to the end), but will label and otherwise designate your pages according to the new scheme. You can even individualize the page labels and automatic page numbers that might appear.

To begin a section, first be sure that the page on which you want to start is prominent in the document window. Its label should appear in the **Page Number** field, lower-left on the horizontal scroll bar. The easiest way to get it there is to double-click to select its page icon in the Document Layout palette. Then open the Page menu and choose **Section**. A Section dialog box like that shown in Figure 10.32 is displayed. Click an **x** into the **Section Start** checkbox.

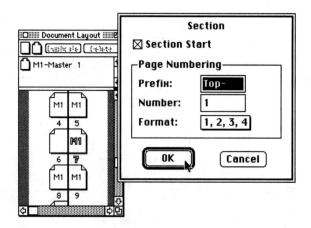

Figure 10.32 *Enabling section numbering.*

Now, under **Page Numbering**, you'll see a field for **Prefix**. You can leave this blank or type up to four characters into it. If you do type in a prefix (as **Top-** was keyed in here), the prefix will become part of the page label that appears on the document **Page Number** field—and that prints out if automatic page numbering has been set up on a master page.

At the next field, **Number**, leave the value at **1** if the section numbers/letters are to start at **1** or **A**. Change to another value if you want numbering to start further into the sequence. Note that for section lettering, **1** corresponds to **A**, **2** to **B**, and so on.

Finally, at the **Format** field, notice that a drop-down list allows for five numbering schemes, including Roman numerals, as well as lettering.

Sectioning pages

Select the first page of the section

Open the Pages menu and choose **Section**

Click an **x** into the **Section Start** checkbox

Make other modifications in the dialog box to
   suit the section

Once applied, the section numbering will be in effect through all subsequent pages until another section start is applied at a downstream page. You can remove section numbering by selecting the first page of the section, opening the Section dialog box and clicking the **x** to clear the checkbox.

Automating Jump Lines

Have you been forced to play this game, "continued on...continued from" ? It works like this. You prepare a story that must be jumped to a later page (in QuarkXPress, create a text box and use the Linking tools). You link the jumped text to the later page, continuing the story. You set up the little jump notices that say "continued on....," "continued from..." with the appropriate page numbers. Everything is in order.

Then something changes. Unexpectedly, the story is now jumped to another page. So you go back and sort out the changes in the "continued on..." and "continued from" lines. Or you forget to, and complaints of confusion stream in days or weeks later.

Because publication design and layout is a dynamic process, jump lines are easy to establish and easy to mix up. Why not automate them? Here's how.

QuarkXPress, as you've seen, can automatically number and track pages. It can also number and track jump lines. The key here, as with page numbering, is to enter the appropriate code. It is also necessary to position the jump message in a layer above the text box.

To set up a "continued on" jump line for a text box that has been linked to another page, use the Text Box tool to drag out a small Jump-Line text box. Then key in your jump message, typing in place of the page number the key-stroke **Command-4**. Next, drag the Jump-Line text box so that part of it is lying above the story text box.

In laying Jump-Line text boxes over stories, you should be careful of the interplay between text boxes. So, set **Runaround** on the jump-line box to **None**, and if necessary, move the box so it is just barely overlapping the text box underneath.

To set up a "continued from" jump line, proceed as above with this excep-tion. In place of the page number, type the keystroke **Command-2**.

Creating automatic jump lines

Use the Text-Box tool and make a small text box after the story text box is created

Key in the continuation notice excepting the page number

For a "jump to" notice, key **Command-4**; for a "jump from" notice, key **Command-2**

Drag the jump box until it overlaps the text box

As Figure 10.33 shows, the jump-line page numbers, when in place, will follow the "to" and "from" relationship set up in the text chain and visible in the arrows between linked boxes.

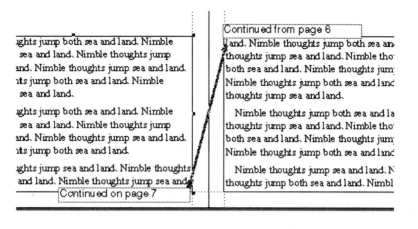

Figure 10.33 *Automatic jump-line page numbers in place.*

Onward

For all publications, document flow is a prevailing concern. Some of the most powerful features of the program are devoted to handling this. As master pages and style sheets are formed and modified, applied and reapplied, your publication takes form rapidly, with each step saving crucial production time. Automating task such as page numbering and sectioning will multiply the effect of your labors. Using these techniques once will certainly sell you on their strengths.

For more effective and varied text, inline graphics, and grouping anchoring elaborate your work into more typographically dynamic pieces.

Working these techniques into a variety of publications of greater complexity sharpens your abilities with them and with the program in general. In Chapter 11, we'll explore how to apply these powerhouse features to assembling and refining documents as we go to work on catalogs and books.

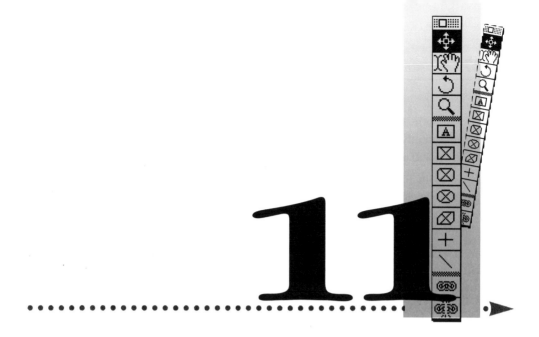

On the Job: Catalogs, Manuals, and Books

What you will learn in this chapter:

- ❖ How to apply style sheets to a catalog
- ❖ How to apply master pages to a manual
- ❖ How to use sectioning in a book
- ❖ How to apply absolute leading to in-line graphics

Book-length documents present special challenges. Two kinds of publications that frequently cross into this realm are manuals and catalogs. They require as much flow control as more literary tomes—and often much more organization.

Millions of customers who rely on catalogs would shun them if they did not provide quick and easy presentation. Repairs would cease, installations of all sorts would be stymied, and eventually many operations would falter altogether, if manuals failed to make reference information clear and accessible.

The strong, clear organization required by these types of publications can be achieved when style sheets, master pages, and the other document flow features covered in Chapter 10 are used to advantage.

In this chapter, we'll apply skills toward the construction of both a catalog and a manual. We'll use the methods that make a publication into a unified piece. In doing so, we'll see just how these functions guide the elements in the document.

A Catalog

Many catalogs rely heavily on pictures. Others lean on the printed word to make the sale. But always, text must adhere to a consistent format established early in the catalog. Giving the armchair customer clear, visual cues makes possible even enticing the quick scan as well as a detailed reading. For some readers the name of the product will catch the eye. Others will be engaged by the description or the price. All these things must be readily discernable, usually by type style, size, and format, as well as by position in the main body of text. As you may have guessed, in such type-crucial situations, style sheets can play a major role.

We'll now join a book catalog in progress. Our task is to set up an early page that will serve as a prototype for subsequent pages and will establish the type styles and formats to be used throughout the catalog. To do this, we plan to add heading boxes and establish style sheets for the titles and author names. We'll set the text to fit and include rules to further delineate each item.

Starting the Catalog Page

We set up the document by keying in pica values in the New dialog box as shown in Figure 11.1. It employs a small-format page, 40 by 50 picas, facing, with three columns established automatically and separated by a pica and a half (recall the XpY form of measurements, where X is number of picas and Y is the number of points). The Automatic text box is used because we're given a continuous text file that includes titles, authors, and catalog item blurbs, which will run sequentially.

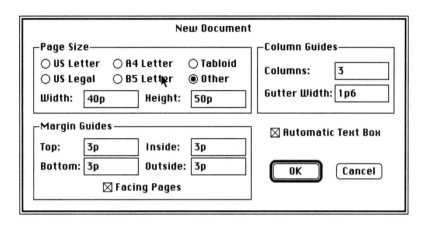

Figure 11.1 *Document set-up for a catalog.*

Before starting to work on the first full listings page, Page 4, we call up the Document Layout palette, open the Document menu and choose **Show Masters**. Then we double-click on the **M1** master to bring it into the main window. We want to fix in place the large text box so it won't inadvertently be shifted as we add and adjust other elements on the pages. Using the Item tool, we click on the text box already in place, and under the Item menu we choose **Lock**.

Next, returning to document Page 4 by double-clicking on its icon in the Document Layout palette, we use the Text tool to drag out a long, horizontal text box across the top of the page. In it we key in the page heading, **Inside Tips**, selecting the Helvetica font at 18 points in the Measurements palette, and applying small caps. Then in order to reverse out the text, we select **All** (**Command-A**) and set the color of type to White through the Style menu. Choosing **Modify** at the Item menu to bring up the Text Box Specifications, we set the color of the background to **Black, 100%**.

With the Text Box tool, we drag out another box to serve as a heading for listings that will appear below it. We key in the text, and at the Measurements palette, we adjust the font to Helvetica, size to 14 points, and style to Italic. Then we make horizontal scale and tracking changes for each box to achieve the preliminary layout shown in Figure 11.2, showing the upper part of the page with guides visible. Since each of the two text boxes lies on a layer above the Automatic text box (always the first down, lowest layer on the page), we don't have to worry about any untoward text collisions. The text destined for the columns will be pushed down once it's been placed there.

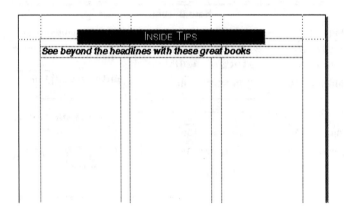

Figure 11.2   *Layout of prototypical early page.*

We choose the Content tool and click it over the large Automatic text box to insert a cursor. Using the **Get Text** command of the File menu, we move through the dialog's file and folder listing to find the word-processing file that will provide text for this page. After we double-click on the file name, the text flows into the columns below the heading. See beyond the headlines with these great books, as shown in Figure 11.3.

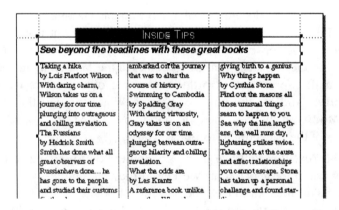

Figure 11.3   *Text pushed down in columns below a Heading text box.*

Using Style Sheets

Notice how uninviting the columns of text seem. Our task now is to set up style sheets that will be applied to emphasize each of the book titles and author names. But first we'll set up a style sheet for the body text as a whole.

We choose the Caslon 540 Roman font at 12 points at the Measurements palette. Experimenting with the appearance of the text lines, we decide a few tries to set them a bit tighter than normal. So we reduce tracking by setting a -5 value at the Measurements palette. The body text is acceptable now. Presumably the type attributes for it won't change, even as we adjust the other lines. But publication design, like life, is full of uncertainties. So, we want a precaution against inadvertent changes. We definitely want the means to change all the body text should the need arise.

N O T E

These body text descriptions will soon become separated paragraphs, barricaded into relative isolation from one another by the formatting of title and author name. Later, changing even just one characteristic of each paragraph would be tedious, frustrating, and unnecessary. By establishing a style sheet for all the descriptive text, we'll be able to do things like pull all the body text tighter or reduce leading throughout the document with just a single change at the style sheet.

So with our cursor planted soundly within the Caslon, 10-point text, we open the Edit menu and choose **Style Sheets**. At the first dialog box, we click **New**. At the Edit Style Sheets dialog box, we approve of the features of our listing text, type in the name **List Text** as shown in Figure 11.4, and click **OK**, returning to the first dialog box. We click the **Save** button.

Now it becomes clear we'll be working with style sheets, so we open the View menu and choose **Show Style Sheets**. The little palette appears with **List Text** showing prominently.

We set to work on doing the whole of the first book listing. Beginning with the book title, we select by triple-clicking. At the Measurements palette, for type font we choose **Helvetica**; for size, **15 points**, for style, **bold**. We increase the tracking to **+10**. At the Style menu, we choose **Horizontal/Vertical Scale** and key in **90%** for Horizontal in the small dialog box that appears. Next, employing the same approach we used to create the List Text style sheet, we go by way of the Edit menu to the dialog boxes off the **Style Sheets** command to create another style sheet. This one we name **Title**. We save as before.

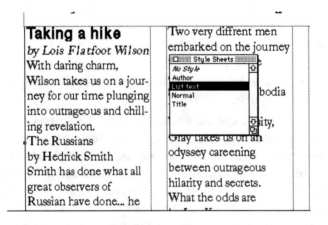

Edit Style Sheet

Name:

List text

Keyboard Equivalent:

Based on: *No Style*

Next Style: *Self*

Caslon 540 Roman; 12 pt; Plain; Black; Shade: 100%; Track Amount: -5; Horiz Scale: 100%; Alignment: Left; Left Indent: 0"; First Line: 0"; Right Indent: 0"; Leading: auto; Space Before: 0"; Space After: 0"; Next Style: Self;

Character

Formats

Rules

Tabs

OK   **Cancel**

Figure 11.4 *Establishing a new style sheet based on selection.*

To create a style sheet for the author's name, we select the name and italicize it and we increase the tracking before establishing the new style sheet. Author (which varies from body text at this point only in that it is italicized). Now we've set the first paragraph as shown in Figure 11.5. The resulting style sheets, represented in the adjacent palette, will serve as formatting and styling tools for all the listings to follow in the catalog.

Next we go to each title and name in turn, clicking a cursor into the line and then clicking the Style Sheet name in the palette to apply it. When finished this way, the page looks like the one shown in Figure 11.6.

Taking a hike
by *Lois Flatfoot Wilson*
With daring charm,
Wilson takes us on a journey for our time plunging
into outrageous and chill-
ing revelation.
The Russians
by Hedrick Smith
Smith has done what all
great observers of
Russian have done... he

Two very diffrent men
embarked on the journey

Style Sheets
No Style
Author
List text
Normal
Title

bodia

ity,

Gray takes us on an
odyssey careening
between outrageous
hilarity and secrets.
What the odds are

Figure 11.5 *A prototypical listing and style sheets palette.*

Figure 11.6   *Result of applying style sheets to entries.*

It is at this moment that we see what was overlooked. For one thing, paragraph spacing between list items is much too scant, failing to set the entries apart. We'll need to add more. Also, the leading over the title, name, and entry text, which spreads them out indiscriminately, can be reduced for a more unified appearance. Also, we'll need to do something to keep widows and orphans from forming. To implement these changes, we'll be going back to edit all the new style sheets, including the List Text.

NOTE   When creating a style sheet based on selected text, you might easily neglect to apply the style sheet to that selection. The lapse wouldn't show up immediately, of course, because the style sheet and selection would match. But should you later make changes to the style sheet, you'd notice that the original selection hadn't changed. The correction for this is simple. Apply the style sheet to the original selection, including that text in any future changes.

To make our revisions we go first to the Author style sheet (through the Edit menu). At the Edit Style Sheet dialog box, we click on Format (for paragraph format). At the **Format** dialog box, we click to engage the **Keep with Next Paragraph** button. This keeps the name from dragging behind the description as the latter jumps to the next column. Remember, we're setting up style sheets for all the other listings in this catalog as well. We want to anticipate what might happen even with problems we don't see on this page.

Next, we go to the Title style sheet, and by the same route, we click on **Keep with Next Paragraph**, as well as **Keep Lines Together**. The latter is important because we don't want a two-line headline to become widowed and decapitated. We also type over the **auto** value currently in the **Leading** field. In its place goes 12 points to match the leading of the list text.

Although the **Keep with Next Paragraph** feature should work all the time, you may find it helps to resize the text box to force it to finally take effect.

Final Work on the Page

Back at the page, everything looks good, except that all the listings are cramped together. The solution to this will be simple: We return to the List Text style sheet, Edit dialog box. There we go to the **Space After** field and key in **2p** for two picas. That should loosen up the paragraphs a bit, and, indeed, it does, as shown in Figure 11.7.

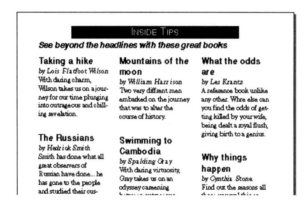

Figure 11.7   *Effect of 2 picas in the style sheet's Space After box.*

Another adjustment or two of leading and box size, and we've almost completed this layout. Still, something more is needed to set off each listing. After a bit of experimentation, we hit on an answer: **Rules** will be chosen to sit above each listing. To apply them, we go to the Edit Style Sheet dialog box for the Title style sheet. Clicking on the **Rules** button, we find ourselves at the Paragraph Rules dialog box. Here, in the dialog box settings shown in Figure 11.8, we choose a **Rule Above**, a double-line rule of 2-point thickness, to be set two picas from the first baseline of the Title paragraph.

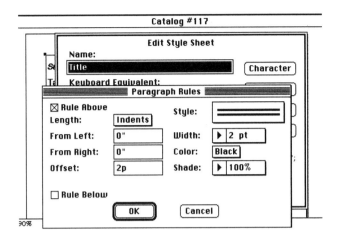

Figure 11.8 *Adding **Rule Above** to the style sheet.*

Saving this revised style sheet in the usual manner adjusts all the listings to the form shown in Figure 11.9. Our catalog styles are now in place and working. The rest of the catalog can be dealt with by applying these styles throughout, selecting each title or name and clicking on the style sheet in the Styles palette. If the word processor supplying the text has the capability, style sheets can be transferred through the text to the word-processing program. That could also free QuarkXPress for other duties, if the work flow demanded them, while the word processor was applying styles to text to be imported to the QuarkXPress document.

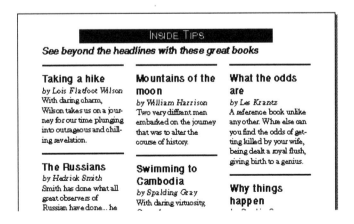

Figure 11.9 *The catalog layout established.*

A Manual

Documentation is a workhorse in the publication world. The ultimate in functionality and logical presentation, some documentation breaks with tradition and is full of illustrations and white space. Manuals have changed looks significantly in recent years. But to most people, a manual has a distinctive look and feel. Effective manuals serve primarily as reference works and sometimes secondarily as training aids. They draw their strength from logical organization and clear subdivisions.

In the manual we'll be constructing, the information we're presenting must be divided into four sections, each clearly marked yet consistent with the others in format. We want readers to be able to locate each section quickly and to be well oriented when they are within a section. To clarify points within the text, small graphics will be included at certain points. To accomplish all of this, we'll be using techniques for master pages, sectioning, and anchoring in-line graphics.

Starting the Manual

The page format we've decided on is 44 picas wide by 54 picas high, with single-column facing pages, margins of 6 picas at top and bottom, and 3 picas on either side. Since this will be a book-length project, we select Automatic textbox when choosing the other features at the New dialog box. Pica is the measurement system preferred. Through the Edit menu we reach the General Preferences dialog box and set both horizontal and vertical measures, in picas.

Our plan for the layout includes text boxes 25 picas wide abutting the right margin on both verso and recto pages, a style consistent with that of many reference guides. Recall that we have Automatic text box engaged. To modify the text boxes in a way that will affect the entire manual, we'll need to work on the master page.

So, at the Document Layout palette, we double-click on the **M1** master icon, which appears alone in the palette. The master page spread comes into view within the main window.

To pull each text box narrower, we grab the middle handle on its left side and drag to the right, monitoring the value **Width** in the Measurements palette all the while, until it indicates 25 picas as shown in Figure 11.10. Next we begin work on the basic layout of the first section, A. In setting this up we'll be setting a format to be followed for all the sections.

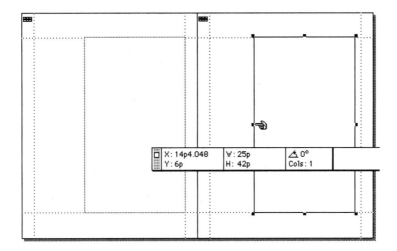

Figure 11.10 *Using the Measurements palette to monitor precise text box adjustment on master pages.*

This manual should be easy to use, so a section indicator will be located in each of the outside margins, as in a thumb index. At the verso page, using the Text Box tool, we drag out a vertical box 10 picas long and 2 picas wide. Selecting the **Kabel Bold** font at 30-point size in the Measurements palette, we type the letter A and then center it with **Command-Shift-C**. **Command-A** selects the text, and at the Style menu the color is set to **White**. Using the Item menu to open the Text Box Specifications dialog box from the **Modify** command, we set the background to **Black**, the vertical alignment to **Center**, and the text offset to **Zero**.

To include a section title at the top of each page, we use the Text Box tool to create another text box on the verso page into which we type the section title, **Installation**. We reverse out the text in this box, as we did earlier, and adjust the box for size, with the aid of the Measurements palette, to line up with the text box below it. We apply tracking at the palette by clicking on the **Increase** arrow to spread the text across the box, at a value of **70**.

We create a placeholder text box for page numbers with the Text Box tool, formatted and adjusted to match the others. We position the box in the lower outside corner of the verso page. But when next with the cursor in the placeholder box, we type **Command-3** to insert the page number symbol **<#>**, an interesting thing happens.

Even though we reduce the type size to 18 points and set tracking to zero, it seems the page number symbol **<#>** won't fit in the text box. This creates a problem, since enlarging the box would interfere with our design. We'd like the boxes to match in width and alignment. At this point we need to look ahead for the moment. Our largest page number will contain two digits, and we'll have a section prefix attached to it. So on the document page we'll need a page label as long as this, A-32. So, determined to preserve the page number text box size, we select all of the text in it and experiment with the Horizontal scale off the Style menu. At **50%** we find our prototype number A-32 fits in the box. This then is the page number text box we keep.

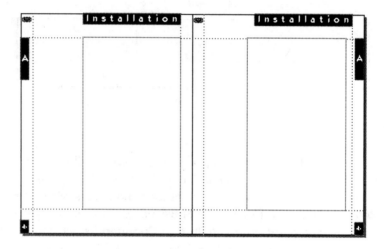

Figure 11.11 *The completed master page spread for Section A.*

Finally, with the Item tool, we select all the text boxes, and then, at the Item menu, we use the **Duplicate** command. Copies of each text box appear. Then we move them to the mirror-image locations on the recto page. Our master spread is now complete, as shown in Figure 11.11.

Working with the Sections

This is one of four sections. We want similar layouts with different labels for each section. So we will create three new masters based on this one: here's how. First, at the Document Layout palette, we select the **M1** icon in the palette; then we click the **Duplicate** button in the palette. A new master icon, **M2** - Master 2, appears. Now, to work on the Section B master page, we double-click on the **M2** icon. A spread identical to **M1** appears on the screen.

Although its appearance is currently exactly that of **M1**, the name in the page number space at the lower left clearly indicates this is indeed **M2**. To change the heading title and the section designation, we select the **A** within the section box and key in **B**, then select the box containing **Installation** and key in **Basics**. Figure 11.12 shows the program window as we work on the verso side. We follow the same pattern on the recto page of this **M2** spread.

One last revision will complete the master page layout for Section B. Since we want the pages of the manual to create that thumb-index effect along the margin, we move the text boxes in the margins—the B boxes—down just the length of the box. We do this by selecting the box on each side and, at the Measurements palette, keying in a value equal to the current location of the text box (**6p**) plus the length of the box (**10p**). We put this **16p** into the **Y Coordinate** field. This shifts the box down by one box length and creates the thumb-index effect shown in Figure 11.13.

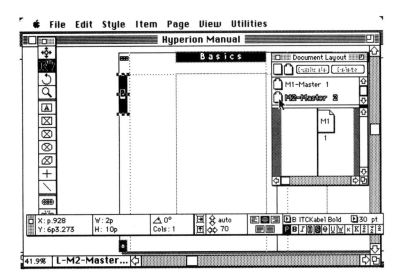

Figure 11.12   *Changing one section master to another.*

Similarly, we create and adjust master spread **M3** for **S**ection C and **M4** for Section D, basing both on **M1**, keying in the corresponding section letters, and shifting the section box down by an additional 10 picas for each in turn.

As a final precaution, we return to the master **M1** spread, and, with the Item tool chosen, give the **Select All** command (**Command-A**) and, at the Item menu, choose **Lock**. This prevents accidental movement or deletion of master items. For each of the other masters, **M2** through **M4**, we do the same.

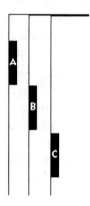

Figure 11.13   *Creating a thumb-indexed book.*

Now everything is in place for sectioning. All that remains is setting up page numbering to follow our plan. Recall that we decided numbering would begin anew with each section.

We're informed that the entire manual will run about 160 pages, and that the first six pages will be devoted to the usual front matter—table of contents, and so forth. Eight more pages will be devoted to back matter. These front and back pages will each have a layout differing completely from any of the master pages.

We'll handle these pages in order. First, we put in the front pages blank. They'll be laid out when the rest of the book is complete. This is a simple move. We open the Pages menu, choose **Insert**, and at the dialog box make the selections shown in Figure 11.14, typing in **6** for pages, clicking the **Before Page 1** button, and choosing **Blank Facing Pages** from the Masters drop-down list. Next to the dialog box shown in Figure 11.14, you can see the result as displayed in the Document Layout palette.

Now, note that we'll be setting up pages as the text comes in. As we're given each text file, we'll import it to a single document page (based on **M1**, **M2**, **M3**, and **M4** for Sections A, B, C, and D, respectively) and let the **Automatic Text Box** function take over. The text has already been formatted in the word processor, and aside from adding a few in-line graphics that have been requested, we'll accept it as is.

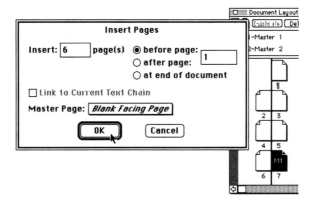

Figure 11.14 *Inserting six plain blank pages in front of Section A.*

WARNING

QuarkXPress behaves somewhat unexpectedly when you add pages from a certain master and then paste or import text into any of them. Suppose a text overrun occurs from the box in which you paste it, and the **Automatic Text Box** function is engaged. If a page from a different master sits downstream of the paste-in page, the text will be blocked from automatically forming new pages to handle the overrun. You may have to link text manually to overcome this blockage.

For Section A, we click the Content tool to put a cursor in the text box on Page 7. Then we open the File menu and choose the **Get Text** command. After locating the word-processed file, Section A, we double-click, and in flows the text. After 23 more pages are created, we find ourselves at Page 30, which will be the end of Section A in our document, as shown in Figure 11.15.

Our next step is to put the first page of Section B in place, and then import the text for that section and let **Automatic Text Box** take over again. Since we need only insert one page, we'll turn to the Document Layout palette, where this is easily accomplished. We select the **M2** icon, the master for Section B pages, and drag it next to Page 30, where Page 31 would go. There the new page is inserted, as shown in Figure 11.16.

Proceeding as with Section A, we use the **Get Text** command to import the formatted Section B text, and let QuarkXPress automatically set it in 31 instantly-appearing pages. This puts us at Page 62. We continue, inserting the first page of Section C and importing its text, and doing the same for Section D.

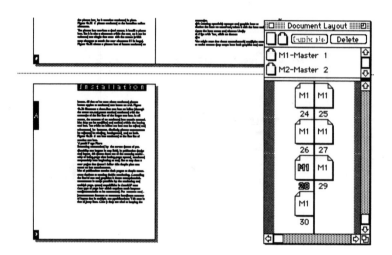

Figure 11.15   *A successful importing into the Automatic text box in Section A.*

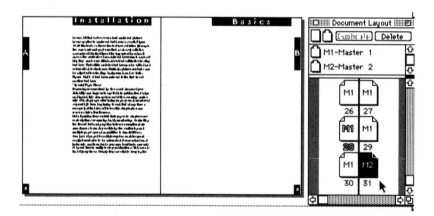

Figure 11.16   *Inserting the first Section B page from the M2 master.*

We still haven't got the sections quite the way we'd like them; remember, the pages are still numbered in a sequence running through all sections. It's our plan to number each section independently. To do this, we'll invoke the sectioning abilities of QuarkXPress. Our efforts begin at the first page of Section A, at what is now Page 7. Using the Document Layout palette, we locate the **Page 7** icon and double-click on it to make the page active and selected. We confirm this by checking the page indicator field at the lower-left of the window.

Now we're ready to section. This part goes simply. We open the Page menu and choose **Section**. At the dialog box, we click an **x** into the **Section Start** checkbox and key in a section designation of **A-** in the prefix field. We leave the numbering at Arabic (1, 2, 3) and click **OK**. The result is shown in Figure 11.17, with the dialog box. Notice that the page number in the corner of the layout has taken on the section designation, as has the page indicator. A small asterisk appears superscripted at the page number in the Document Layout palette and at the main window's page indicator box, to indicate this is the start of a section.

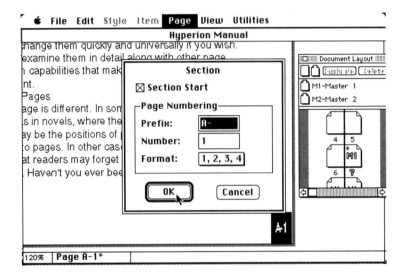

Figure 11.17   *Section A page numbering put into effect.*

While the indicator will shift to reflect new section numbers, the Document palette always maintains its count in absolute terms, starting from Page 1 and running through the final page of the document.

We proceed in similar fashion to correlate page numbers with Sections B, C, and D, keying in **B-** and so on in the Section dialog box.

The final set of pages will be for back matter. We'll set these up as we did the first pages. Eight pages have been allotted. We move our view to the last page (the last page of Section D, known to the Document Layout as Page 152, and elsewhere as D-38). At the Page menu we choose **Insert** and key in the values shown in Figure 11.18, specifying a set of **Blank** facing pages. Eight new empty pages fall into place, waiting for the time when the index and other back matter is ready.

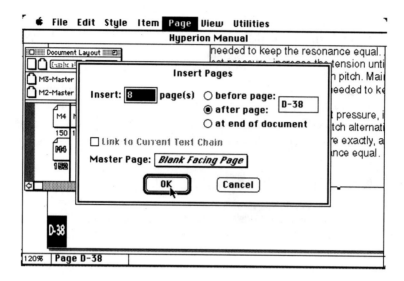

Figure 11.18 *Inserting the back pages after the last section.*

The Manual's Fine Points

Our work making up this manual is nearly complete. There are a few points to deal with on individual pages, and now we attend to them.

In addition to the text, we've been given graphics files that should be inserted into various lines of text so that readers can have instant visual confirmation of the process being described. There are to be no separate illustrations in this book. In this case, these are graphics representing symbols described in the text.

Using the usual techniques for importing graphics, we create a picture box for each and import through the File menu's **Get Picture** command. Now we want to anchor each graphic in its appropriate location within the paragraph. Using the Item tool, we click on the first picture box , selecting it. Then we copy it to the clipboard with a **Command-C** keystroke. Next, we choose the Content tool, click it into position within the paragraph's text and paste with a **Command-V** keystroke. The picture appears in-line. We follow the same procedure for the other symbol . Figure 11.19 shows both picture boxes to the side of the text box and their duplicates in place within the text.

You'll notice that the picture is in-line with the baseline. But a problem has arisen. Even though the graphic is small enough to fit within the lines at regular leading, extra space has been added above it. This is because the leading was set at a relative value to the characters rather than an absolute value. This is indicated in the Measurements palette with a + sign in front of the leading value (shown in Figure 11.20). In this case the leading is not simply a positive 6 points, but rather 6 points over the type size of 12 points. Of course the graphic is recognized as having a larger point size than 12 because its height is greater than the highest ascender of type in each line; and with 6 points added to this greater height, that extra spacing results.

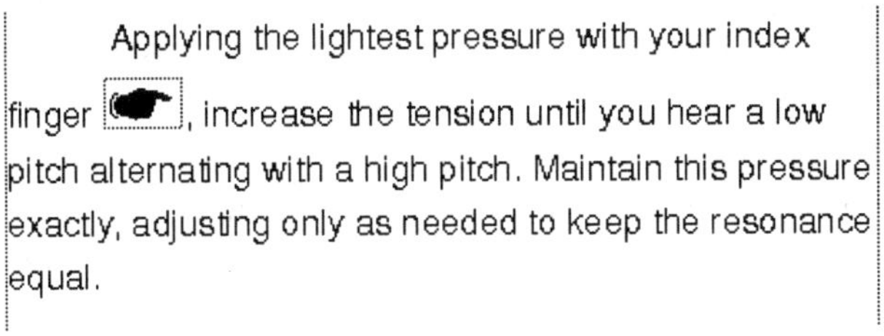

Applying the lightest pressure with your index finger 🖝, increase the tension until you hear a low pitch alternating with a high pitch. Maintain this pressure exactly, adjusting only as needed to keep the resonance equal.

Figure 11.19   Graphic anchored in text line.

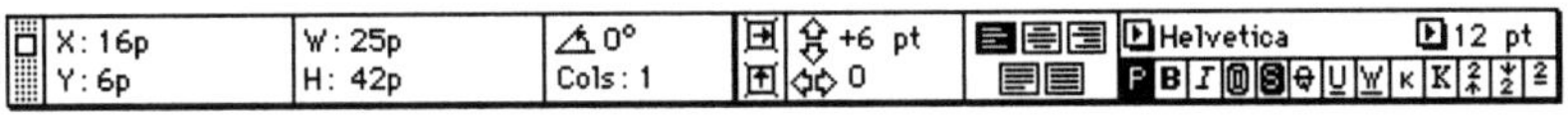

Figure 11.20   Relative leading indicated in the Measurements palette.

To fix this, we select the entire paragraph and, at the Measurements palette, select the **Leading** field and key in an absolute **18 points**. The result is the regular spacing shown in Figure 11.21. With several more adjustments of this kind, we finish our work on this manual and hand the results over to await indexing, table of contents, and other front matter.

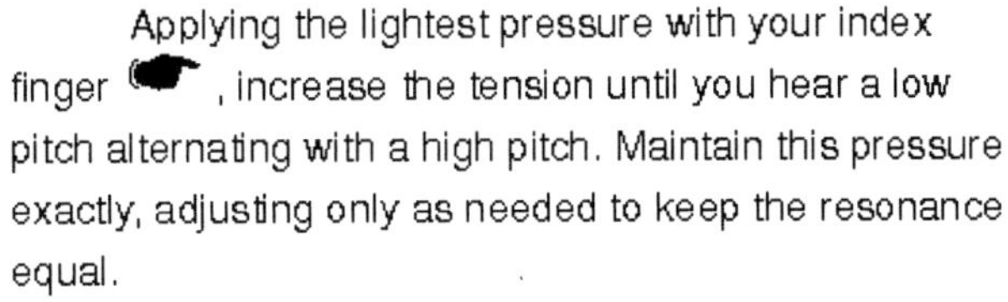

Applying the lightest pressure with your index finger 🖝 , increase the tension until you hear a low pitch alternating with a high pitch. Maintain this pressure exactly, adjusting only as needed to keep the resonance equal.

Figure 11.21 Paragraph adjusted to absolute leading.

Onward

Assembling this catalog and manual has employed skills that apply to all types of books. Ironically, some longer books will be simpler to lay out because they don't require sectioning or multiple master pages and style sheets. The basics of automatic page creation, however, apply to all such volumes. In-line graphics and the methods of page layout seen here are fundamental to refining the appearance of any book-length publication.

Having already looked at graphics, their place in pictures, and how we can adjust them, we've still seen only part of the picture, so to speak. Further modifications to the images themselves are possible in QuarkXPress, which will greatly affect which images can be used as illustrations. They can change the impact of any images brought into the document. These refinements are as significant to the picture side of a document as what we've seen is to the text side. In Chapter 12 you'll see just how to perform these manipulations.

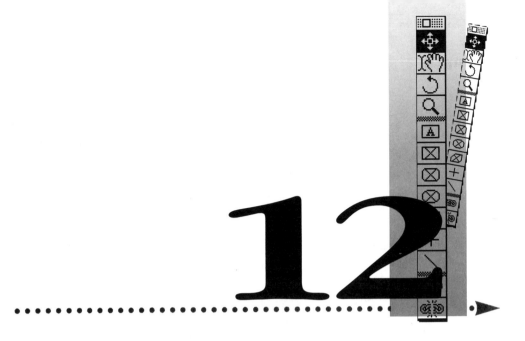

Manipulating Images

What you will learn in this chapter:

- ❖ Working with grayscale images
- ❖ How to adjust contrast
- ❖ How to prepare halftones
- ❖ How to maximize resolution
- ❖ The effects of sizing, contrast and halftone screens on image quality

On the printed page an illustration appears as it does because techniques for handling the image have been tempered with judgment. Color, shading, sizing, and skewing adjustments, which can be applied to all kinds of images from software-generated line drawings to scanned photographs, are some of the more obvious image controls. These can be exerted on a wide range of imported graphics. A certain smaller group of file formats provide opportunities to perform even more varied manipulations of image quality. In this chapter we'll look into these manipulations and their effects on the final printed image.

Complex graphics vary, each one within itself, in tonal values and contrast (as in photographs, for instance). Adjusting these features for optimum reproduction determines when the clarity and subtleties of an illustration come through on the printed page, and when they are lost. In these cases, QuarkXPress offers other methods of manipulation and image editing, as well. Some of these are often the province of graphics software.

In particular we'll be looking into the two aspects that have the greatest effect on the printability of an illustration, *contrast* and *halftones*. This discussion takes us out of the realm of line-art and pictures as placeholders and simple stand-ins for illustrations in a layout. We now move into actual image fine-tuning. Here we work with the image, which will eventually be printed directly from the document and the files it manages. So, examining and enhancing the image becomes important.

Contrast and When It Matters

To put it most simply, the contrast of an image is the relation between its dark and light parts. Take your black felt marker (say Black P98, Chartpak) and draw a square on a piece of white paper, and you'll establish a vivid contrast. Draw the square with a gray marker (say Cool Gray 5 P185, Chartpak), and the contrast of the image is reduced. Draw each square on gray paper stock and a still lower contrast results. Switch to black paper, and you'll lose all contrast.

The kinds of graphics files for which contrast is adjustable in QuarkXPress are grayscale images. That means the image consists not just of black and white areas, but also variations (grays) in shades between those extremes. Sometimes these variations are described as highlights, shadows, and middle tones.

If the graphic you're importing into QuarkXPress contains grayscales, and you plan to print it for best possible effect, then you'll have use for these controls. Typically but not exclusively, these grayscale images are found in many tagged image file formats (TIFF) and certain bitmapped picture formats. The TIFF is a particularly favored format that travels well from one application to the next.

What is important about these and other eligible formats is that they have the capacity for conveying grayscale information. They can describe images in black, white, or various shades of gray. Recall the shading values we've applied through the Style menu. Those were shading reductions applied uniformly over an image. Here, we're looking at the shades of gray varying within an image.

OK, if contrast is already established in the imported image file, what can QuarkXPress possibly do about it? Simply, the program remembers the imported image's shades of gray information for each bit and has controls to determine how those shades will be translated into the document image document. Consider that someone seeing a photographic print might say, "I like it, but it should be lighter." By this is meant take every shade of gray and convert it to a lighter shade of gray. Or take every dot or bit within the image and make that bit lighter than it was. In this case 100% black bits might become 80% bits, 10% bits might become 8% bits, and so on. This is a simple translation to a less black image.

Suppose, however, the person said, "I like it, but it needs more contrast." One way to accommodate this request would be: for every bit that is black, or some shade of gray between 51% and 100% black, make it black; and for every bit that is white or some shade of gray between 0% and 50%, make it white. The effect here would be considerably different. In the case of simple reduced shading of the previous paragraph, the result would simply be a lighter image. On the other hand, in the adjustment just described the result could be lighter or it could be darker, depending on the relative grayness of bits within the image. This second case is one example of adjusting contrast.

Figure 12.1 demonstrates the difference between the shading and contrast adjustments just described. The top box contains an image with a gradient of shading varying from left to right, 100% black to white. The middle box contains the same image adjusted to 50% of the original shading. Notice how the overall effect is a washing out of the black as all shades are reduced to half their original values.

The box at bottom contains the same top image, but here the contrast has been adjusted as described in the preceding paragraph, using 50% black as the contrast cut-off criteria. Darker than 50% black is turned to 100%, while lighter than 50% is turned to 0%. Notice that the left half of the original image has turned completely black, and the right hand has turned completely white. This is extreme contrast adjustment and just one of countless possible contrast adjustments.

Figure 12.1 An original grayscale image, shown also at
50% shading, and with extreme contrast.

It's helpful to note that contrast adjustments are applied relative to the shading of the imported image. As in photographic darkroom developing, you can darken just the light shades, or lighten just the dark ones, or the reverse, or darken or lighten the middle tones, or combine various effects. Obviously, the particular contrast enhancements you choose or devise will depend on the image and the effect you desire from it. Let's see how.

Adjusting Contrast with Preset Controls

QuarkXPress provides controls that make preset adjustments of contrast in grayscale pictures. You've already seen one kind of adjustment in the form of the **Negative** command under the Style menu. This handles grayscale, in addition to other factors such as color complements and so forth. Recall how applying this command made white-on-black images turn into black-on-white images. In the strictest sense the contrast did not change, since the relative shades were simply interchanged. But the effect was inverted grayscale values.

Whenever an image is imported into a picture box the values of its grayscales are considered normal. If fact, if you look under the Style menu when a picture is active and the Content tool is selected, you'll see a checkmark by the command, **Normal Contrast**. Should you change the contrast, then later wish to reclaim the original contrast setting, you can choose this command to do so.

Figure 12.2 shows a scanned photograph that has been imported into a picture box and is set at its original contrast, that is, the contrast at which the scanning software saved the original image.

Adjusting an image to original contrast

Select picture with Content tool active
Open the Style menu and choose **Normal Contrast**

Figure 12.2 *An image at **Normal Contrast** setting.*

One of the simplest and starkest contrast adjustments possible is that of the third picture box in Figure 12.1, where all dots that form the image are forced to be either black or white. QuarkXPress provides a similar control through a predefined command in the Style menu. The effect of this command is to change a grayscale picture into one with just two levels of shading, black and white. This effectively turns grayscale images into line art, like a black marker drawing on white paper. In this case, the program must make a decision: which shades are replaced with white and which with black.

The predefined command, **High Contrast**, does this by setting to white all shades lighter than 30% black. It likewise sets to 100% black all shades greater than 30%. Figure 12.3 shows the Figure 12.2 picture after it has been selected and had the **High Contrast** command applied to it. Notice that all grayscale variation has been eliminated. This is the most drastic of contrast adjustments.

Figure 12.3   *The image of Figure 12.2 at **High Contrast** setting.*

Adjusting an image to black and white contrast

Select picture with Content tool active
Open the Style menu and choose **High Contrast**

Another contrast setting can change an image by forcing each of its grayscale bits to assume a gray value of one of six levels, instead of just the two (black and white) of the **High Contrast** command. This is a stepped contrast, listed on the Style menu as **Posterized**. Its effect is to take the variable grays that exist on an image and change them each to the nearest of six levels of gray, 20%, 40%, 60%, 80%, 100% (Black), and 0% (White). Applying this command to the earlier image results in the picture of Figure 12.4.

Adjusting an image to stepped contrast

Select picture with Content tool active
Open the Style menu and choose **Posterized**

At first this image may look similar to the one shown in Figure 12.2. But notice carefully the flattening out and loss of detail that occurs in many areas.

Figure 12.4 *The image of Figure 12.2 at* **Posterized** *setting.*

Customized Adjustments to Contrast

If your bent urges you toward even more picture contrast control, you may want to turn to a dialog box that provides the means to graphically set up a relationship between the contrast of the imported image, the one displayed in the document and the one printed through QuarkXPress. The result will be a contrast-adjusted image of your own design. Controls for this option are reached by choosing the **Other Contrast** command under the Style menu.

What you'll see is a dialog box titled Picture Contrast Specifications. All the controls of this dialog box are used in drawing a graph that defines a new image contrast. This new contrast will be applied to the original image shading. In the dialog box a chart of original versus altered shadings appears with the horizontal axis labeled Input and the vertical axis labeled Output. Together they plot a relation that converts from one contrast to another. If you choose **Other Contrast** for a picture to which a preset contrast control has been applied, you'll see that control's effect on shading values plotted in the graph.

Figure 12.5 shows the Picture Contrast dialog box for **Normal Contrast**. Note that the graph portrays a one-to-one relation between **Input** and **Output**. The straight diagonal line indicates an increase of **Input** shading is matched exactly by an equal increase of **Output**. A 100% black bit will be replaced by a 100% black bit, a 37% black bit by a 37% black bit, and so on. That represents no change over the original image contrast—in other words, **Normal Contrast**.

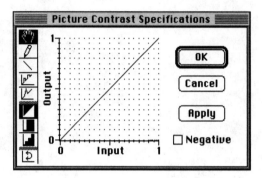

Figure 12.5   *The Picture Contrast Specifications plot of **Normal Contrast** setting.*

Notice also that at the dialog tools you'll see the button bearing a similar diagonal line engaged. The Picture Contrast dialog box is an alternate way of applying the same settings as the commands we've just looked at in the Style menu. It's also a way to examine what conversion is actually performed by **High Contrast** and **Posterized Contrast** as shown in Figures 12.6 and 12.7, respectively. Of course to do so you need some ease at reading graphs. Notice the buttons engaged for each of these likewise mimic the plotted graph of contrast **Input/Output**.

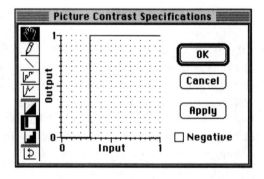

Figure 12.6   *The Picture Contrast Specifications' plot of the **High Contrast** setting.*

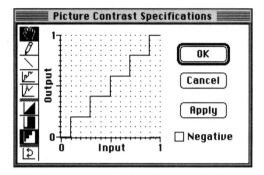

Figure 12.7 *The Picture Contrast Specifications' plot of the **Posterized** setting.*

The button at the bottom of the dialog tools can be used to invert whatever **Input/Output** relation is established in the graph. This inversion tool flips the curve upside down around its center. For instance, when applied where a high input shading might have resulted in a high output shading, the inversion process will plot a new relation, which results in a low output shading. The combinations of effects are endless, but Figure 12.8 shows the result of applying the **High Contrast** button, then the **Inversion** button.

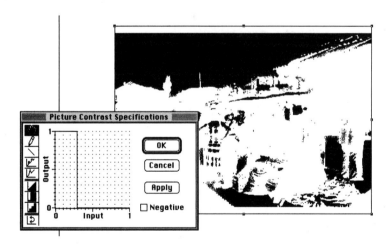

Figure 12.8 *Plot of applying first the **High Contrast** button, then the **Inversion** button.*

The **Hand Icon** button at the top of the dialog tools provides a means to shift the graph within the confines of the chart. Note that when you do so the graph will be reformed. The **Pencil Icon** button below it engages a Freehand Drawing tool with which you can draw any shape graph to produce any desired relation in contrast. Using it, as using all the first five tools, gives the impression of tugging on the plot already drawn. The third tool down provides a means to draw straight lines in the graph. Figure 12.9 shows the effect of using it to draw a graph that peaks and accentuates low percentage input shades, then drops and falls to zero of high percentage shades.

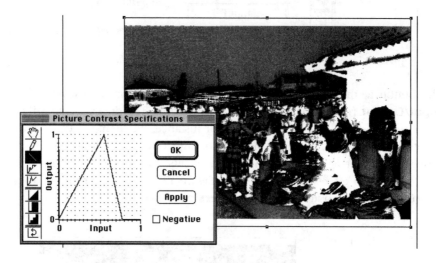

Figure 12.9 *Effect of one hand-drawn contrast plot.*

The fourth and fifth buttons select the plot and provide handles by which the graph can be pulled for fine-tuned adjustments. Button four provides handles between the 10% input marks; button five, handles at the 10% marks for pulling spikes or valleys.

There is also a checkbox in the lower-right corner, which applies the same **Negative** command encountered earlier on the Style menu.

Together, the tools of the Picture Contrast dialog box provide all the controls of QuarkXPress over relative image shading levels. The possibilities are countless. You can accentuate normally low percentage features and mute high percentage ones. Add to these capabilities the shading controls, and you'll have most of the control for enhancing and highlighting images in the document.

Making a custom adjustment of contrast

Select the picture with Content tool active

Open the Style menu and choose **Other Contrast**

At the dialog use the first five tools to draw or modify a contrast graph

Use the last four tools and buttons to apply or invert a contrast graph

Click the **Apply** button and revise as necessary, repeat as needed

---

Halftones

Ink is not silver nitrate. Or, put another way, printing is not photography. What appears on film, or on screen, will not reproduce acceptably in print unless modification is made to convey the information inherent in the image. Continuous-tone illustrations are reproduced by translating them through a screen that results in another image known as the halftone. By virtue of halftones, images with grays are represented in a medium that deals only with black and white (or full color and no color). Therefore, we have photographs in newspapers, magazines, and books. A close look at any such photographic reproduction will reveal the arrangement of black dots that fools the eye into seeing gray (or color tints).

The pattern of these dots is produced by photographing the continuous-tone image through a screen, which breaks the grays into dots of varying size. A collection of big dots overlaps to produce black. Smaller dots and pieces of dots simulate grays. Figure 12.10 shows an image of relatively continuous tones on the right, and it's screened halftone counterpart on the left. Notice how the dot formation in the halftone creates an impression of gray. Note how the dots are all smaller than a certain size. This maximum dot size is determined by the grid-like screen through which the image is captured. Further examination of the halftone in the figure also reveals that the dots fall into a pattern that is made up of lines at 45° to the horizontal. This screen can then be described as 45 lines per inch, dot screen, at 45°. A screen can also consist of lines of varying thickness instead of dots of varying size. So the parameters for a screen are (a) lines per inch, (b) the pattern, and (c) the angle of screen rotation.

Figure 12.10 *Continuous tone image and its halftone counterpart.*

The screen is what determines and creates the halftone image from an original image. Of course, there is always some loss of image clarity when a screen is applied. But the result is an image that can be conveyed through a printing press.

QuarkXPress achieves the screening effect digitally. The result is halftone pictures that can be sent to all sorts of printers and imagesetters to display a rendition of the shading present in continuous tone illustrations. The controls for halftoning, like the contrast controls, come in two forms and are found in commands on the Style menu as shown in Figure 12.11.

Unless otherwise specified, the program applies a default screen to any picture image. This is represented by the Style menu command, Normal. You might find your default is set to a dot pattern of 60 lpi at 45°. To apply a preset halftone setting to any picture image, first select the picture with the Content tool. Next open the Style menu and choose any of the four screens displayed with icons there.

Note that even after making these changes you probably won't notice them on your monitor. QuarkXPress doesn't display halftones unless specifically requested. Screen redraw times are considerably lengthened when halftoning is displayed. However, you can specify halftone display through the final screen command in the Style menu.

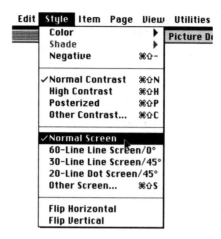

Figure 12.11   *Halftoning screen controls on the Style menu.*

Applying preset halftone screening to an image

Select picture with Content tool active

Open the Style menu and choose one of the screens in the
    lowest box

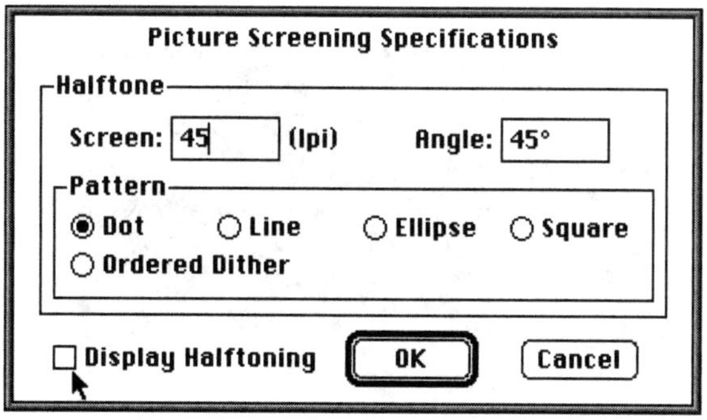

Figure 12.12   *Dialog box for custom halftoning
adjustments from the **Other Screen** command.*

You can examine an existing screen applied to a picture, or specify a screen of different parameters by opening the Style menu and choosing **Other Screen**. A dialog box titled Picture Screening Specifications will appear as in Figure 12.12. Note that both angle and screen lines per inch are adjustable here, as well as pattern type. Also presented is the checkbox control at the lower left of the dialog box for displaying the halftone on your monitor display.

Figure 12.13 shows the two preset dot screens of Normal (here 60 lpi/45°, on the left) and the coarser fourth choice on the screen commands (20 lpi/45°, on the right) applied to the same illustration shown earlier. Figure 12.14 shows the two preset line screens 60 lpi/0° (on the left) and 30 lpi/45° (on the right) applied to the illustration. Notice how the lines per inch of the screen has a drastic effect on the quality of the image, and how the choice of dot or line has a subtler, but distinctive effect.

Figure 12.13   Halftones of normal screen and 20-lpi dot screen/45°.

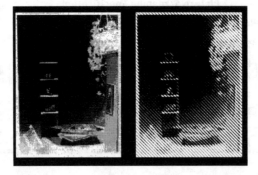

Figure 12.14   Halftones of 60-lpi line screen/0° and 30-lpi line screen/45°.

Resolution

Aside from contrast and screening, a much simpler, but significant, aspect of image manipulation always has an effect on the illustrations that are included in a document file: This is enlargement and reduction, or sizing. You've already seen how to size an image. But here, let's consider what happens to image quality as a result of sizing.

To understand the effect of sizing on the types of images we're looking at in this chapter (bitmapped and grayscale) you should note that these images are like mosaics, with hundreds and thousands of little dark or light bits tiled into patterns that we recognize as images. The size of these bits is originally determined by the device and software that puts them into a graphics file. This system may be the graphics-generating program operating in your computer, or it may be a scanner system. The bits are positioned into place in a rectilinear grid, like tiles laid into a floor.

In simple bitmaps the bits are either black or white. In grayscale bitmaps, however, the bits can be black, white, or some shade of gray. As bitmapped images are enlarged, these pieces become apparent. At small dimensions the clarity of a bitmapped image can appear quite sharp. In fact, reducing the size of an image is sometimes the best way to improve its apparent quality.

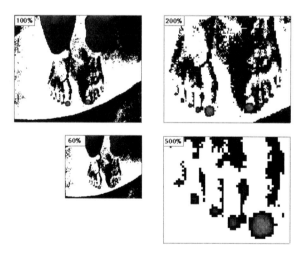

Figure 12.15 *Resolution effects of resizing bitmapped art.*

Enlarged several hundred percent, however, the same image can show the underlying pattern of the bitmap grid in a way that distracts from the image itself. Figure 12.15 shows a scanned painting that has been both enlarged and reduced. In this case you can see the effect on resolution becomes clearly noticeable at 500%. Because each image varies, the effect of enlarging or reducing size will vary greatly from image to image. It's wise not to assume you can enlarge to any size. Rather, consider original size and fineness of the bitmap before committing a piece of digital art to a large size.

Onward

Images within pictures can be modified and manipulated in ways relating to resolution, contrast, halftoning, and shading, as you've seen. Almost all that we've said about black images applies just as well for images to which you apply color. The effects you can apply in layout and printing will make a wider range of images valuable to you. The imperfectly scanned photograph, the file from a graphics program that's just a bit off, now come into reach.

The next step is to see when and how these techniques are applied to layout. With the wide range of magazine designs that have come into acceptance, image manipulations of the types we've just explored become especially useful. In Chapter 13 we'll see how these manipulations prove their worth in producing a magazine layout.

On the Job:
Magazine Pages

What you will learn in this chapter:

- Drawing and applying contrast curves
- How to adjust graphic contrast within a layout
- How to balance graphics and text flow in an article
- How to adjust halftone screens on the page

307

Nowhere are illustrations more pressed to their limits than in the contemporary magazine. Maximum impact is the goal. This demands that photographs, drawings, and paintings buoy up and carry articles along. In fact, stories without strong, effective visuals are frequently shunned.

Ironically the most visual subjects sometimes require using original images never intended for reproduction in publications. In these cases, you may need to work a little magic to coax the medium of photography to show itself favorably in the medium of print.

When illustrations are destined for output directly from a electronically published document, image manipulation and software halftoning come into play. In this chapter we'll be laying out a strongly illustrated magazine piece. We will prepare grayscale pictures in a document for final output with the text they accompany. To do this we'll make use of QuarkXPress's image manipulation techniques, especially those encountered in the previous chapter. In this project we'll be interested in adjusting these digital images to optimum quality for output through an imagesetter.

Assembling the Elements

The pages we're working on are 50 picas by 65 picas high, have top and bottom margins of 4 picas, inside margin of 2.5 picas and an outside margin of 3.5 picas. The grid is made up of three columns separated by a 1 pica gutter. For our document we've engaged the Automatic Text Box feature, and text chaining. Though we'll be adding other elements, they'll go on layers above the automatic box. By assuring that text runaround is engaged for these, we'll let the program help in arranging the text through the labyrinth of pictures to be laid out.

The story here is about various locations around the world. Scanned digital TIFF files of photographs are the graphics we have to work with. Obviously, in final camera-ready copy photographic prints are in many ways to be preferred to scanned files. The resolution of scanners (technological marvels that they are) at this writing often lags behind that of the photographic process. But working from digital files, a great deal can be accomplished.

Since this will be a highly graphic piece we're going to build it from the pictures out. That is, we'll establish the illustrations on three pages allotted to the story, adjust them for optimum reproducibility, then include and typeset the body of the story and other text. We have four TIFF files and one text file. We'll also need to generate headline text and captions.

Our first move is to make a rough pictorial layout. This story is allocated the spread of Pages 32 and 33, and Page 34. We have four scanned photographs to incorporate into the layout. In order to work with these images we choose to make an adjustment to the document's preset image resolution.

N O T E

Note that though we're making adjustments to an image in the picture, QuarkXPress is really only providing a representation of the actual graphic file. That graphics file, which will be called on during printing output, still resides outside the document. Normally, TIFF pictures are displayed at a low document image resolution, which is what we see on screen. This is a preferred state if you wish to avoid lengthy redraws of the screen each time the TIFF picture is altered, or when the view is changed. (Just how lengthy these redraws will be depends on your computer system.)

In order to make the adjustments we have in mind, we prefer to see the images at the fullest resolution of our monitor. So, opening the Edit menu we choose **Preferences**, then **Application** in the submenu. At the dialog box that appears we move to the **Display** section. There we open the listing under Gray TIFF's (which determines how grayscale tiff files will be imported) and choose **256 levels.** Now every Grayscale TIFF image we import will be displayed at highest resolution.

We choose to incorporate the first image large on the page spread in a prominent position, starting near the upper right, and running across the fold. To bring this about we choose the Rectangular Picture Box tool and draw a large picture box into which we import the TIFF file, from the File menu's **Get Picture** command. Using the keystroke, **Command-Shift-Option-F**, with the picture selected and the Content tool active, we proportionally enlarge the image to fit the box. Then we use the Picture Grabber Hand tool (dragging with the Content tool in the box) and the box handles for more adjustment to put the cropped image in place over the fold. We've deliberately done a bleed (extending the image past the end of the page) to the right to add to the sense of expanse in the image. On the left side we've pulled the picture box so far that it covers a column there, making it a four-column-plus picture box.

We're not satisfied with the contrast of the image, so we open the Style menu with the image selected and choose **Other Contrast**. In the dialog box we click the **Spike Points** button; handles appear on the straight 45° line of the Normal Contrast graph. We begin to distort the graph by pulling on these points, especially at the dark (to the right, the high input value) end.

After some experimenting, pulling a point and then clicking the **Apply** button we settle on the image setting showing in Figure 13.1. Next to it is the contrast graph that we've adjusted. You'll notice the pointer hand pulling on one of the lighter end graph points at the lower left. In order to create more distinctness among the darkest shades we've dragged points in opposite directions at the dark (or high) end of the plot. This has the effect of pulling things out of the shadows. We've also whitened out the lightest (or lowest) end of the graph.

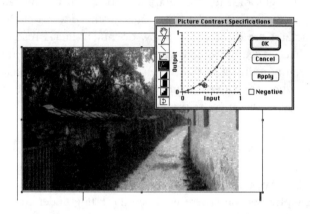

Figure 13.1 *The adjusted contrast graph for an imported image.*

Another photograph also figures into the piece early, so we position it on the spread as well, in a picture box somewhat smaller and lower at the left on Page 32 where its portrait orientation fits well. We similarly size and crop it to bleed off the left edge of the page. Figure 13.2 shows this photograph at normal contrast.

Figure 13.2 *The normal contrast image.*

We decided that this scanned image needed a couple adjustments, so we again chose **Other Contrast** and modified the **Input/Output** contrast curve of the picture by using the Pencil Line tool. With the tool we redraw the graph, clicking the **Apply** button as we go to monitor the effect of the contrast distortion on the image. Reconstructing the contrast curve this way we manage to accentuate contrast in certain tone levels and subdue it in others. Our changes bring out some of the features we value in the scanned subject. After several tries, we're able to increase certain dark tones slightly, and to darken slightly some of the lighter features. By the point this is achieved we have the Picture Contrast graph of Figure 13.3 producing the enhanced image shown beside it.

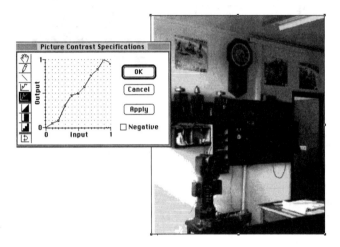

Figure 13.3   *Effect of point-wise manipulation of contrast.*

On Page 34 of this magazine we use the Picture Box tool again to draw out two boxes into which we import two more image files at the top and bottom of the page. Again we size the images and crop them, pulling on the box handle of the top picture to bleed it off the page to the left. With each of these grayscale images we encounter a need to darken the higher percentage shades and lighten the lower ones.

We do this with a method that often proves effective for us. In the dialog box presented through the **Other Contrast** command using the Pencil tool we tailor each end of the Normal Contrast graph by redrawing the curve there into a taper. This bends the overall graph into an S shape. The gradual climb of the curve at the light end brings out the whites; the reverse curve at the dark end brings out the blacks.

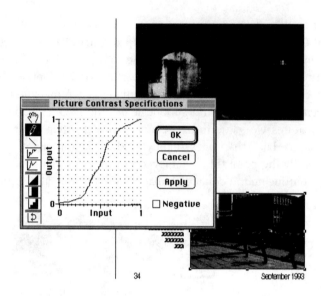

Figure 13.4 *An S contrast graph applied to each of two images.*

In Figure 13.4 you see both images. Between them you can see the Picture Contrast graph we applied to each one. This kind of grayscale contrast adjustment, which exaggerates the lights and darks, often proves useful in heightening contrast without losing middle tones.

Setting the Text

Now we decide to set the text in place. Recall that this document is based on a master page spread that chains text from one page to the next in three columns. Note also that the picture boxes now in place have been created with an automatic text runaround feature active. With the Content tool active, we insert a cursor in a column of the text box of Page 32, then import through the **Get Text** command. The text flows, in serpentine fashion, in the column spaces around the first picture, then over to Page 33 and under the second picture, then on to Page 34, between the third and fourth pictures.

We next go to work on the typography, setting the typeface and size in the Measurements palette, establishing a new hyphenated specification with H&J's dialog box, engaging this specification and indenting the first line of each paragraph through the Paragraph Formats dialog box. We also use the Text Box tool to create a new text box for the headline at the upper left of Page 32. Into this we type the heading, then format lines both flush left and flush right to give a staggered effect. The headline text box now joins the picture boxes in pushing the body text down into available column space.

We now make adjustments to the lead paragraph, formatting the first several words in all caps through the Measurements palette, and removing the first line indent for this paragraph only through the Format dialog box.

A captions box is needed. We decide to describe both paintings in one caption, so we draw a small box to fit in at the bottom of the second column next to the photo on the lower left. We key in the description, then choose a bold sans serif font and align left using the Measurements palette. We also make adjustments at the Text Box Specifications dialog box, removing the text inset and vertically aligning to the bottom of the box.

Everything on Pages 32 and 33 seems to be coming into place when we discover that the text and pictures are much too close. So using the Content tool, we select each picture box in turn and open the Item menu to choose **Text Runaround** where we increase the offset to 8pts all around. Now things are in order, except that the left side of our caption doesn't appear to be in line with the story text. This occurs because its text box was created after the picture box and so resides on a layer above it. Since the picture box runaround will affect only those text boxes below it, we'll have to rearrange the layers. We select the picture box with the Item tool and, opening the Item menu, choose **Bring to Front**. Now the spread, seen in Figure 13.5, is acceptable, and we turn to the last page of the story.

Figure 13.5 *The spread of Pages 32 and 33, all text pictures adjusted.*

On Page 34 we see the text already in place. Here we likewise increase the text runaround of the picture boxes. We create a similar caption box by copying the one from Page 32, pasting it in here, then selecting the text, aligning right from the Measurements palette, and keying in the new caption. Figure 13.6 shows a close up of this page, story and pictures complete.

Figure 13.6   *The final layout of Page 34.*

Halftone Considerations

As far as layout and page makeup go, we've completed the story. But remember that this is a special case. If we had simply left space for photographs to be pasted in, we'd be done; that is, we'd be done if the graphics were line drawings (which print easily).

On the surface, all appears finished. But consider this: we have grayscale images to be output directly from this QuarkXPress document file. How well they appear in the final film, negative, or paper output depends on the output device (imagesetter, laser printer, etc.) and on the ways we prepare them within the document.

Whether we've chosen it, halftoning is already applied to each image. By default, a halftone setting will be in effect for each image unless we override it. The display of halftones on the monitor is normally switched off by QuarkXPress. What we've been looking at doesn't reveal the halftones that will be applied eventually to the pictures when the document is printed.

In order to see the simulated effects of halftoning we Open Style menu and choose **Other Screen**. At the dialog box that appears we click on the **Display Halftone** checkbox. Without making any other adjustments we click **OK**. The result is a screen representation of the default halftone.

N O T E Many good monitor displays may not reach the clarity of an image-setter (120 dpi is not quite 133 lpi). But for the moment we put a wary faith that what we see is some indication of what we'll get. Experience is the most reliable way to correlate screen images and the specific output device being used.

Figure 13.7   *Monitor display for Normal halftone and chosen halftone.*

Each picture is a special case, so we go from one to another, noting that the ultimate output device that will receive this document is capable of 133 lpi. At each we try different halftone screens. Some effects show up more dramatically than others. Figure 13.7 shows the Normal Screen version (at 60 lpi) of the picture on the left, and next to it the picture at the screen setting we choose for vividness. With the pictures thus set to match the output device, we have finally completed layout and are prepared for printing.

Onward

These preparations make use of functions often invisible in QuarkXPress—invisible, that is, until you see the printed page. Several other features affect the quality and success of final document output. Some affect whether you spend weeks or just days on a project. Others determine what files you can gain access to. Still others affect the size and color of your page proofs and final output.

In the remaining chapters we turn to these features. For instance, we'll explore the ways to avoid the episodic turmoils of publication production. If you must prepare issues of a publication regularly, you can use QuarkXPress features to avoid duplication of effort and to speed production. In Chapter 14, we'll see how.

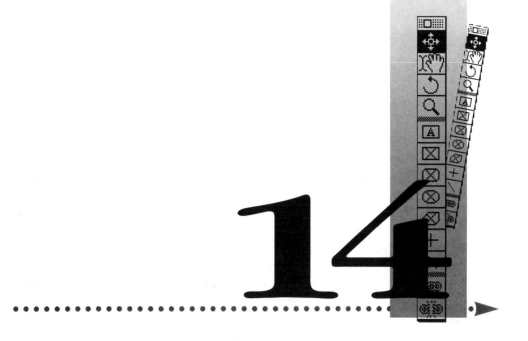

Multiple Editions and Multiple Documents

What you will learn in this chapter:

- ❖ How to transfer elements between documents
- ❖ How to move pages between documents
- ❖ How to change type formats automatically
- ❖ How to produce and use publication templates

Once is not enough. Nowhere (perhaps almost nowhere) is this more true than in desktop publishing and electronic design. Certainly, there are many one-of-a-kind books and advertisements and other unique productions produced through desktop software. But so often, documents, sections of them, or elements from them find their way into new projects. Sometimes, projects derive directly from the original document, as in subsequent magazine issues. Other times, pages, layouts, or arrangements resurface into new layouts.

One sure way to expand your resource base and cut down on redundant efforts is to master the secrets of working with multiple documents and multiple editions of the same document. In this chapter we're going to examine ways to re-apply whole pages, to update, to return to existing documents, to set up and reuse documents in new forms and later editions.

This exploration will take us into methods that use QuarkXPress features to transverse the boundary between document files. By using the program's ability to open as many documents as the memory of your system can accommodate, you'll see how to create superdocuments in which all the elements of any document are readily available to any other. The features that make this expansive work possible include thumbnails, templates, special searching and replacing, reverting, and library creation and use.

Across the Document Boundary

First, take note that the techniques of crossing file boundaries in an application depend on which files can be accessible from within the program at any one session. QuarkXPress can present a host of documents, all of which simultaneously open in their own windows. Previous limits have been exceeded to the ultimate. Now only the hardware of your computer will limit the number of open documents. Therefore, provided enough memory is made available to the program, any number of files can be open at once.

Couple this with an ability to move items from one document to the other, and you possess the ability to share directly unlimited numbers of elements. Suppose a document exists that contains elements you'd like to use, perhaps in modified form, in a second document you're creating. Periodicals, for instance, often spawn special collections or booklets. Many of these offspring are based on copy and designs taken from their parent periodical. If your need is to transfer elements or layout pieces from one such document to the other, you'll find the steps to do so surprisingly simple, even simpler than cutting and pasting.

To copy items from one document to another, first bring both document windows into view within the program window. One way to do this is to open the View menu, then the Window submenu, and choose **Tile Documents**. This command fits all open document windows into the program window space. In cases where many documents are open, you may need to close some other windows to use this command effectively. Or you might wish to size the windows manually to make them each provide a view of the areas in question.

Next, make certain the source document's window is active by clicking on it or using the Windows submenu's document list. Now select the items to be transferred. This means using the Item tool, of course. Then drag them out of the source window to the destination window and release the mouse. Duplicates of the items will be deposited into the destination document.

Duplicate drags between documents

Bring both document windows into view

Select the items in the source document

Drag them across the window boundaries into the destination document and release mouse in position

---

Figure 14.1 shows such a transfer in progress. Here the handshake illustration has been selected in the window holding the "Info News" tabloid, on the left. It is being dragged into the "Data Guide" booklet, on the right. Notice that the items appear in the "Data Guide" window at the larger view size selected for it. Once the midpoint of the selection crosses the window boundary it jumps automatically to the adjacent window and conforms in all ways to the window parameters in effect there. While being dragged, the image may seem to disappear from the source document for a moment. But when you release the mouse button as has just been done in the figure, the pictures appear visible in both documents.

Notice that these item duplications can be carried out with more than two documents. You can put three or more documents within the program window at once and drag items between any of them. In fact as you drag an item it will appear momentarily within whichever window you've pulled the mouse tool. Keeping the mouse button depressed as you continue dragging, you'll see the item leave that document window, enter the next, and so on until you release the mouse button where the item will be deposited. Note that you can select a collection of items and drag a duplicate of the whole collection to a different document.

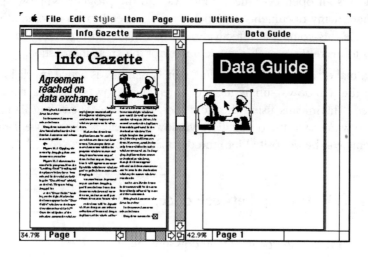

Figure 14.1   Copying elements by dragging from one document to another.

WARNING

Working between multiple windows you would do well to exercise caution when you delete. It's natural to notice the duplicate items sitting selected in the destination window. You might imagine that pressing the delete key will remove them. However, consider that only items within the active window are acted on. In dragging duplicates from source to destination windows, though the items appear selected and the mouse arrow can be seen in the destination window, the source window remains the active one. So the items in the source will be the ones immediately affected by a **cut** or **delete** command.

Thumbnails

On the page level exists another means for working between documents. It allows for whole pages to be duplicated or transferred from one QuarkXPress file to another. This means can also be used in reorganizing pages within a document, as an alternative to the Document Layout palette. Curiously enough, you gain access to this control through a View menu selection. The choice is Thumbnails, immediately following the page views. This choice does more than change to the Lilliputian view. It engages a feature for visually moving pages directly.

To use it within a document, begin by opening the View menu and choosing **Thumbnails**. The document will appear in an extremely small size view. In this state only the pages are accessible. If you try to select or manipulate the items on those pages, you'll find you are locked out of such actions. To actually duplicate a thumbnail page, simply bring it into view within the window, click on it to select, then drag to a new location and release. You'll find that the mouse cursor changes to placement cursors similar to those provided in the Document Layout palette. You can use them in a similar way to insert pages, to widen spreads, and so on.

When you position the mouse tool before releasing, you'll see one of several placement cursors when moving pages there. The box cursor indicates the spread will be enlarged with the new page. The small bar-arrow cursors indicate which page will be pushed aside and downstream to make way for the new page. QuarkXPress will rearrange pages as necessary to accommodate the new positioning.

The **Thumbnails** feature offers some clever variations for page movements. To select a range of pages, click at one end of the range, then hold down the **Shift** key and click at the other end. The entire group of pages will be highlighted and can be moved together. To select a scattered assortment of pages click on one, then hold down the **Command** key to click on the others. When you move one page the others will follow, and the group will be inserted where the cursor is placed.

Moving duplicate pages within a document using thumbnails

Select the pages by clicking, Shift-clicking, or Command-clicking

Drag to new location and release

Copying a page from one document to another is a similar process, much like copying items from document to document. With both document windows showing, make each active in turn and select the Thumbnails view for each. Next click the source document to make it active and click on the page (or pages) to be moved. Drag it across the window frames and into the destination document. Following the same tool cursor strategy as in the Document Layout palette, you release the mouse button when the page is in position. QuarkXPress will rearrange the pages to fit.

Recall that each document created in QuarkXPress is set up in one page size. So, what happens if you try to drag a page from a small page document to one of large format? QuarkXPress simply creates a new page (or pages) of the destination document size, then puts all the elements from the source document in place seated in the upper-left corner. But note that if you try to drag from a larger page document to a smaller page document, the program cancels the attempt with a dialog notice.

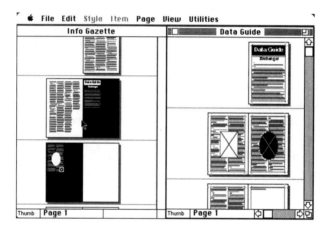

Figure 14.2   A thumbnail copy from a small page-size document to a larger one.

Figure 14.2 shows the result of dragging Pages 1 and 3 (selected with **Command-click**) from the smaller format (6 by 9 inches) document on the right. It has been dragged to the larger format (tabloid, 11 by 17 inches) document (after Page 2) on the left. Notice that the contents of each of the smaller duplicated pages, which are highlighted after the drag, appear tucked into the upper-left corner of newly created, larger pages.

Bringing new pages to the document this way will also bring over any master pages, hyphenation, and justification specifications, and differently named style sheets that are applied within these copied pages.

> ## Copying pages between documents
>
> Select each document in turn and choose **Thumbnails** from the View menu
>
> At the source document window select the pages by clicking, Shift-clicking, or Command-clicking
>
> Drag into the destination window and release

Blind Replacements and Updating

Consider the guidebook that needs revision, or the magazine being readied for a regional edition, or that once-approved project that must suddenly reflect a sheaf of last-minute changes from the editorial department. In all these cases we're dealing with content, which remains largely the same, except for the miscellaneous change. Of course, miscellaneous changes can number into the hundreds easily on a project of any size. Still, when revision is preferable to redoing, you're looking at an updating effort.

You've already seen that QuarkXPress provides a search and replace feature that makes quick work of changing "this year's totals" to "last year's totals" or "delivering all artwork to the art director, Hal Stinson" to "delivering all artwork to the production editor, Amelia Peter." But by extending this feature you can easily make global (that is, document wide) changes in subtler and more typographic fashion.

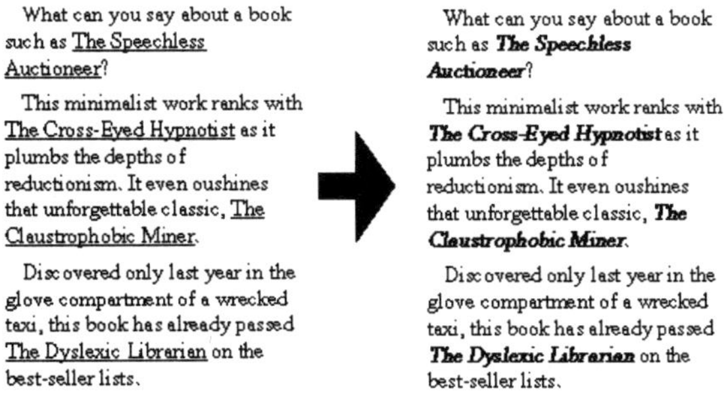

Figure 14.3   *A blind change of type formatting through the Find/Change dialog box.*

For instance, suppose the text file you're given includes the names of several books. It was prepared by a person who always uses underlining to indicate titles. If the standards of your publication require another type style, say bold italic, for each book title, you can easily make the change of style automatically for any title that might be already designated within the text. This would be the kind of change indicated in Figure 14.3.

To automatically change the type features within text, open the Edit menu and choose **Find/Change**. At the dialog that appears click to remove the X from the checkbox marked **Ignore Attributes**. An expanded Find/Change dialog box will appear, which additionally allows changes of font, size, and type style.

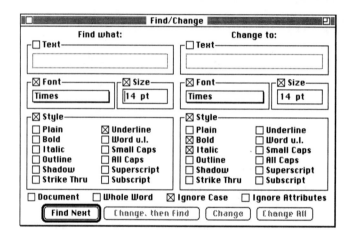

Figure 14.4 *Blind Change dialog box that made the changes in Figure 14.3.*

Under style you'll find that the checkboxes can be clicked blank, X-ed, or grayed. In this case gray means: deliberately ignore that feature during the search. In this expanded search you proceed exactly as with the simple text find/change routine, clicking **Find Next**, then **Change** or **Change All**, as appropriate. Figure 14.4 shows the blind search and change that automatically converted the underlines to bold italics in Figure 14.3.

Note that no text is entered into either field for text. This tells QuarkXPress we're looking for a change of whatever text has the attributes indicated in the rest of the dialog box. Note that you could also change font or font size, or use the box to search for attributes. One such search might be to locate each bolded word in a document, or each phrase in All Caps.

N O T E Notice that for the Find/Change dialog box to recognize attributes such as bolding, italics, and so forth, these must be applied within the program. For instance, a font that is set to plain but is bold or black itself will be treated as plain text.

Fixing Mistakes and Reverting

A word about mistakes. We all make them; the computer makes them; the software makes them; at times the person-computer-software team makes them. Of course, it's in our interest to keep all wrong turns to a minimum. But clearly, there is no progress without error at getting there. The key to success is knowing when to attempt to fix the mistake and when to just do it over.

In preparing a layout you may encounter a situation in which you've made a number of adjustments since last saving the document. Maybe some elaborate text style and formats have been applied; perhaps a layout or series of image adjustments has been achieved. And sometimes after doing all this, you conclude the document or page just isn't right.

Going backward to undo every move or format change is one way to fix things. But QuarkXPress provides another, more extreme, method. If indeed you haven't saved the document since the beginning of these changes, then all you need do is give a single command, and the program clears the changes and returns the last saved version of the document to the window. The way to do this is simply open the File menu and choose **Revert to Saved**. A dialog box will appear, asking for confirmation. Clicking **OK** brings up the earlier version to replace what was just in the window.

Now, if you care to work more aggressively, you can deliberately experiment with changes to your document with an eye to this command. The key is not to save until you're sure you want to go forward from that point. If you don't like the results of an experiment, then you tell QuarkXPress to **Revert to Saved.** Realize of course that once done, reverting can't be undone. So you'll want to be confident that the earlier version was the one preferred when you give this command. The changes you make between saves are kept in the computer's short-term memory, while the saved versions are, of course, kept on disk files.

Another approach to project development relies on your ability to use the **Save As** command under the File menu. As has been mentioned in an earlier chapter, by simply saving documents under different names you can create a bank of possibilities to draw on for a final decision. This method works well for various drafts or versions, which the names can reflect, such as Layout #1, Layout #2, and so on.

Multiple Editions and Templates

If you plan repeated access to a document and use it as a basis for developing future documents, you'll want to treat it as special and set in stone. That is, you'll want to assure that it won't be inadvertently changed. This way you can use it many times, confident of your starting point. A file that serves as a starting point for others is known as a *template*. Some templates can be created and used as the basis of issue layout in a regularly reappearing publication. Others can provide a form or report that is built on to produce a final document.

Templates serve as handy repositories for all the work that will be applied issue after issue. Here you can preserve ready access to layouts, page organization, special graphics, headings, logos, master pages, style sheets, hyphenation and justification specifications, custom colors (more about these in Chapter 16), and all the elements that go into the look of a publication or other document.

You can make a template from scratch, creating a prototype document using dummy text and pictures to get a grasp on how it will appear. Or, more practically, you can create an actual issue being sure to save all the layouts, specifications, style sheets, and preferences you might want for subsequent issues. In either case, you can then strip out the changeable text and graphics (deleting with the Content tool), leaving boxes in place as appropriate.

One way to set up a template is to generate the document and save it in the usual way (with the **Document** radio button engaged in the Save As dialog box). Then, when it's time to produce the current issue, the template document can be opened, and the **Save As** command given with a new name. For instance, you might open the template document. The Global Investigator and then make changes pertinent to the March issue, saving this new version as Global I—March, and leaving the template document unchanged. Then when the next month's production began, you could open The Global Investigator again, make changes, and save it as Global I—April.

A most important point here is to be sure not to inadvertently save changes onto the original template document, except when you want to change the template. The best practice in this case is to immediately choose the **Save As command** after opening the template, and to generate a new document by giving it a different name, even before a single change is made to the template.

Making Templates from the Save As Dialog Box

A second way to set up a template is to apply a feature available through the Save As dialog box. To use this, key in a new file name and click the **Template** radio button. In the case of the template file mentioned above, the file saved would be labeled The Global Investigator. Figure 14.5 shows The Global Investigator file being saved as a template named Data Guides.

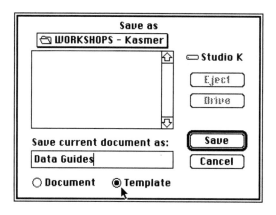

Figure 14.5   *Saving a file as a template.*

A template file can be opened, but not altered. When you try to save it after opening, you're presented with a Save As dialog box, which prompts you to save the current document as a normal document type. Note that you can also generate a new template from an existing one, saving the template in document file format, then modifying, and finally saving the modified document as a template under a different name.

Onward

Many of these highly effective tools are so simple to use that it's easy to overlook how much work they can save you. But in developing multiple documents and editions, you get to put your efforts to work again and again, with the payoff being that your best efforts can be applied to every project they can benefit.

Providing for updating documents, using templates, and transferring elements and pages between documents are the bases for handling numbers of projects. These methods will prove invaluable when meeting production demands.

Electronic publishing extends beyond the wide spaces of QuarkXPress, of course. And many elements from various sources will be coming into the complex document. There are a number of ways of dealing with these elements from the larger world. In Chapter 15 we look into what can be done to manage graphics and text within and among documents, and how to handle some special transfers.

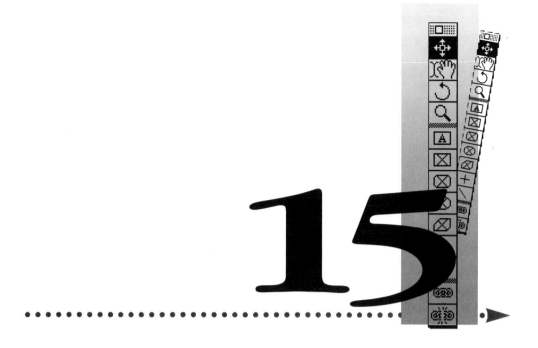

Transfers Within and Without

What you will learn in this chapter:

- ❖ How Libraries exist with documents
- ❖ How to transfer elements between documents and libraries
- ❖ How to export text content
- ❖ How to export XPress tags
- ❖ How to create and use EPS pages
- ❖ How to work with screen captures

A versatile platform, the QuarkXPress document provides such a ready means for assembling, modifying, and creating design elements, we are tempted to use it to store and organize page elements. While a standard document can be adapted to this purpose, other means in the program are more suited to the task. The *XPress Library* is a special kind of document designed exclusively for compiling and retrieving text, graphics, and other items. The advantages it offers include naming and search capabilities.

Those images and texts, and even partial layouts, can travel into and out of documents in a variety of forms. Diverse elements in page layouts eventually require some understanding of exporting features.

In this chapter we turn to the sophisticated ways we can control the flow of elements through documents. We'll look into the applications of libraries. We'll also see how to export text, graphics, and layouts by command and through auxiliary software.

The Library

Library. It's a word that conjures up apprehension in many otherwise courageous, worldly, and sophisticated adults. Dusty books secreted in dimly lit, tottering stacks under arcane numbering systems. Lost souls drifting desperately through impossible mazes. Fortunately, a QuarkXPress library is somewhat different. In one sense it's just a kind of Rolodex for design elements.

You can use an XPress library to store any item that can be placed on a document page. If you put pictures in a library, all their specifications will be stored in the library with them. If you place a text box in one, formatting and style features will likewise be stored with the text box. In effect, a library is a specialized QuarkXPress file designed for storing items. It occupies a window, like a document, and many libraries may be opened at once. Items can be interchanged between libraries, and between them and documents. The total number of open documents and libraries are limited only by the memory available to the computer.

If you think of a library as a specially arranged document, you'll soon get a grasp of its usefulness. Bringing a library window onscreen can be accomplished in virtually the same way that documents are brought onscreen. To open an existing library, start at the File menu and choose **Open**. The dialog box that appears can then be used to locate and select the library, in the same way a document is opened.

The library will appear at the right side of the program window, normally as a long, vertical window resembling the Document Layout palette. You can size and move this window just like any other in the Macintosh

You can use the File menu's **New** submenu to make a new empty library into which you'll drag collected entries. At the dialog box that appears, first key in a name in that field, then click on the **Create** button.environment.

Creating a library

Open the File menu, and submenu **New**, choose **Library**

Proceed to locate a place for the file through the folder windows, and key in a name for it

Click the **Create** button

Opening a library

Open the File menu, and choose **Open**

At the dialog, proceed to locate the file through the folder windows, or key in the name

Click the **Open** button

How do you gain access to items in a library? Use the same approach you apply to transfer items from document to document. Simply select a library item and drag it to a document window, or to another library window. The item so dragged will be duplicated in the destination window, following the same behavior as items dragged between document windows. You can drag items from library to library to build different specialized sets of working collections.

You can likewise drag an item from a document to a library to put a duplicate of it there. Within the library every item (or selected group of items) will appear as a thumbnail, just as each of the various collections of information appears as a book within a library building.

> ## Using items between documents and libraries
>
> Position the windows of both in the program window
>
> Click on the source window to activate it, then the item(s)
>
> Drag to the other window and release to copy the item there

Everything that applies to moving a single item also applies to several items that have been selected together. In such cases however, the item selection will appear as a single thumbnail within the library. This is actually a handy way of temporarily grouping items for reuse.

Figure 15.1   Items as thumbnails within a library.

How do you deal with the thumbnails within a library? In Figure 15.1 you can see a library with three items (a text box and two pictures) that have all been dragged in at different times from a document. When you drag an item or item collection to a library, a pair of small triangles serve as markers to indicate where the item will be placed. Also, the cursor becomes a pair of spectacles. By moving the mouse tool along you can choose where in the list to drop the new item when you release. Just observe the location of the triangle pair.

Positioning entries within a library

While dragging the item(s) note the appearance of double triangles

When the triangles mark the desired insert point release

The familiar functions of **Cut**, **Copy**, **Paste**, and **Delete** are available within the library under the program's Edit menu. Using them you can, for instance, take an entry from a library by clicking on its thumbnail, and then giving a **Cut** command. Locating the Item tool elsewhere, you can give the **Paste** command to relocate it elsewhere within the library, or to paste a copy of it within a document. Note that you can select any thumbnail entry from a library by using the mouse, regardless of which tool has been selected from the Program Tool palette, and copy it by dragging it out of the window.

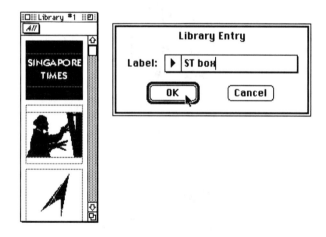

Figure 15.2   *Labeling a library entry after double-clicking on it.*

A feature particularly helpful with large library collections is the ability to name each library thumbnail. To do this for a thumbnail, you double-click on it, and a Name dialog box appears. Key in the name and click **OK**. In Figure 15.2 the text box at the top of the library has been double-clicked to produce the dialog next to it where a label has been typed.

Naming library entries

Double-click on the entry to call up the Library Entry dialog box

Key in the name

Click **OK**

You can locate any thumbnail by using the library's scroll bar. But when you've named thumbnails, you can also locate them by opening the drop-down list and choosing from the alphabetical listing of names you've given, as in Figure 15.3. Doing so displays the thumbnail by itself in the library window, or it displays every thumbnail bearing the same name. To return to a view of all the thumbnails, you can open the list and choose **All**.

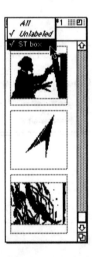

Figure 15.3 *Choosing a library entry from alphabetical name list.*

QuarkXPress saves the library file when you close the window. However, you can instruct the program to automatically save the library each time an item is added to it. The control to engage this automatic saving is a checkbox in the Application Preferences dialog box. To locate it, open the Edit menu, choose **Preferences**, then the submenu **Application**.

Sending Text Outside QuarkXPress

Of course, when using the QuarkXPress platform for developing designs and typesetting, we often send information out of the document by printing through QuarkXPress. There are other ways to send export information established within the document. For instance, elements can be exported in the form of files that can be handled through other software.

Text is the usual grist for the document layout mill. However, text that has been processed within the document may also be sent out in a form that can be used in other programs. For instance, you may wish to make the final text from your publication available to other staff members who have access only to word processing software. In such a case, you'll need to export the text.

In QuarkXPress one control enables you to send out text in various file formats, whole stories or in part. As you might guess, this is the outbound counterpart of the **Get Text** command, and like **Get Text**, the exporting command is found under the File menu. It's labeled *Save Text*, and presents a dialog box like the Get Text dialog. The options are similar. But realize we're going the other way now. In the Get Text dialog you have the option of importing different file types. This allows for pulling text into the QuarkXPress document platform from a variety of sources. This variety is limited only by the available filters present in the XPress directory.

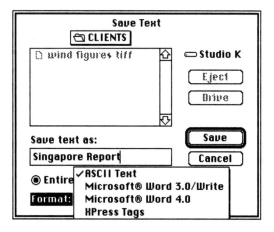

Figure 15.4 *Choosing an export file format from the Save Text dialog box.*

In the Save Text dialog, you can export through these same filters. But now the process leads not to a single QuarkXPress document, but to any of the word processor types represented by available file filters. As before, your options include the universal plain text format known as ASCII. Recall that this is plain text at its plainest, with no style or formatting attributes included. Other export options include Microsoft Word, MacWrite, and other formats. Figure 15.4 shows the Save Text dialog box with a file type being chosen from the drop down list at the lower left.

If there is a chance that you might ever need to re-import a story that has already been formatted in QuarkXPress, you'll want to consider another format, which is at once universal and yet particular to QuarkXPress. This is a special text file type in standard ASCII format. What makes it universal is the standard file type. What makes it particular to QuarkXPress are special codes included within the text file. These are character and paragraph tags that QuarkXPress understands, which are actually spelled out in the text. They signal QuarkXPress to automatically apply formatting and styling when the text is imported. This file format is found under the listing, XPress Tags, in the file type drop-down list of the Save Text dialog box.

Saving formatting information in an ASCII text file

Place the cursor within, or select, the text to be exported

At the File menu choose **Save Text**

At the dialog box use the drop-down list to choose **XPress Tags**

Click **OK**

In Figure 15.5 at the left you can see a text box to which the **Save Text** command was applied with XPress Tags. To the right of it is the text file opened in Microsoft Word. Notice that all the text of the box is found in the text file, but accompanied by a number of arcane-looking notations enclosed in pairs of angle brackets. In fact, with a little attention these notations can be decoded. For instance, preceding and following each title within the text you can see the phrase, **<BI>**, which indicates to switch on, then off, the bolding and italics for the words between. You could, through rather simple deductive reasoning, go through the entire comparison and derive the meanings of nearly each code.

What can you say about a book such as **The Speechless Auctioneer**?
This minimalist work ranks with **The Cross-Eyed Hypnotist** as it plumbs the depths of reductionism. It even oushines that unforgettable classic, **The Claustrophobic Miner.**
Discovered only last year in the glove compartment of a wrecked taxi, this book has already passed **The Dyslexic Librarian** on the best-seller lists.

```
<v1.60><e0>
@Normal=[S"",'Normal"]<"L"h"Standard""kn0"k
t0"ra0"rb0"d0"p(0,0,0,0,0,0,g,"U.S.
English")"t(0,0," "):
Ps100t0h100z12k0b0c"Black"f'Helvetica">
@Normal:<"h"off'"p(0,10.8,0,0,0,5.76,g,"U.S.
English")z14f'Times-Roman">What can you
say about a book such as <Bl>The Speechless
Auctioneer<Bl>?
This minimalist work ranks with <Bl>The
Cross-Eyed Hypnotist<Bl> as it plumbs the
depths of reductionism. It even oushines that
unforgettable classic, <Bl>The Claustrophobic
Miner<Bl>.
Discovered only last year in the glove compart-
ment of a wrecked taxi, this book has already
passed <Bl>The Dyslexic Librarian<Bl> on the
best-seller lists.
```

Figure 15.5   *Formatted text at left and same text exported with XPress Tags.*

Again, the advantage of the XPress Tags file type is in its ability to re-import formatting and character attributes intact. So, you can work on typesetting within a document, export text in XPress Tags format for editing, then reimport for final copyfitting without losing a bit of your typesetting effort. Of course, in this case the editor must work around these codes and regard them as unalterable.

Consider also this interesting twist: Once a familiarity is gained, typesetting codes can be applied directly outside of QuarkXPress, in nearly any word processor. In fact, the use of typed of codes has been a part of traditional typesetters' jobs for decades.

Sending Page Layouts Outside the Document— Encapsulated Postscript (EPS)

Just as text can be sent out of QuarkXPress to be used in other programs, so can layouts, within certain limitations. In one such way the designers of QuarkXPress included the capability of exporting everything on a page at once. The approach they used was saving an entire page as a graphic image file.

The type of graphic image saved through this method is an *Encapsulated Postscript*, or EPS. Postscript as you may know is a programming language specifically designed for high resolution printing. Several programs such as Adobe Illustrator and Aldus FreeHand work with EPS files. Because this format of file is precise in its description, it offers a means of accurate and smooth output.

QuarkXPress can save single pages as EPS files. This means an entire page can be turned into a graphic. The command for doing this is found in the File menu, **Save Page as EPS**. In theory, the use of EPS files to preserve elements in a document page with this command should provide exact replicas that can be printed or manipulated from a variety of programs. You could even lay out a page in QuarkXPress, export it as EPS, paste it into that other desktop publishing program, PageMaker, and then print from the PageMaker document.

However, because of the complexities of EPS files, you might want to proceed cautiously and try the process out yourself before committing yourself to using it in your projects.

N O T E

For instance, that whatever fonts are used on the page so exported must be available to the receiving program. Likewise, high-resolution graphics should accompany the EPS page just as they would for printing.

Sending Layouts Outside QuarkXPress— Screen Capture

One method is often overlooked for bringing images outside of program documents, yet it's available for use with any software. This is the *screen capture*. A relatively blunt way of taking an image on the screen and saving it as a bit-mapped file, screen capture is a method that always works. The reason screen capturing is often neglected is simple. In screen captures you are always limited to the resolution of the screen. For comparison, consider that a good monitor might have a resolution of 120 dots per inch (dpi), while a standard laser printer will generate 300 dpi, and an imagesetter upward from 1200 dpi. We're talking about a substantial difference in quality. Jagged letters and stair-step lines are real possibilities here.

OK, now consider the advantages: You can always, always, always capture the screen. Now, it's up to you to decide if the capability of taking an image from a QuarkXPress document offsets the lowered quality that image will present. There are many occasions, perhaps most times, that the degraded image is unacceptable. But, for those situations when some visual information on the screen must be retained or transferring some layout or image to another program is vital regardless of lower resolution, the screen capture is the way to go. For instance, if you are faxing a page that is set up in QuarkXPress, the resolution on the receiving end will be limited to 100 dpi or 200 dpi anyway.

What happens in a screen capture (also known by the ungracious terms of screen dump or screen shot)? Well, the image on the screen is duplicated bit-by-bit in a file, which can be used just like any other bit-mapped file. The image can be brought into any software document that will read this type of file, such as a graphics, paint-style program. From there it can be edited and printed. A screen capture can be imported into a QuarkXPress document as a graphics file through the Get Picture dialog box. You can even import a screen capture of the scene in a program back into that program's document. (That's how several of the adjacent comparison illustrations shown in this book were created.)

How do you capture the screen? One method is built into the Macintosh platform on which QuarkXPress works. Other methods make use of dedicated screen capture software. If you use the Macintosh method, the bit-mapped image will be saved to files labeled consecutively, Screen 1, Screen 2, and so forth.

The Macintosh capture method works through a keystroke command, and is universally available. To copy and save a screen image to a file, press **Command-Shift-3**.

Capturing a screen image

Prepare the screen as desired

Press **Command-Shift-3**

Some capture programs work through the clipboard. Normally the clipboard and its contents are out of view. However, you can gain viewing access to this Macintosh feature through QuarkXPress. Seeing the clipboard can be useful at any time when you lose track of what you most recently **Cut** or **Copied**, whether screen shot or not. To take a look at the clipboard contents, open the Edit menu and choose **Show Clipboard**. A window will appear labeled Clipboard.

Figure 15.6 *A portion of a screen capture in a picture box.*

Recall that the clipboard is where text or graphics are put when the **Cut** or **Copy** commands are given. You bring out a copy of the clipboard contents by issuing the **Paste** command. In Figure 15.6 you can see a portion of a captured screen in which a QuarkXPress document is open, and within it a shot of a document layout. For orientation, notice that the screen shot is enclosed within a picture-box double frame of 20% Black.

Likewise, you can paste the clipboard screen capture into other files through other software. For instance, you could paste the captured image into a graphics program. Or the image could go into a word processor, if the program has the ability to receive graphics.

Other than using this method to transfer monitor-quality images, you might find it handy to capture some settings such as those in a dialog box, or as a quick way of providing background information when troubleshooting a document.

Alternatives to the use of the **Command-Shift-3** keystroke are the various screen capture software packages that save the screen shot to an automatically generated file. These usually offer a number of file format options. They also allow you to crop the picture before it's saved and to include the mouse tool within the captured image.

Whichever way you go, the side door graphics from screen captures are quick, reliable, and relatively easy ways to document what you see on your monitor.

Onward

Handling text, images, and layouts is what electronic paste-up is all about. Through exporting and screen captures, you now have techniques for side-stepping the file format incompatibilities. Through libraries you have a means of managing your graphic resources in ways that need not be tied to any one document. You never need to be at a loss for controlling the movement of design elements either into or out of QuarkXPress documents.

Next we move into an area that is more an art than a science—managing color from our documents. QuarkXPress offers a feature that some competitors are just beginning to add. That ability—which includes the ability to mix, to apply, and to separate colors into the various plates needed for printing—is what we're going to explore in Chapter 16.

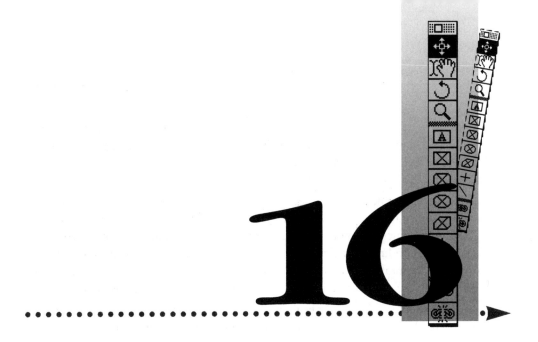

Color

What you will learn in this chapter:

- ❖ What are color models
- ❖ How to use the color wheel
- ❖ How to choose process and spot colors
- ❖ How to prepare color separations
- ❖ Blending colors
- ❖ Trapping colors

Working with color documents can be difficult. Matching colors is a subtle skill. There are schemes and models that make it easier, but predicting how a color produced using one scheme can be replicated in another is mostly a matter of judgment and expertise.

Imagine contacting a painter by telephone after you've created the perfect color. You try to describe the color and how to mix it. Your painter colleague is good at mixing colors, but has a different set of colors than you have. Eventually the painter produces a color. But does it match your blend? This is akin to the challenge of translating a color from your monitor to one on the printed page. Fortunately there are a number of approaches that try to meet this challenge.

This chapter is about how QuarkXPress can help you get colors from the screen to the final print run. First we'll look at various schemes QuarkXPress uses to handle colors and how you can make use of them.

Screen Color versus Print Color

Recall the colors we applied from the Style menu back in Chapter 6. These preset colors were just a snowflake on the iceberg of colors that are available. With a good monitor and enough memory in your system's graphics card you can see millions of colors on the screen. But here's the most amazing part of all: Every one of these millions of colors generated on the screen is made from just three primary colors.

This may jog a memory going back to elementary school. By adding red, green, and blue light together you can make virtually every other color in the spectrum. You might recall a teacher discussing rainbows, or that science class with prisms.

The images on your monitor—it is just a highly controlled light source after all—are derived from an additive system. With no light added, you see black. With red added, you see red. With red, green, and blue added together in equal shares, you see white. That is the basis of one color model, the *RGB model*, (the Red-Green-Blue model).

N O T E

You can see for yourself that these colors truly are added to make up the color monitor display. Take a magnifier (5x or better works well) and focus it on a white part of the screen display. You'll see that indeed what you're looking at is not pure white, after all, but a tight-knit combination of red, green, and blue dots. In fact, these dots are so closely knit that the eye sees them combined as larger spots of a different color altogether, the one they all add up to, white. Of course, you can go on to dissect each color on the screen with the magnifier as your tool. You can see a similar effect on the color wheel described next.

If you're working on a quality color monitor, it is probably based on the RGB model. For this reason, a whole class of video monitors came to be known as RGB monitors. To see the RGB model at work in your system, open the Edit menu and choose **Colors**. At the dialog box titled, Colors For, you'll see the familiar preset colors in a listing. Now click on the **New** button, and a dialog titled, Edit Color, will appear. Be sure that the model RGB is selected from the Model drop-down list.

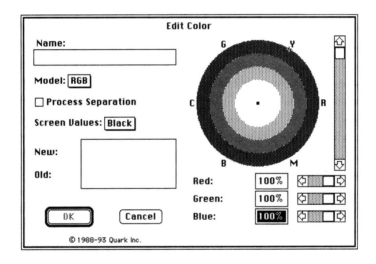

Figure 16.1 *The Colors dialog box with color wheel indicating white.*

As shown in Figure 16.1, this is where you can design your own color, or modify one already in place. To see how the RGB model works, note the wheel at the right of the box. This is the color wheel. It represents, in its fashion, all the colors of the spectrum. At this point you'll see within it a small black box in the center. The three fields below the wheel show 100% each of red, green, and blue. This, as we have just seen, creates the color, white.

Each position on the wheel represents a different color. You can verify this by dragging the tool (a pair of crosshairs seen in the figure in the upper-right of the wheel) with the mouse button down. The values of the additive colors will be shown in the **%** fields below the wheel as you move. Note that the Crosshairs tool in Figure 16.1 is in the position representing yellow labeled with a "Y" outside the wheel (100% green and 100% red). But because the mouse has not been clicked, the original value, white, is still the one represented in those values. To the lower left of the dialog above the **Cancel** button is a box that displays the color currently selected on the wheel, (opposite **New:**) as well as the original color that is being edited (opposite **Old:**). These solid color bars provide a large, contiguous area for you to see more clearly how the colors (on the monitor) appear.

As you drag along the edge of the wheel with the mouse button down, you select colors that are composed of varying percentages of two colors and 0% of the third. The center of the wheel is, as mentioned, white. Positions between the center and the circumference represent assorted nonzero combinations of red, green, and blue. Note that you can also adjust colors by moving the sliders adjacent to each primary color percentage field, or by typing in percentage values in those fields. In these cases the new color will appear in the New:/Old: color box at the left.

Producing a color

At the edit menu, choose **Colors**

At the dialog, click **New**

Use the mouse tool to click at a color on the color wheel

Or

Type in values of percentage of each color in the field boxes

Or

Use the sliders to combine colors

Monitor the resulting color at the color bar

Click **OK** at the Edit Color dialog box, then **Save** at the Color dialog box

You can also add varying amounts of black to any color you're editing. This is done through a vertical slider bar to the right of the color wheel. At its uppermost position, the slider adds no black, at its lowermost, 100% black.

NOTE You can make use of the color wheel and colors even if you use a black-and-white monitor. Of course you'd lose your visual feedback. However, if you knew the percentage combinations of the colors you wanted, you could prepare them in the Edit Color dialog box like a colorblind painter systematically mixing from labeled tubes of paint.

You can experiment with the RGB system, as well as use it to provide custom colors to your layout document. Later, QuarkXPress can separate the colors for the individual runs they'll need to make through your printer's presses. But here's the rub: While the monitor uses an additive system to make colors, ink by its very nature uses a subtractive system. This means that as light—white light that contains the whole of the visible color spectrum—falls on a color of ink, we see that particular color because all the other colors are subtracted out of the light, and only the visible one is reflected to our eye.

There is enough translation difficulty between one ink-based color model and another. But translating between a subtractive model and an additive model requires a mental leap, and when all is said and done, a good eye and experience.

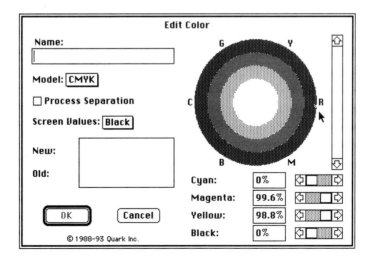

Figure 16.2 *The color, red, as viewed in the CMYK color model of the Edit Color dialog.*

The prevailing color model used by printers is one in which the colors cyan, magenta, yellow, and black are blended to produce a desired color. This model, CMYK, is based clearly on a different foundation than the RGB model. However, ultimately, they both perform the same function. That is, they both represent colors that are not present by a combination of colors that are present. You can choose a color in any model, then switch to a different model. Figure 16.2 shows the dialog box for the color, red, which was chosen in the RGB model (by setting the slider controls to 100% Red, 0% Green, and 0% Blue), but that now appears in the CMYK model. Note the values that produce red are a combination of two colors in this model. Yet we're still looking at the same color. Just its representation has changed. You can select any available model through the drop-down list of the **Model** field.

Keep in mind that we can use the Edit Color dialog box to create or change colors. These new colors will then be available to be applied through the Style menu to the items in our document.

Other Models and Printers

Another color-mixing scheme provided in the Edit Color dialog box is one that allows you to choose a pigment (hue), then its proportion (saturation), and its brightness (black or lack of it). This is the *HSB model*, an approach that brings us back to tubes of paint pigments. Again, you can choose this scheme from the drop-down list for Model.

Note, as in Figure 16.3, where a green color has been mixed, that you'll find similar sliders under the color wheel as in the RGB and CMYK models. But now the top slider/field will be the determiner of color; the second slider will determine tint; and the last will serve the same function as the vertical black-adding slider to the right of the wheel. As you move the Hue slider, the small color marker will move around in a circle. As you move the tint slider, the marker will move radially toward or away from the center of the wheel.

As you may know, other widely accepted color models exist that are somewhat less scientific in their approach, but more generally understood. These are the commercial color-matching systems. QuarkXPress offers use of three such systems through the Model drop-down list. They work on the premise that a large number of color swatches can provide for many, if not most, of the choices needed in color layouts.

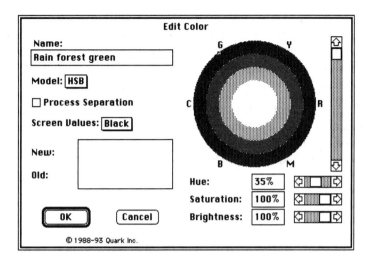

Figure 16.3   *The Hue-Saturation-Brightness color model presented in the Edit Color dialog box.*

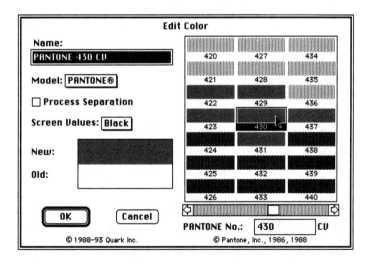

Figure 16.4   *The Pantone matching system presented in the Edit Color dialog box.*

Three widely known systems here—Pantone, Trumatch, and Focoltone—are each different commercial products as are three others offered in the list: Pantone Process, Pantone ProSim, and Pantone Uncoated. But they're all represented in the same way. Figure 16.4 shows the Pantone matching system as presented in the Edit Color dialog box. In this scheme you scroll through the swatches in the box that has replaced the color wheel. When you find a color that matches what you'd like to include in the document, you click on it and then **OK**. Most of the colors are designated by number, but some are indicated by name (That's indication of an evolved, rather than strictly designed, approach).

You might work from the color books associated with these models. In this case, you can choose color from printed swatches in the book and click on its number in the dialog box. Note again that these matching models can be viewed and edited through the color wheel models, and vice versa.

Color Separations

If we had a tube of paint for every color we wanted to produce, there would be no need for blending. Likewise, if a magic color printer worked directly from the QuarkXPress document, we could simply assign colors, click the **Print** button and watch thousands of color-matched copies stream from the presses. While this is currently somewhat possible on the small scale through color-proofing output printers, the reality of large-scale printing is that we often need to reduce our color demands to simply followed instructions in which a limited number of colors are used to create the full range in our documents.

The key to most color printing is that there are two types of colors that printers work with. One is *spot color*, consisting of the designated colors for which the premixed ink can be found to match. This is often the case with color-matching systems like the Pantone system described. The other type is *process color*, a means of separating nearly any color into its component colors within the CMYK model. Most colors can be separated in this way into a four-color equivalent.

The way QuarkXPress handles these separations is to print a separate version of each page to correspond to the separate printing plates that will apply to each of the CMYK colors in the presses. In the final print run of such a separation, each page may be printed on four times to produce the range of colors needed. But you need to designate which colors will be treated as process color. To do so, click to engage an X in the **Process Separation** checkbox in the Edit Color dialog box. Then whenever you print separations, QuarkXPress will know to organize this color into its cyan, magenta, yellow, and black components before separate printing of each. Putting into effect the separation of a color, as well as including new or edited colors in the Style menu, requires an additional step—clicking the **Save** button in the Colors For... dialog box.

Note that a document can be output as separations of spot color as well as process colors. Both spot and process colors can be output from the same document concurrently. The final step to this color separation process from QuarkXPress is during printing. You can take care of this when you give the **Print** command at the File menu. What's necessary is simply to choose **On** in the Separations drop-down list of the dialog box. When the pages are printed to a PostScript printer, each separated color will come out on its own page, ready for the printing department to prepare for the presses.

Trapping Colors

When multiple colors are printed onto the same page in the printing press, they come together. The way they come together is determined by how the inks from each of the plates align when they meet the paper. Things are imperfect in printing presses as they are in most of life, so, QuarkXPress provides for the the imperfect ways ink colors meet. It uses a widely acknowledged approach known as *trapping*. If your document includes a red square over a blue background, for instance, QuarkXPress will remove the blue behind the square, in order that the colors don't mix in intended ways. This way the red prints over white and appears as red as you intended.

However, when the high-speed presses are finally turning your document into ink-and-paper reality, the red square might not line up exactly over the cutout. When this happens, the white (in this case) can peek through, creating wholly unplanned visual effects. The most obvious proof of the inaccuracy of multicolor printing can be found in the extreme example of Sunday comic strips of many newspapers, where a character's eyes can be found migrated mysteriously toward one temple, like a flounder's.

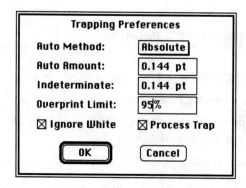

Figure 16.5 *The Trapping Preferences dialog box.*

To compensate for this kind of effect, QuarkXPress automatically overprints slightly, to overlap the adjacent colors. This trapping method is adjustable, if you prefer, through two dialog boxes. One is documentwide. It's reached through the Edit menu by choosing **Preferences**, then the submenu Trapping. Figure 16.5 shows this dialog box.

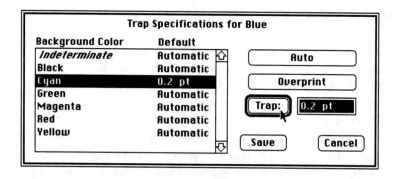

Figure 16.6 *Applying a trapping value to the color blue.*

The other way to adjust trapping is color by color through the Color dialog box under the Edit menu. Here, by clicking **Edit Trap** button, you'll reach the Trap Specifications dialog box for the color you've selected. In the example of Figure 16.6 the Cyan component of the color, blue, is being given a 0.2 point trapping value through the field box next to the Trap button.

The Color Palette and Blending Colors

As you've seen, the lively and subliminal effects of adding color to a publication result in no small way from the designer's scrutiny and attention to detail. Color work can be made a little easier by using a tool through which you can apply colors to items and backgrounds, as you might apply styles to text. In keeping with the spirit of the Measurements palette, the Style palette, and the Document layout palette, QuarkXPress provides yet another, the Colors palette, shown in Figure 16.7. Here you can choose colors and shadings for items, frames, pictures, text, and backgrounds.

Figure 16.7 *The Colors palette.*

Most of the controls in this palette function in a straightforward fashion. With the buttons across the top section you choose which aspect of an item will receive the color. The first button on the left at the top applies to the frame of the item selected, the next applies to the text or picture content within the selected box, and the last applies to the background of the box in question. Note that you can select text passages, words, sentences, and so on and apply coloring to these selections. Tint or shading of color is controlled through the drop-down list and field value to the right of the buttons.

Most of the Colors palette is taken up by the scrolling list of colors. As you create and save new colors, they're added here as well. To apply a color, select the object, click one of the three top buttons to indicate which aspect to color, click on a color in the list, and apply a tint if desired through the drop-down list or value field.

Additionally, there is a control for blending background shades and colors. For instance, you could blend the background of a text box from a 50% black to a 10% black horizontally and produce a box that lightened from left to right. Similarly, you can blend from one color, or one color tint to another.

The control for this is engaged by first selecting the item, then choosing **Linear Blend** from the drop-down list below the first row of buttons in the palette. Next you click the round button labeled **#1**, and then choose a color and tint. Then click the round button labeled **#2** and then choose a second color and tint. If the angular value next to these buttons is 0°, you'll see a blend of color and shade from left to right when the item tool is chosen.

When you apply blends to a text box, be sure to select the Item tool in order to view the effect on screen. With the Content tool selected, you may only see text on an standard background. Also blends applied to picture backgrounds may not be immediately visible when the picture is displayed. To make sure you're seeing the blend onscreen, try nudging the picture with the Cropper Grabber Hand (Content tool selected).

N O T E

The Color palette supplies a quick way to create reverse text boxes. For instance, click the **Background** button and choose **black**, and click the **Text** button and choose **white**.

N O T E

Creating a color blend in background

Select the picture or text box with the Item tool

From the drop down list in the Colors palette, chose **Linear Blend**

Click the **#1** button, and then click a color and a shading

Click the **#2** button, and then click a color and a shading

---

Notice that 0° represents the horizontal. You can change this value to 45° for the oblique, or 90° for the vertical, or any other angle within the circle of 360°, and the blend will run in the direction chosen. The blend feature is handy and adds variation to text or picture backgrounds.

Onward

Color can be an elusive goal. What other aspect of publication production demands so much subjective judgment! Fortunately, with the techniques introduced here, you can begin to produce the colors you want from your documents. Experience and familiarity will prove to be the best guides in the long run.

Bringing your documents to print involves much more than color replication. There are factors of font and image usage that become crucial in the actual printing process, whether you're proofing with a laser printer, or sending final output to an imagesetter. This is also where the large formats meet the reality of small paper sizes. And printing long documents can steal away precious eleventh-hour computer time if you let it.

In the next chapter we explore the ways to make your printing flow as smoothly as possible. We'll look at surprise problems that can be avoided. And we'll see how to get the best results regardless of the output device available for your project.

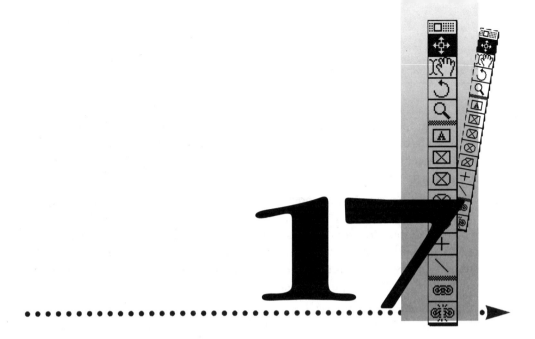

Printing

What you will learn in this chapter:

❖ How to update images
❖ How to track font usage
❖ How to replace font choices
❖ How to output documents to printers
❖ How to automatically collect document data

In printing, the *what-you-see* turns into the *what-you-get*. The print process must successfully translate digital computer files into a film, paper, print, or negative visual master, or all the work of design, layout, typesetting, image adjustment, and so forth, is for nothing.

It sounds so simple, and indeed, printing often requires no more than opening a menu and giving a command. However, it's a little like sailing a ship. When conditions are calm and the course unobstructed, there's smooth sailing. But as the complexity of the document grows, as its form becomes out of the ordinary in any way, as font and picture decisions are made for effective design rather than convenience, the waters may not be so smooth.

In this chapter we're going to look at how you can manage your document files through the sometimes turbulent printing process. We'll see what can be done in advance and how to facilitate the output session. We'll look at font management, picture management, printers, drivers, and dealing with over- and undersized pages.

Checks and Connections

One thing is easily overlooked while a document is being produced: The QuarkXPress program does not act alone. As we're guiding it to lay out and typeset pages, the software calls on other software and files behind the scenes. Several of these lie always within easy reach of the program, within the same folder.

Others are brought in from outside as needed. We introduce some ourselves when we call up a file or insert a disk into the floppy drive. Some of the files used by QuarkXPress are not part of the QuarkXPress software package. But they must be present during printing for our labors to bear fruit. Principal among these are many fonts and graphics files imported into a document.

Image Sources

Consider first large image files we might be using in a document. Scans and elaborate grayscale renderings can occupy large amounts of storage space. When QuarkXPress imports these images, you may remember, it is really importing a screen representation while establishing a link outside the document to the original file. Through this link the program is able to use the graphics file to manage printing of the image at the highest possible resolution.

Now consider just for a moment the things that could happen to complicate this arrangement. When all the information required for printing is contained securely within a single document file, that's one thing. But when QuarkXPress must seek out a graphics file in order to print, well, what if it's been moved? What if an image has been altered in the file, but not on the document? What if the floppy disk from which you imported the image is in a briefcase at 30,000 feet headed for Rome?

To make your printing flawless, you'll want to assure that the sources for all images in the document are available to QuarkXPress when the final print command is given. Note that if you are simply generating laser proofs and picture quality is the least of your concerns, then having the sources at hand for the program is not important. In this case QuarkXPress will use the rendering it uses for screen display. Of course, this is coarser quality, but you may find it acceptable when positioning and cropping are your main concerns.

However, when the time comes to print to the image-setter, or even to print the best possible laser copy, then you'll need to provide the source file to QuarkXPress.

The program tries to keep track of the status of each source for every picture within a document. If a source is moved, QuarkXPress will know. If a source image is modified in some way by outside software, the program knows that, too. You can check on the status for each source, and you can take action to reestablish or update linkages between your document and the source file.

You do both through a single dialog box. To see the status of the document's picture-source files, open the Utilities menu and choose **Picture Usage**. A dialog box similar to the one shown in Figure 17.1 will appear listing the Drive and File path of the source files, the document page on which each is used, file type suffix, and status of the source file.

In Figure 17.1, notice that the status for each of the images on Pages 1, 4, and 21 is **OK**. This means that the program has maintained a link to the files from which these images were imported, and that the images have been unchanged since being imported. QuarkXPress can use the sources without a problem.

However, the status of the Page 8 picture file is Modified. This file was originally imported to the document and later altered in a graphics program. The figure shows how we have used the **Show Me** button to locate this image, **Painter Pict** within the document. To examine a picture on location at the page where it appears, select the file and then click the **Show Me** button. QuarkXPress will scroll through the document to the page where the picture is. This can help you to clarify just which picture is in need of updating or what was the subject of that missing source file.

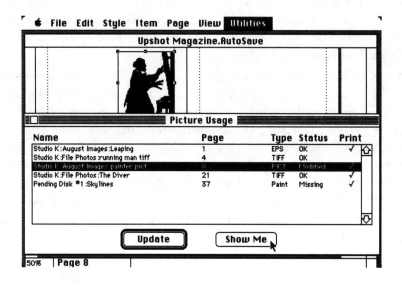

Figure 17.1 *A document's Picture Usage dialog box indicating status of source files and used to locate a picture.*

The picture on Page 37 is listed as Missing; QuarkXPress couldn't locate it. In fact, this image was on a floppy disk, which has since been removed. In this case you might notice that the file path indicates this source file was imported from a different disk, the floppy disk labeled Pending Disk #1. Inadvertently removing a floppy disk source is a particularly easy mistake to make. The other four files associated with this document all derive from the hard drive labeled Studio K, two from the folder, August Images, and two from the folder, File Photos.

A final feature can be of help during printing when large image files are included in the document. The last column, Print, indicates by check marks whether the picture will be printed by QuarkXPress. Notice that all the pictures but one bear check marks in this column. You can switch off a picture selectively here by simply clicking at its check mark. This will suppress the printout of that image. To enable the printout you simply click again to insert a check mark.

Updating

To make sure all the sources are in order and up to date, you'll need to use the **Update** button. Select the file you want to update by clicking on it. Or select several files by the **Shift-click** or **Command-click** methods. Then click on **Update**. All questionable files will be addressed individually in the dialog boxes that appear in turn. In the case of a Modified file, a confirmation dialog box will appear. Click **OK**, and the new source file is linked to the document. In the case of a Missing file, a dialog box asks you to locate the file. You use it just as you would an Open dialog box.

Updating picture sources

At the Utilities menu, choose **Picture Usage**

At the dialog box, select the missing or modified file and click the **Update** button

Follow directions as they are displayed

Fonts in a Document

If there is any one support on which all of desktop publishing rests, it is the availability of fonts. Electronic typefaces are a high form of graphic unequaled in their ability to change the look, effectiveness, mood, and subliminal message of a layout. They are a constantly shifting foundation, however, as new fonts are added and new formats of fonts evolve.

In this commercial arena, a variety of contenders vie for market position. For instance, a current standard has developed around fonts in the Adobe PostScript format. That one type of font should be standard is more an indication of history and marketing placement than of any inherent superiority. Other fine fonts are available from other vendors; among them are the TrueType fonts.

How the Program Deals with Fonts

In some ways, QuarkXPress treats fonts as it does graphics files. Let's consider Adobe fonts for the moment. Generally, they can be displayed on screen only if the font file is present. A file must also be present for printing. It used to be that you needed a font file for each size you wanted to be able to see on your monitor. However, Adobe developed a program that could work in conjunction with desktop publishing, word processing, and other software to produce screen representations of fonts at any size from files of just one font size. This is Adobe Type Manager or ATM.

If you're using Adobe or other PostScript fonts for serious desktop publishing, you are almost certainly using ATM, or a program like it. This program works in the background to assist with printing, as well. To add or remove Adobe fonts, you can start the ATM control panel program, which would reside on your hard drive. Operation is quite simple. You select from a list of fonts in either adding or removing. Having the font files present during printing is essential. Otherwise often ugly substitutions of other fonts are likely.

TrueType fonts can also be added or removed. In fact, similar font installer/removers can be found. Some TrueType fonts can also be imbedded within a document file, so that during printing the document itself provides the font information. This is sure to simplify font and document management as it becomes more common.

Keeping Track of Fonts

Currently, the odds are very good that you'll need to assure the proper fonts are available when printing occurs. Of course, if printing means outputting the document to a laser printer directly from the same computer system you used to create and lay it out, there should be no problem with fonts.

However, if you're sending your file out to a pre-press shop or service bureau for output from their system, watch out! The number and variety of fonts each carries can vary. You would be surprised at how an otherwise thorough shop can be missing that one font you were sure they would have on hand. Even within your own office or studio, you may find that when you move your file to another computer, a different set of fonts may reside on it. These differences, by the way, are not usually obvious. Often just one or two fonts are different or missing.

One wise approach to take in dealing with fonts and your documents is this: make a list of the fonts used in the document. This sounds simple until you start to go through, page by page, trying to note every special heading or, harder still, all the special fonts within the main body text. However, QuarkXPress can do all this automatically. Remember the expanded Find/Change dialog box for dealing with text style revisions? The program presents a similar dialog box whose main purpose is to identify or change fonts already applied in the document.

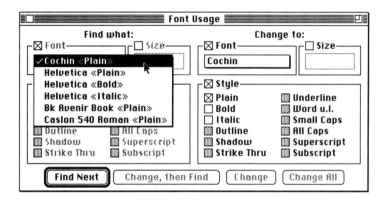

Figure 17.2 *Using a document's Font Usage dialog box to get a list of active fonts.*

To use this feature, open the Utilities menu and choose **Font Usage**. A dialog box will appear. To see a list of every font used within the document, click on the arrow for the drop-down list next to **Font Name** field. You'll see a list of fonts, as shown in Figure 17.2. Preceding each font name, in angle brackets, you'll notice an indication of the style of font present in the document, if the font appears in bold, italic, or plain text. Should one appear in more than one of these styles, then the list will show each style with font name. You can make a note of these. Or you can use the methods for screen capture to provide an instant visual file of the dialog box.

Collecting a list of fonts in a document

At the Utilities menu, choose **Font Usage**

At the dialog box, open the drop-down list at the **Font** field

---

You can use this dialog box to make changes throughout the document. Say you just gained access to the Avenir book font and you want to replace the recurring font, Cochin, in your completed document with it. Following the same procedure as with the expanded Find/Change dialog box, you can make that change in one operation.

Replacing fonts document wide

At the Utilities menu, choose **Font Usage**

At the dialog box, select font and style to be replaced under **Find What**

Select new font and style under **Change To**

N O T E

This dialog box may prove a bit sluggish in displaying current font collection after a change. To be sure you're seeing a current list of fonts after making a change, close the dialog box, by clicking on the close button in the upper-left of the box, and then reopen it from the menu. The newly opened dialog box should accurately reflect the font status of your document.

Readying a Print

Of course, you're going to need to send the QuarkXPress file somewhere in order to get a physical print of the document. Use the Printer Setup dialog box to select the printer and specify how you want the print session to proceed. You can bring up this dialog box by opening the File menu and choosing **Page Setup**.

In the dialog box shown in Figure 17.3 you'll find a heading for Printer Type in which you can prepare QuarkXPress's output through software to the printer of your choice. Orientation boxes and **Paper Radio** buttons relate to printer logistics.

Clicking the **Options** button in this dialog leads to another dialog depending on the printer driver in your system. For a LaserWriter printer for instance, The Image box allows for mirror images, **Flip Horizontal** and **Flip Vertical**, and for a negative image, **Invert**. Note that if you're working with the same printer repeatedly, you need only check the printer set-up initially, and thereafter you can leave it alone until the occasion calls for some variation.

This is a good time to check that all systems are "go" at the printer itself: paper, film, trays in place, cables connected, and power on.

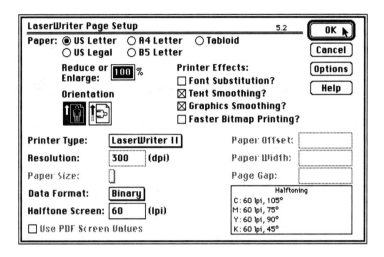

Figure 17.3   *The Printer Setup dialog box.*

To Print

Another gauntlet of choices seems to present itself the first time you open the Print dialog box from the File menu. Will this never end? In fact, the choices before you seldom need all be considered together. As with the Printer Setup dialog box, often when you're doing simple proofing you can find a set of specifications that works, and then use it until there is reason to change. This may mean simply choosing the **Print** command and clicking **OK** immediately at the dialog box.

At times you'll want more control than is already established in the Print specifications. For instance, you can print multiple copies of a document. To do so, simply type in the number in the **Copies** field of the Print dialog box, as shown in Figure 17.4. If your work is focusing on a portion of the document, you can print a range of pages rather than the entire document. Click the **Pages** button to the left of **From**, and key in the starting and concluding pages you want.

Another useful option allows printing of just the odd or even pages. If you're doing a mock-up of a double-sided publication on your proofing printer, you can first order the printing of odd **Pages** button, gather the printed pages, turn them over, reinsert in your paper feeder, and then issue the **Print** command for even pages only. You'll have a double-sided printed document. The control for this is found in a drop-down list under the heading Page Sequence.

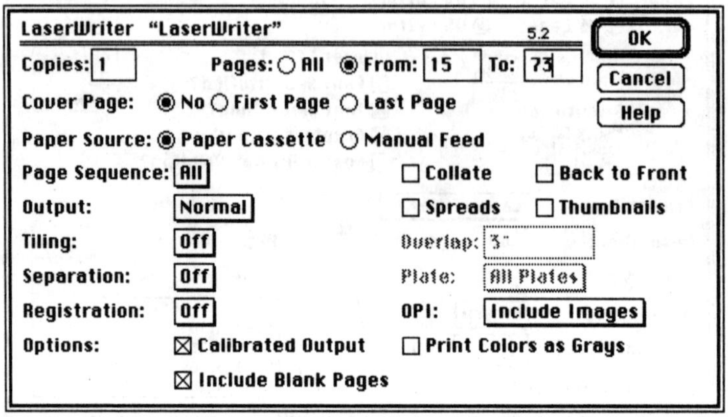

```
LaserWriter  "LaserWriter"                         5.2      OK
Copies: 1          Pages: ○ All  ◉ From: 15  To: 73
Cover Page:  ◉ No ○ First Page ○ Last Page               Cancel
Paper Source: ◉ Paper Cassette  ○ Manual Feed             Help
Page Sequence: All            □ Collate      □ Back to Front
Output:       Normal          □ Spreads      □ Thumbnails
Tiling:       Off             Overlap: 3"
Separation:   Off             Plate:  All Plates
Registration: Off             OPI:    Include Images
Options:      ⊠ Calibrated Output  □ Print Colors as Grays
              ⊠ Include Blank Pages
```

Figure 17.4   *The Print dialog box.*

Printing a double-sided document

At the Print dialog box, open the Page Sequence list and choose **Odd**

Print as usual

Turn the pages over and reinsert in the paper feeder

At the Print dialog box, open the Page Sequence list and choose **Even**

Print as usual

If you want your computer system to do the paper shuffling instead of doing it yourself, you may want to click an **x** in the **Back to Front** checkbox. Similarly, if you're doing multiple copies and you want each set grouped together into a document, then be sure to click an **x** into **Collate**.

Note that in running color separations, the printer staff needs to know how to align each of the color plates. Opening the Registration drop-down list provides the choice of guides in the form of small crosses within circles in the margins of each separation. From these marks, alignment can be controlled for each color printing. Engaging this feature also provides crop marks for trimming excess paper from a page format smaller than the paper format. Open the Registration list and choose **Off Center** if you're concerned that the printers might inadvertently rotate your separation plates upside down.

How do you get a 48-inch-square document page out of a letter-size capacity laser printer? The answer is that it comes in pieces. By opening the Tiling drop-down list in the dialog box and choosing **Automatic**, you can turn on QuarkXPress's ability to section a large on-screen image into a tiled mosaic with a specified overlap.

You can also manually tile pages one at a time. First, at the document window, drag the zero-point crosshairs from the upper-left corner of where the rulers meet, to the point you want to serve as upper-left in that tile. Then, at the dialog box, click on **Manual**. The page will print. Repeat this process until the entire page is printed in pieces.

The heading for the list on Separations allows for choosing **On** to is engage color separations for printing. You can also specify that colors be printed as the corresponding shade of gray, by clicking an **x** into that checkbox. At the Output list is another route to printing simulated proofs. Here, click on the **Rough** button to have pictures print as boxed **x**'s.

Of course, the actual print command for all these specifications is initiated by clicking the **OK** button.

Tiling a page

On the document page point, assure that the rulers are showing

Click at the crosshairs where the rulers meet, and drag to upper-left of desired tile

At the Print dialog box, click to engage the **Manual** choice at the Tiling list

Proceed as usual for printing a single page, clicking the **OK** button

Repeat the process for each section of the page

NOTE If you need to change or upgrade your printer connections, you'll encounter another feature. Note that QuarkXPress and the system work through software installed specifically for each output, or print, device. These are known as *printer drivers.* If you add a different type or model of printer to your system, chances are you'll need to install specific printer driver software.

Collecting Document Data

QuarkXPress provides a feature that will produce a report you can use as a checklist for printing at a off-site location. This function will compile virtually all the details about graphics imported, fonts used, hyphenation and justification settings, style sheets, and document dimensions.

All this data is useful, and sometimes vital, for services that output or print your documents. And to help you met deadlines, this report—which takes the form of a text file—can assure you that you've supplied all the files needed by your document.

To create the report, wait until your final save of the document. Then open the File menu and choose **Collect** for Output. You'll be presented with a dialog box for naming and saving the report.

Onward

Printing, a final step in the desktop publishing process, is crucial on any job, whether it is an 11th-hour final film output or a page proof of your layout in development. Fonts, pictures, and document requirements still need attention at this point. Using the update techniques shown in this chapter makes achieving successful printing a relatively straightforward matter. Of course there will always be surprises. But adaptation is the key to improvement.

You've come nearly full circle now, from the original idea or sketch to finished pages. Your journeys through the processes of QuarkXPress have shown you what is possible and how. What you do with these skills will speak volumes.

There are often faster, more powerful ways of achieving your goals. The last chapter presents special tips, shortcuts, and parting advice for producing better documents more easily with QuarkXPress.

Beyond the Usual Methods

What you will learn in this chapter:

- ❖ Keyboard shortcuts
- ❖ How to access instant views
- ❖ How to select through layers
- ❖ How to make one-stroke hanging indents
- ❖ Finding and using special character sets
- ❖ Setting defaults and preferences

369

Acquire some skills in anything, and more possibilities present themselves. In QuarkXPress, there is no end to the possibilities. The methods and techniques you've encountered and learned to use will springboard you to new levels of skill. If you've used preceding chapters to teach yourself QuarkXPress, consider now how you'll benefit from a few well-chosen refinements.

The aim of this book has been dual: to make you proficient with QuarkXPress techniques while giving you a special mastery of desktop publishing. Showing how things work in this environment has led, in this plan, to showing how to perform essential tasks and how to build unified documents. These methods and examples have been devoted to showing you ways to design and produce practical projects with an elegant software.

This chapter presents shortcuts and suggestions for working with QuarkXPress. It provides a few of the best tips that go beyond the methods presented in previous chapters. Some people call these *power techniques*. We'll uncover ways to save time and improve the product—from producing graphics with your keyboard to presetting program defaults.

Keyboard Shortcuts

When you perform certain procedures frequently, it's natural to want to accelerate performance. Throughout most of this book we've explored the straightforward ways of carrying out tasks in QuarkXPress. By this point, though, perhaps you've identified some techniques you'd like to streamline.

Shortcuts always seem like a great idea at first glance. But they usually impose a price of their own. Sometimes this price is small in return for speeded operation; that's a question of judgment. In accelerating your software proficiency, you may have to remember some offbeat sequence or keystroke. This is hardly a problem when certain procedures come up repeatedly.

But if you've ever taken just a two-week break from a familiar piece of software, you'll know that you can find yourself fumbling to recall certain arcane key combinations that seemed second nature at the time. Another problem—one that this author faces frequently—is switching among a large number of software programs that perform similar functions. The shortcut that works in one may do something completely different in another.

Again, the key to shortcuts is deciding which to learn and which to pass over.

Command Key Shortcuts

The most obvious shortcuts are the Command (⌘) keystroke equivalents of the menu commands. You can find these listed opposite each command when you open a menu. Their form is easily understood. Each command that has a keystroke equivalent will operate when the **Command** key is held down while some other key (or keys) is pressed. For instance, as you've seen you can give the **Cut** command by using the keystroke, **Command-X**—the keystroke abbreviated to the right of the command. These keystrokes exist for somewhat less than half of the menu commands.

Momentary Item Tool

When you're using the Content tool, you may often find yourself needing to use the Item tool for just a moment. For instance, you might want to drag a text box to a new location before continuing to edit the contents.

You can momentarily invoke the Item tool when the Content tool is selected by holding down the **Command** key. You'll see the mouse cursor change to a Four-Arrow tool. Then you can press the mouse button and drag the box to a new location. When you release the **Command** key, the Content tool is once again in force.

Quick switching from Content to Item tool

Hold down the Command key, and proceed as with Item tool

Release to reactivate Content tool

Text Sizing

As you know, the Measurements palette provides a convenient alternative to opening the Style menu to change the size of selected text. However, an even quicker method is available through the keyboard. This method is limited to the size increments available in the drop-down size listing of either the Measurements palette or Style menu; but it's fast.

To increase the font size from the keyboard to the next higher increment, hold down the **Command** and **Shift** keys and press the right-angle bracket key, >. To reduce the size, hold down **Command** and **Shift** and press the left-angle bracket key, <.

Sizing text by keystrokes

Select text and hold down **Command** and **Shift** keys

Press > key to enlarge, < to reduce

Text Box Resizing

One of the most dazzling approaches to manipulating text involves resizing it by directly adjusting its text box. In this method you treat the text as a purely graphic item. To understand this operation, recall that holding the **Command** key while dragging a picture box handle resizes the image content along with the box. Applying the same approach to a text box will resize all the text within the box.

The technique is similar: with either the Item or Content tool selected, you press the **Command** key and grab a box handle (the pointing finger appears), then drag the box to a new size and proportion. If you drag immediately, the outline of the box will move with the drag. If you wait a moment after grabbing the handle until the box flashes, the text inside the box will be seen to expand and contract with the drag. In either case, the text will be readjusted to the new box size. That is, it will be made larger, smaller, wider, narrower, taller, shorter as determined by the change in box dimensions.

Text resizing

Command-drag on a text box handle

(Wait for flash to make text resizing real-time)

Behind the obvious razzle-dazzle of this effect, QuarkXPress is actually adjusting three type features in order to keep up with the box change. And whether the text within a box is of uniform or differing formatting and styling to begin with, the program will adjust each character proportionally in these three features. The features modified include text size, horizontal scaling, and vertical scaling.

You can keep the same proportions of text and text box by holding down the **Option** and **Shift** keys while Command-dragging.

> **Text Proportional Resizing**
>
> **Command-Option-Shift-Drag** on a text box handle
> (Wait for flash to make text resizing real-time)

Click Zooming

Without a doubt, two of the most useful views are Actual Size and Fit in Window. Adjusting items life-size, then pulling back to look at the whole page (spread) is frequently called for during page layout. In addition, magnifying quickly to say 200% is often important when placing items precisely. Using the menu, you can switch between these views by choosing commands. But you can see that **Command-0** at the keyboard will force a Fit in Window view.

You could likewise use **Command-1** to force an Actual Size view. Switching back and forth like this will display the entire page, then an actual size view. The area shown at actual size will depend on what has been set up. If an item is selected, actual size will center on that item. Otherwise, the actual size will revert to the previous actual size view.

However, there is another way you can use size changes to control movement around the page or spread. By pointing with the mouse cursor and then clicking while holding down the **Option** and **Command** keys, you will force the view to 200% on the first click, then to 100% on the second click. By using the tool as a centering pointer, you can position any part of the Fit in Window view in the center of the Actual or 200% views. So, rather than move across a spread with the grabber hand, it's often faster to simply give a **Command-0** keystroke, putting the whole spread into Fit in Window view, then to locate the part of interest with the Mouse tool, and click back to 200%, or 100% view.

N O T E

If you continue to **Command-Option-Click**, you'll toggle between 100% and 200% views.

Centering views with the mouse

From any view, position the cursor at desired center
Command-Option-Click to 200%
Command-Option-Click again to Actual Size

Selecting Through Layers

If your layout calls for items of about the same size to be layered, or for many items to be layered all in a pile, you will probably encounter the inconvenience and frustration of being unable to reach a particular item to make some modification. The tedious solution is to move items out of the way, sending them to the back in a revised stacking order. Then after making the modifications, you restack the items in their original layering order.

But there is a better way. With either Item or Content tool selected, hold down **Command-Option-Shift** at the keyboard. Point at the stack and click once for each layer you want to descend. Items within the stack will become selected singly, one after the other, from the top down. They will not move out of stacking order, but will simply become accessible. After you've selected the appropriate item, you can proceed as usual, while you modify it.

Selecting through the layered items in a stack

Hold **Command-Option-Shift** and point into the stack
Click once to select the topmost item, click again for each
    backward layer

Simple, Direct Word Counting

There is a simple way to get a word count from QuarkXPress; it's easy to use, but it is obscureas we've seen. To determine the number of words in a story, use the Spelling feature.

Here's how it works: Put the text cursor in the story. Open the Utilities menu and choose **Spelling**. Then at the submenu, choose **Story**. Before actually checking spelling, the program will present an informational dialog box indicating the total number of words, the number that appears only once, and the number that the spell checker cannot match with its list. Click **OK**, and the Check Story dialog box will appear. If you don't care to run the spelling check, simply click **Cancel**.

Running a word count

Insert the text cursor

Open the Utilities menu, choose **Spelling**, then **Story**

Quick Page Moves

The **Up** and **Down Arrow** keys can be made to do more than on-line shifts in QuarkXPress. To move the cursor one paragraph using the keyboard, hold the **Command** key while pressing either **Arrow** key. The screen will respond accordingly, moving the cursor to the beginning of the paragraph behind it, or to the beginning of the paragraph ahead of it.

Moving through pages by keyboard

Command-Up Arrow and **Command-Down Arrow** for paragraph moves

Command-Left Arrow for beginning of story

Command-Right Arrow for end of story

In similar fashion, you can move to the beginning of a story or the end by holding the **Command** key as you press the left arrow or right arrow, respectively.

One-Step Hanging Indents

We've discussed ways to adjust paragraphs from the Paragraph Formats and Tabs dialog boxes, including establishing hanging indents. There is a direct, character-based method for hanging indents. It requires simply that you place a hidden character to serve as a marker. Under this invisible marker the remainder of a paragraph will indent. You can put this marker in the first, second, or a later line, and the lines following it in the paragraph will indent under it.

To create an instant hanging indent this way, insert the text cursor within the line above those you wish to indent, at the point where they ought to indent. Hold down the **Command** key and press the backslash key, \. The rest of the paragraph's lines below this will indent immediately.

Inserting a hang-below character

Position cursor in line above desired indent line

Key in **Command-**

This creates an invisible character whose effect will be applied until the character is removed. To remove it, select the space at which you've inserted it and press Backspace.

N O T E

Note also that if you move the characters on that line so that the invisible "indent here" character moves too, then all the lines below in the paragraph will move to the new indent position, following the marker.

Adding Typographers' Quotes, Common Marks, and Symbols

If you are typing in QuarkXPress and choose to type in quotes, they will appear in nonspecific typewriter fashion (") as you type from the keyboard. For typographically standard open quotes with most fonts, hold the **Option** key while typing the open bracket ([ ). For comparable closed quotes type **Option-Shift-[.**

Following the same approach, you can produce registered marks (**Option-r**), copyright marks (**Option-g**), and bullets (**Option-8**).

The Macintosh offers a similar scheme with full alternate character sets that can be typed through the **Option** key and the keyboard. The exact characters produced may depend on the font chosen. But in each case the method is to hold down the **Option** or the **Option-Shift** keys while typing a standard key.

Producing alternate character sets

Hold down the **Option** key (or **Option** and **Shift** keys) and press a standard key

---

You can view these character sets through a desk accessory that is standard on the system. (As you may know, desk accessories are miniprograms available through the Apple menu at the extreme left of the menu bar.) The accessory to use for alternate character sets is Key Caps. Pressing down the **Option** key in Key Caps will display the characters that will be produced in conjunction with it.

You can remember the keystroke, then retype it back at the QuarkXPress text box. Or you can click on the character you want in Key Caps, then copy it from the Edit menu. Returning to the text box, you can then paste in the copied characters.

Setting Defaults and Preferences

Throughout earlier chapters we've encountered the effects of defaults and preference settings. You've seen how changing the settings in preferences will change defaults for the document that's open at the time. But as you work you'll want to begin from a set of preferences that match your approach to projects.

The Application Preferences dialog box is reached through the Edit menu, and resets certain defaults for the program. These apply whenever it is run subsequently. The other four Preferences dialog boxes—General, Typographic, Trapping, and Tools—also reached through the Edit menu, apply only to those documents open at the time of resetting.

You can establish the defaults to be in effect whenever the program is started. To do so, simply clear the program window of any document windows by closing all open documents. Then set up the specifications in each Preference dialog box and exit the program immediately without opening a document. When you next start QuarkXPress the newly set preferences will be in effect for all new documents.

Setting start-up defaults for any preference

With QuarkXPress running, assure that all documents are closed

Set up specifications under the Edit menu, Preferences

Exit the program

Where To?

You had some goal when you first picked up this book—perhaps to acquire enough skills to complete your project at hand; perhaps to gain a solid grounding of skills in software destined to be your constant work companion for years to come; perhaps to gain a firmer grasp of desktop publishing. If you've come though the previous chapters, you've hopefully arrived here, in control of dozens of now-familiar tools. Probably you have a much wider reach with which to execute many more design and layout decisions.

This book attempts to show and pass onto you the controls of QuarkXPress. It also demonstrates practical methods for using these tools. Your work may be like many others in the background of a publication or multimedia production. But remember that readers and viewers appreciate your well-attended efforts. Extra effort and attention to detail makes a difference that shows. I believe that using QuarkXPress can only improve your results in the long run.

Your enhanced proficiency need not end here. One certainty in the technology of publishing and design is that no one knows it all. No one source can tell it all. If your goal calls for you to seek out other sources, by all means proceed. You'll find a few select recommendations in Appendix B.

If this book has encouraged you to look further into the program to see how to do something you've never tried before, it has served a noble purpose. Experimentation is the best way for you to find what works best. You will be the final judge of of what works and what doesn't.

As QuarkXPress is becoming second nature to you, now is the time to let your own energy, spirit, and experience show through your projects. It will be the sincere pleasure of this author to help you teach yourself this program. Hundreds of clients and trainees have taken away skills and advice from my workshops and training seminars, but I never tire of hearing from them. I invite you to join them in sharing your thoughts and experiences about QuarkXPress, the book, or publishing and design. You may write to me at Studio K, Box 3562, San Diego, California 92163, or care of the publisher. There are always new workshops and new books. I invite you to look for them.

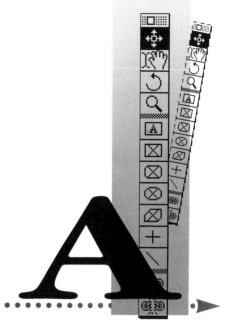

QuarkXPress Methods At-a-Glance

In the chapters you'll find the full explanations of the methods and techniques for using the program. In this appendix you'll find the At-a-Glance summaries for 112 of those methods. All are listed according to the chapters in which they appear. They provide a ready reference to the chapter context in which each summary emerges.

Chapter 2

Moving an object in the Macintosh

Select with click

Drag to new location

Release

Scrolling window views

Click Scroll Bar arrow

or

Drag scroll bar box

or

Click in scroll bar outside box

Sizing objects

Position pointer (on side or corner handle) until it becomes a sizing tool

Drag to new shape and size

Chapter 3

Starting QuarkXPress

Locate QuarkXPress icon

Double-click on it

Viewing pasteboard with pages

Option + Fit in window

Precision percentage views

Double-click value in percentage view display

Key in new percentage

Return key

Selecting tools from the keyboard

Command-Tab to move downward through buttons, or to show palette

Command-Shift-Tab to move upward

Modifying through Measurements palette

Select Item & Locate attribute in palette

Highlight attribute value & type in new value

or

Select new value from drop-down list

Press **Return**

Magnifying view with Zoom tool

Position tool over point to anchor

Click repeatedly until magnification is achieved

Reducing view with Zoom tool

Position tool over point to anchor

Hold **Option** key and click repeatedly until reduction is achieved

Precision magnification with Zoom tool

Choose rectangular area to magnify

Position Zoom tool at one corner

Drag diagonally to create enclosing box

Release

Using the Grabber Hand tool

With any tool but the Zoom selected, hold the **Option** key

Press mouse button and drag page through window view

Using the Selecting box

With Item tool drag a box to enclose any part of item(s)

Positioning with the Measurements palette

Select item

Key in new location as **X** and **Y** values

Selecting scattered items

Hold **Shift** key and click on each item

(De-select with second click)

Selecting a range of pages in Document Layout

Click on page at one end of range

Scroll to other end in Document Layout

Hold **Shift** key and click on page at other end

Selecting scattered pages in Document Layout

Hold **Command** key and click on each page

(De-select with second click)

Moving to adjacent pages by Grabber Hand tool

Hold **Option** key and drag pages through window view

up to higher numbers

down to lower

sideways on spreads

Moving to a page by Document Layout

In the palette scroll to locate page icon

Double-click to bring page into window

Moving items to distant pages in the document

Select item(s) and at Edit menu choose **Cut**

Locate destination page

At Edit menu choose **Paste**

Chapter 4

Making a text box

Choose Text Box tool

Choose rectangular area in which to place box

Position Text Box tool at one corner of chosen area

Drag diagonally until box fits area chosen

Clipboard text transfers

Select the text with Content tool and at the Edit menu choose **Cut** or **Copy**

Select the recipient text box with Content tool

(Set insertion cursor or selection if necessary)

At the Edit menu choose **Paste**

Importing text

Assure that text box is selected with Content tool active

At File menu choose **Get Text**

Select file in dialog listings

Exporting text

Assure that text box is selected with Content tool active or a selection of text is highlighted

At File menu choose **Save Text**

Click Entire Story or **Selected Text** button

Select file format in dialog listings

Name text and choose destination

Selecting text by powerstrokes

Use the Content tool to do the following

One word: double-click

One line: triple-click

One paragraph: quadruple-click

Kerning at the Text palette

Position I-beam text cursor between letters

Use Palette arrows for incremental changes (10 units each)

or

Key in kern value and press **Enter**

Adjusting columns at the palette

Select text box with either Item or Content tool

Select value in **Cols:** field at palette

Key in new value and press **Enter**

Chapter 5

Using the Grabber Hand tool

With any tool but the Zoom selected, hold the **Option** key

Press mouse button and drag page through window view

Basic QuarkXPress character codes

New line	**\n**
New paragraph	**\p**
Tab	**\t**

Quick copying between documents

Display both documents concurrently (View menu, Windows list, **Tile**)

Select item in source document window

Drag to destination document window and release

Word counting through spell checking

Put the cursor in the story of interest

Open the Utilities menu and open the Check Spelling list

Note the count and click **OK**

When the Check Story dialog box appears click **Cancel**

Chapter 6

Importing a graphic

Activate a Picture Box tool and draw a box

Assure the Content tool is selected

At the File menu choose **Get Picture**

Locate the graphic file in the dialog box and double-click

Making a Polygon Picture box

Using the Polygon tool, click at each angle in turn

Return to the first click point and double-click

Using the picture grabber tool

Position the Content tool over the picture box

Drag the image through the window

Reshaping, resizing the picture image

Command-drag the picture box handles

Instant fitting of image within picture box

Command-Shift-F

Instant fitting of image proportionally within picture box

Command-Shift-Option-F

Reversing type

Select text

Open Specifications dialog box, set background to Black, 100%

Open Style menu, choosing **Color** as **White**

Using the Rotation tool

Select the box

Click a fulcrum point

Drag out a rotation lever

Pull the lever around the point

Creating a guideline

Assure that the rulers are displayed

Point on the rule, oriented as the guideline will be, and drag out a line

Establishing text runaround

Assure the Runaround item is selected and above the text layer

At the Item menu choose **Runaround**, select the Mode and set the offset spacing

Adjusting a manual image

Drag the side or handle into place

Add or remove handles by Command-click

Establishing a text chain

Using the Linking tool click on the first box in the chain

Click on every other box in order

Linking a text box in an existing text chain

Using the Linking tool click on the box before the insertion point

Click on the new text box

Breaking a text chain

Select the Unlinking tool

Click on an arrowhead or tailfeather

Removing one box from a text chain

Select the Unlinking tool

Shift-click on the unwanted box

Chapter 7

Pulling a guide that extends across a spread

Point the cursor in the Horizontal ruler above the pasteboard

Pull directly down

Momentarily switching to the Item tool

With any but the Zoom tool engaged, hold down the **Command** key

Instant opening of the Specifications dialog box

Using the Item tool, select and double-click on the item

Scaling a box proportionately by sight

Draw a line through and beyond the opposite corners of the box

Or create and position an empty picture box with diagonals showing through Show Guides

Resize the box by dragging one corner along the line

Converting a picture box shape

Select the box

Open the Item menu, then the **Box Shape** submenu, and select the replacement shape from the list of shapes

Adjusting a polygon picture box

To change the shape of the box, drag an angle point or side

To add an angle point, point along a side and **Command-click**

To remove an angle point, point over an existing point and **Command-click**

Locating nonprinting character codes in text

Open the View menu and choose **Show Invisibles**

Adjusting indents

Select the paragraph(s)

Call up the Paragraph Formats dialog box, locating the ruler above the paragraph)(s)

Slide the triangular markers into place as follows: first-line indent, small top marker; left-indent, small bottom marker;

right-indent, large marker
Or, key values into corresponding fields

Creating hanging indents

In the Paragraph Formats dialog box, drag the left indent over
Drag the first line indent back leftward of the left indent

Chapter 9

Finding the midpoint

Drag a box between two extremes
The item handles at the sides will fall at the midpoint

Chapter 10

Applying a master page through the Document Layout

At the Document Layout palette, select the page or pages
Press **Option** while clicking on the master page

Moving to a master page

Open the Page menu and choose **Display**
At the submenu, choose the master page
or
At the Document Layout, double-click on the master page icon

Locking items

Select the items
Open Item menu and choose **Lock**

Adjusting position or size of a locked item

Select the item

Enter new values in the Measurements palette

Adding a master page

At the Document Layout palette, drag a Plain Master Page icon down into the Master Page list

Move the arrow cursor into position on the list and release button

Removing a master page

At the Document Layout palette, click to select the master page icon

Click the **Delete** button

Changing the format of a master page

At the Document Layout palette, click to select the master page

Option click the replacement master format

Renaming a master page

At the Document Layout palette, click on the name next to the master page

Key in the new name

Establishing automatic page numbering

At the master page, prepare a text box

Press **Command-3**

Applying a style sheet to text

Select the paragraph(s) with the Content tool, or insert cursor

At the Style Sheets palette, click on the style sheet

or

At the Style menu, choose **Style Sheets**, then select the desired style sheet

Importing style sheets

Open the Edit menu and choose **Style Sheets**

At the Style Sheets dialog box, click the **Append** button

In the dialog box that appears, locate the document containing desired style sheets and double-click

Creating a style from a text selection

Select the model text

Open the Style Sheets dialog box and choose **New**

At the Edit Style Sheets dialog box, key in a name, and click the **OK** button

At the Style Sheets dialog box, click **Save**

Basing one style sheet on another

Proceed as usual, creating a new style sheet or editing an existing one

In the Edit Style Sheets dialog box, open the Based On drop-down list and choose an existing style sheet

Grouping items

To group items, select them all.

Then open the Item menu and choose **Group**.

Anchoring a graphic or text box in line with text

Select the item with the Item tool

Copy or cut it

Use the Content tool to click an active cursor in the text line

Paste it

Creating special drop caps and graphic inserts

Anchor the item as usual and select it with the Item tool

Open the Item menu and choose **Modify**

At **Align with Text**, click on **Ascent**

Expanding a page spread

At the Document Layout palette, select a master page

Drag the cursor to the outside of the spread icons and click

Sectioning pages

Select the first page of the section

Open the Pages menu and choose **Section**

Click an **x** into the **Section Start** checkbox

Make other modifications in the dialog box to suit the section

Creating automatic jump lines

Use the text box tool and make a small text box after the story text box is created

Key in the continuation notice excepting the page number

For a "jump to" notice, key **Command-4**; for a "jump from" notice, key **Command-2**

Drag the jump box until it overlaps the text box

Chapter 12

Adjusting an image to original contrast

Select picture with Content tool active

Open the Style menu and choose **Normal Contrast**

Adjusting an image to black and white contrast

Select picture with Content tool active

Open the Style menu and choose **High Contrast**

Adjusting an image to stepped contrast

Select picture with Content tool active

Open the Style menu and choose **Posterized**

Making a custom adjustment of contrast

Select the picture with Content tool active

Open the Style menu and choose **Other Contrast**

At the dialog box use the first five tools to draw or modify a contrast graph

Use the last four tools and buttons to apply or invert a contrast graph

Click the **Apply** button and revise as necessary, repeat as needed

Applying preset halftone screening to an image

Select picture with Content tool active

Open the Style menu and choose one of the screens in the lowest box

Chapter 14

Duplicate drags between documents

Bring both document windows into view

In the source document select the items

Drag them across the window boundaries into the destination document and release mouse in position

Moving duplicate pages within a document using thumbnails

Select the pages by clicking, **Shift**-clicking, or **Command-clicking**

Drag to new location and release

Copying pages between documents

Select each document in turn and choose thumbnails from the View menu

At the source document window select the pages by clicking **Shift**-clicking, or **Command**-clicking

Drag into the destination window and release

Chapter 15

Creating a library

Open the File menu and submenu **New**, choose **Library**

Proceed to locate a place for the file through the folder windows,

Key in a name

Click the **Create** button

Opening a library

Open the File menu and choose **Open**

At the dialog box, proceed to locate the file through the folder windows, or key in the name

Click the **Open** button

Using items between documents and libraries

Position the windows of both in the program window

Click on the source window to activate it, then, and the item(s)

Drag to the other window and release to copy the item there

Positioning entries within a library

While dragging the item(s) note the appearance of double triangles

When the triangles mark the desired insert point release

Naming library entries

Double-click on the entry to call up the Library Entry dialog box

Key in the name

Click **OK**

Saving formatting information in an ASCII text file

Place the cursor within, or select, the text to be exported

At the File menu choose **Save Text**

At the dialog box use the drop-down list to choose **XPress Tags**

Click **OK**

Capturing a screen image

Prepare the screen as desired

Press **Command-Shift-3**

Chapter 16

Producing a color

At the edit menu, choose **Colors**

At the dialog box, click **New**

Use the Mouse tool to click at a color on the color wheel

Or

Type in values of percentage of each color in the field boxes

Or

Use the sliders to combine colors

Monitor the resulting color at the color bar

Click **OK** at the Edit Color dialog box, then **Save** at the Color
dialog box

Preparing colors for separation

In the Edit Color dialog box, display the color to be separated

Click an X into the **Process Separation** checkbox

Prior to printing in the Print dialog box, choose **On** in the
Separations drop-down list.

Creating a color blend in background

Select the picture or text box with the Item tool

From the drop-down list in the Colors palette, choose **Linear
Blend**

Click the **#1** button, click a color and a shading

Click the **#2** button, click a color and a shading

Chapter 17

Updating picture sources

At the Utilities menu, choose **Picture Usage**

At the dialog box, select the missing or modified file and click the **Update** button

Follow directions as they are displayed

Collecting a list of fonts in a document

At the Utilities menu, choose **Font Usage**

At the dialog box, open the drop-down list at the **Font** field

Replacing fonts document wide

At the Utilities menu, choose **Font Usage**

At the dialog box, select font and style to be replaced under **Find What**

Select new font and style under **Change To**

Printing a double-sided document

At the Print dialog box, open the Page Sequence list and choose **Odd**

Print as usual

Turn the pages over and reinsert in the paper feeder

At the Print dialog box, open the Page Sequence list and choose **Even**

Print as usual

Tiling a page

On the document page point, assure that the rulers are showing

Click at the crosshairs where the rulers meet, and drag to upper left of desired tile

At the Print dialog box, click to engage the **Manual** choice at the Tiling list

Proceed as usual for printing a single page, clicking the **OK** button

Repeat the process for each section of the page

Chapter 18

Quick switching from content to Item tool

Hold down the Command key, and proceed as with Item tool
Release to reactivate Content tool

Sizing text by keystrokes

Select text and hold down **Command** and **Shift keys**
Press > key to enlarge, < to reduce

Text Box Resizing

Command-drag on a text box handle
(Wait for flash to make text resizing real-time)

Text Box Proportional Resizing

Command-Option-Shift-drag on a text box handle
(Wait for flash to make text resizing real-time)

Centering views with the mouse

From any view, position the cursor at desired center
Command-Option-Click to **200%**
Command-Option-Click again to **Actual Size**

Selecting through the layered items in a stack

Hold **Command-Option-Shift** and point into the stack

Click once to select the topmost item, click again for each backward layer

Running a word count

Insert the text cursor

Open the Utilities menu, choose **Spelling**, then **Story**

Moving through pages by keyboard

Command-Up Arrow and Command-Down Arrow

Or Command-Left Arrow for beginning of story and Command-Right Arrow for end of story

Inserting a hang-below character

Position cursor in line above desired indent line

Key in **Command-**

Producing alternate character sets

Hold down the **Option** key (or **Option** and **Shift** keys) and press a standard key

Setting start-up defaults for any preference

With QuarkXPress running, assure that all documents are closed

Set-up specifications under the Edit menu, **Preferences**

Exit the program

A Short List of Resources for Electronic Publishing and Design

People who use desktop publishing programs come from a wide variety of backgrounds. So, I am often compelled to recommend a range of books to match their needs. The listing that follows is by no means exhaustive. It does include a selected group of books and publications found to be useful to my clients and students. If you're looking for general advice to help with electronic layout and typesetting, some of these references may prove useful to you, as well. If you're in need of more specific recommendations, you may contact me by mail (Studio K, Box 3562, San Diego, CA 92163).

Books

- *Great Pages* by Jan V. White. Detailed but off-the-cuff remarks on publication design, typography, and approaches to page design, useful to both desktop and traditional designers. White is particularly adept at putting into words what other designers point, sketch, and murmur about.

- *Editing by Design* by Jan V. White. A wry energy drives this book, which very successfully bridges the gap between the graphic design and editorial sides of the publishing. The book offers methods of editorial planning, layout, and printing, with emphasis on practical details of publication design.

- *Designing for Magazines* by Jan V. White. A counterpart to White's *Editing by Design*, but with emphasis on examples, this book seeks to show what designs succeed and why.

- *Newsletters from the Desktop* by Roger C. Parker. Good at breaking down the newsletter (and some of desktop publishing process) into component parts. Parker's titles have gained wide popularity, perhaps for their directness and easy reading.

- *Basic Desktop Design and Layout* by David Collier and Bob Cotton. This very visual book is full of examples in progress. Though not a step-by-step reference, it does provide insight into the design and development process by giving snapshots of various effects.

- *Graphic Design Cookbook* by Leonard Koren and R. Wippo Meckler. The temptation in this 100% layout book is to believe that you can perhaps just copy the ideas directly to your project. In reality, it serves best as a page-through wake-up call to your creativity, getting you thinking rather than giving you direct answers.

- *Publishing Newsletters* by Howard Penn Hudson. Though slanted toward manual layout and traditional typesetting, Hudson's book provides the lowdown on all aspects of bringing out a newsletter from basic planning and production through marketing.

- *How to Do Leaflets, Newsletters and Newspapers* by Nancy Brigham, et al. This down-home, grass-roots, large-format book carries lots of line drawings that convey the start-to-finish process of newsletters and newspapers. The advice is solid, with a kitchen-table, tight-budget slant.

Periodic Publications

❖ *Publish.* Though its focus seems to have wandered, this magazine has followed desktop publishing since the early days and continues to do so. It alternates between generic desktop wisdom and product-specific information.

❖ *Magazine Design and Production.* No-nonsense production technology coverage that views desktop publishing as a peripheral part of the larger process.

❖ *The Newsletter on Newsletters.* Comments and updates on the newsletter business by the author of *Publishing Newsletters.*

Index